MARC SHELL

Elizabeth's Glass

◆

WITH
"The Glass of the Sinful Soul" (1544)
BY *Elizabeth I*

AND

"Epistle Dedicatory" & "Conclusion"
(1548)
BY *John Bale*

◆

University of Nebraska Press

Lincoln & London

D1363735

Library of Congress Cataloging
in Publication Data
Shell, Marc.
Elizabeth's Glass : with The glass of the
Sinful Soul (1544) by Elizabeth I.
and Epistle dedicatory and Conclusion
(1548) by John Bale / Marc Shell.
p.   cm.
Includes transcription of Elizabeth I's
translation of Marguerite of
Navarre's Le miroir de l'âme pécheresse.
Includes bibliographical references
(p.   ) and index.
ISBN 0-8032-4216-6 (cl)
1. Elizabeth I, Queen of England,
1533-1603–Literary art.
2. Christian poetry, French – Translations
into English – History and criticism.
3. Women and literature – England –
History – 16th century.
4. Christian poetry, French – Translations
into English.
5. Great Britain – Kings and rulers –
Biography.
I. Elizabeth I, Queen of England,
1533 – 1603.
II. Bale, John, 1495-1563.
III. Marguerite, Queen, consort of
Henry II, King of Navarre, 1492-1549.
Miroir de l'âme pécheresse.
English.   1993.   IV. Title.
DA356.S54   1933   942.05'5 — dc20
92-5554   CIP

Frontispiece:
Elizabeth as Princess, c. 1546, age
thirteen or fourteen. Royal Collection,
St. James's Palace. © Her Majesty
Queen Elizabeth II.

For Susan

You know a kingdom knows no kindred.
— Elizabeth I to Henry Sidney (1565)

Contents

INTRODUCTION: "No Man Bastard Be"

JOHN BALE (1548)

ELIZABETH I (1544)

Illustrations

Preface

The which book is entitled, or named, *The Mirror
or Glass of the Sinful Soul*, wherein is contained how she
(beholding and contemplating what she is) doth perceive
how of herself and of her own strength she can do nothing
that good is, or prevaileth for her salvation, unless it be
through the grace of God, whose mother, daughter, sister,
and wife by the scriptures she proveth herself to be.
— Princess Elizabeth to Queen Catherine Parr,
December, 1544

E lizabeth's childhood, so goes the story, must have been unhappy. She disappointed her father (Henry VIII) by not being born a boy, was bereaved when her mother (Anne Boleyn) was beheaded for sibling incest, was declared a bastard and eventually exiled from the court by her father, and had four stepmothers (Jane Seymour, Anne of Cleves, Catherine Howard, and Catherine Parr). After her father died, the orphaned Elizabeth's ten-year-old half-sibling (Edward, son of Jane Seymour) became king. Her one-time step-uncle (Thomas Seymour) became her stepfather by marrying, in indecent haste, one of her stepmothers (Catherine Parr). This uncle-father, for his subsequent seduction of Elizabeth or an attempt to marry her, was executed by his own brother (Edward Seymour, "Protector of England").

Elizabeth had seen a good deal of sin and suffering by the time her manuscript "The Glass of the Sinful Soul" was published in Germany in 1548 as *A Godly Medytacyon of the Christen*

Sowle. Elizabeth was then fourteen years old. She had completed the manuscript when she was eleven.

In the next few years, the Protestant monarch Edward IV died. Elizabeth's other half-sibling (Mary Tudor) became the Catholic monarch and arranged for the eighteen-year-old Elizabeth to be sent to prison at the Tower of London and then to custody at Woodstock. Written with a diamond on her window at Woodstock some time in the mid-1550s are the lines "Much suspected by me, / Nothing proved can be, / Quoth Elizabeth prisoner."[1] Yet despite the insecurity of this existence, Elizabeth succeeded to the throne of England in 1558, at the age of twenty-five. And although her legitimacy was never legally established, she became, so goes the historical account, one of the most powerful and influential rulers that Europe would ever see.

This brave tale of triumph over adversity is well known (the unseemly incestuous details are usually omitted from elementary school texts, however, along with any mention of the "Glass"). Do not reviewers in the United States, mired in the Horatio Alger tradition, still praise those books about "Good Queen Bess" whose publishers patronizingly target the "eleven-year-old marketplace," precisely because such books provide their readers — or their readers' parents — with a moral role model for "juveniles" growing up in unsettled circumstances?[2]

The comforting explanation of the accomplishments of Elizabeth's mature years in terms of the precariousness of her early years is not, of course, without some scholarly justification. And that explanation has informed books about Elizabeth marketed

1. Elizabeth, *Poems*, p.3.
2. Marianne Partridge's review ("Good Queen Bess") of Diane Stanley and Peter Vennema's *Story of Elizabeth I of England* is an example.

for adults. Here the aesthetic requirements of biographical and historical narrative seem to have encouraged authors to emphasize, often *in vacuo*, the tension between adversity and triumph in order to clarify, or seem to clarify, the connection, crucial to the analysis of national politics in Britain, between Elizabeth's personal life and her public presence.

In this context there arises a need for a reexamination of the family of the brilliantly educated and precociously intelligent preadolescent Elizabeth in relationship to the subsequent politics of nationhood in the Elizabethan era. Exactly how the circumstances of the young Elizabeth's private "adversity" are linked to her later public "triumph" is no easy matter to discern. We are not father confessors or psychoanalysts who look into the souls of our subjects. At least we are not Elizabeth's. But even as we acknowledge the limits of possible knowledge in this arena, we can begin, by considering the significance of the long-overlooked speculum of the sinful soul that Elizabeth herself provided during these formative years of her life, to make reasonable speculations. For Elizabeth's "Glass," understood in historical context, mirrors the way ordinary kinship, which is the precondition for what Elizabeth calls "fornication"[3] and incest, might for her be transcended by one or another kind of extraordinary spiritual or political kinship.

Ordinary kinship, or its legal figurations, Elizabeth had known in situations where one person is both sibling and lover/spouse (as Anne Boleyn was to George Boleyn or Catherine of Aragon to Henry VIII) or both parent and lover/spouse (as

---

3. "But thou, which hast made separation of My bed, and did put thy false lovers in My place and committed fornication with them, yet, for all this, thou mayst come unto Me again, for I will not be angry against thee. Lift up thine eyes, and look up, then shalt thou see in what place thy sin had led thee, and how thou liest down in the earth" (Elizabeth, "The Glass of the Sinful Soul," fol. 36v; reproduced below, pp. 114–44).

Thomas Seymour to Elizabeth herself). Extraordinary kinship and its apparent transcendence of the incest taboo Elizabeth would have known from its Christian formulations. These formulations, which she expresses in her speculum, include the doctrine of universal siblinghood, according to which all human beings are siblings, so that every act of sexual intercourse is incestuous; they also include the doctrine of the quadruply affined *sponsa Christi*, according to which, as Elizabeth suggests in the letter to her stepmother Catherine Parr that she attached to the 1544 manuscript of the "Glass" (quoted in the epigraph above), one human being is at once the parent, sibling, child, and spouse/lover of another being. Extraordinary kinship Elizabeth would also come to know—and perhaps even foreknow—in the developing British and generally European doctrine of nationhood. The interconnection of Christian kinship and nationhood, as well as Elizabeth's own life and work, constitutes the subject of this book.

Elizabeth's Glass provides a modernized transcription and photographic reproduction of the manuscript of Princess Elizabeth's interpretive translation of a poem by the spiritual libertine Queen Marguerite of Navarre; it includes also John Bale's "Epistle Dedicatory" and "Conclusion" to Elizabeth's translation, as well as my own introduction and ancillary scholarly material. Bale's essays, with their focus on the idea of consanguineous and spiritual lineage, have not been reproduced in any printed form since 1590, so far as I know.

§

Many people helped out with the preparation and encouragement of this project. Graduate students at Harvard University, the State University of New York at Buffalo, and the University

Preface

of Massachusetts at Amherst attended seminars with such titles as "Fictions of Kinship in the Renaissance" and asked fruitful questions. Roger Strittmatter and Derek Alwes, graduate assistants at the University of Massachusetts, helped me compile the Glossary of Proper Names in Bale. Barry Weller read over the manuscript and made important suggestions for improving it. Murray Schwartz, until recently Dean of the Faculty of Humanities and Fine Arts at the University of Massachusetts, provided time away from my administrative duties as head of the Department of Comparative Literature.

I am thankful to the British Library, the Bodleian Library, the Houghton Library, and the Scottish Record Office, which generously provided photographic material and access to rare books and manuscripts.

I have learned most from my beloved children, Jacob and Hanna. They have taught me not to underestimate the intelligence and perspicacity of children or to misconstrue the importance of their scholarly pursuits and spiritual accomplishments. As I would not misjudge the talents and ambitions of my own children, so I do not underestimate those of the Princess Elizabeth.

Introduction

"No Man Bastard Be"

If your first spring and auther
God you view,
No man bastard be.
— Elizabeth I, Englishing of
Boethius,
De consolatione philosophiae

Marguerite Angoulême, queen of Navarre, devout and free-thinking sister to King Francis of France, first published in 1531 her remarkable religious meditation of some 1,700 lines, *Le Miroir de l'âme pécheresse.*[1] Marguerite had been an acquaintance of Anne Boleyn since 1516.[2] And after Anne, Henry VIII's mistress since 1527, married the English king in 1533 and gave birth in the same year to Elizabeth, Marguerite in 1534–35 renewed her association with the well-educated and reform-minded English queen.[3] At about this time, it seems likely, Marguerite sent Anne a copy of her book.[4] Anne was beheaded in 1536. But in 1544 her daughter, then eleven years old, made an English translation of Marguerite's *Miroir,* most likely from a 1533 edition that she found in her mother's collection.[5] Elizabeth called her translation "The Glass of the Sinful Soul."

Elizabeth sent the manuscript, together with a letter and an elaborate needlework cover embroidered by herself, to her stepmother Queen Catherine Parr as a New Year's gift for 1545.[6] Catherine, herself the author of such religious meditations as *The Lamentacion of a Synner* (1547) and *Prayers, or Meditations* (1545), may have amended the manuscript — as Elizabeth had asked her to do in her covering letter[7] — and probably added some new material of her own. Catherine then probably sent the manuscript and revisions to John Bale, her friend — and Elizabeth's.

Bale was an ardent reformer, scholar, and playwright.[8] And he was a powerful Protestant polemicist, publishing in Marburg (Germany) in 1546–47, for example, two tracts defending the martyr Anne Askew. In his capacity as nationalist scholar and theologian, Bale "mended" some of Elizabeth's "Glass of the Sinful Soul," adding to it a long "Epistle Dedicatory" and "Conclusion" and prudently retitling the work *A Godly Medytacyon of the Christen Sowle.* In 1548, just a few months after the death of Henry VIII, Bale published not only the first part of his *Illustrium majoris Britanniae scriptorum* and his *Kynge Johan* but also, with the Marburg publisher Dirik van Straten, Princess Elizabeth's "Glass." He included in his edition a few multilingual biblical translations by the princess and a woodcut depicting her kneeling before Christ (Illustration 1).[9]

Queen Elizabeth herself probably did not think too badly of her work. Bale's 1548 edition was reprinted in 1590 in London by Roger Ward. In the interim it was re-edited by James Cancellar in 1568 or perhaps 1570 (when the Roman Catholic Mary Stuart, Queen of Scots, was in the power of the Protestant Elizabeth, Queen of England) and again in 1582. Cancellar substituted for the original preface a larger one of his own. His 1568–70 edition was reissued in 1582 in Bentley's *Monument of Matrones.*

There has been no readily available edition of Elizabeth's translation of Marguerite's poem since 1590. The facsimile of the 1544 manuscript reproduced below was published in a rare 1897 edition by Percy W. Ames, previously obtainable at only a handful of research libraries.[10] And the sixteenth-century publications, in the *Godly Medytacyon,* of Bale's dedication and conclusion have remained until now the only printings of those works.

The "Glass" is to this day the only translation of one of Queen Marguerite's most beautiful and enigmatic meditations. Elizabeth I wrote a fair number of literary works, and most

The Conclusyon.
At all tymes God.is with the iust/
Bycause they put,in hym their trust.
Who shall therfor, from Syon geue,
That helthe whych hāgeth,in our beleue
Whan God shall take,frō hys the smart,
Than wyll Jacob,reioyce in hart.
Prayse to God.
FR tsiis Bm.ss.d.6 wp.2T im.27.

Imprented in the yeare of our lorde
1548. in Apryll.

1. Princess Elizabeth kneeling with a book in her hand. Woodcut.
From Elizabeth, Godly Medytacyon of the Christen Sowle *(1548).*
Reproduced by permission of the Folger Shakespeare Library.

have been published, some in good scholarly editions. Why has this particular work, listed in the oldest bibliographies, been virtually ignored?[11] The answer to that question is finally inseparable from the real subjects of the "Glass" — the queen, her family, and the nation. These are the subjects also of most of this Introduction. Other attempts at explanation are worth dealing with briefly, however. Some scholars say that Elizabeth's is a poor translation;[12] others, that the original is a poor French poem;[13] still others, that the "Glass" is merely the effort of an immature young girl.

Yet this text is the combined work of two or three of Europe's greatest women monarchs (Marguerite, Elizabeth, Catherine). As published, it includes important writings by a key theologian of the English Reformation (Bale). Moreover, it can shed light on the history of handwriting,[14] on the education of women[15] as well as the larger role of women writers in the sixteenth century,[16] and on such common genres of writings by women as devotional literature[17] and translation[18] and such rare ones in the Elizabethan period as poetry.[19] Have not the works of less brilliant or influential people proved useful to scholars and cultural historians in these and similar fields? Surely, too, almost any work written by a reigning monarch and published in several editions during her lifetime is likely to have had some literary and/or political influence.[20]

What is most interesting about the "Glass" may go some way toward explaining its relative obscurity. Elizabeth's work expresses, as we shall see, an ideology both important and discomforting in its personal and historical aspects. Its treatment of bastardy and incest, for example, has potentially disconcerting ramifications for ideas of liberty and politics generally and illuminates the historical rise of the English nation and biographical role of Elizabeth herself. For the most profound themes of the "Glass" involve the reworking and expansion in nationalist and secular terms of such medieval theological notions concerning kinship as universal siblinghood, whereby all men and women are equally akin, and dormition, wherein the Virgin Mary plays at once the role of mother and daughter as well as wife.[21] Above all, the "Glass," whose French original had a subtitle about the human conflict between flesh and spirit (*Discord étant en l'homme par contrariété de l'esprit et de la chair*), concerns the transmutation of the desire for or fear of physical incest into the desire for or fear of spiritual incest. It thus reflects the beginnings of a new ideal and real political organization, which, partly out of Elizabeth's own concerns with incest and bastardy and partly out of political exigencies of the time, England's great monarch introduced as a kind of "national siblinghood" to which she was simultaneously the mother and wife.

The "Glass" is a reflection of Elizabeth herself. (She wrote to Catherine Parr, "The part that I wrought in it" was as "well spiritual as manual.")[22] But interpretation and contextualization of that glass help to elucidate — in terms both of individual psychology and of national politics — not only how a preadolescent young woman of 1544 formed her spirit but also how that spirit informed the political identity of the English nation (as Bale predicted it would) and participated in producing the modern nation state.

2. INCEST, BASTARDY, AND THE BIRTH OF A NATION

It is, or it is not, according to the nature
of men, an advantage to be orphaned at an early age.
— Thomas de Quincey, *The Caesars*

In 1544, the year she wrote the "Glass," the eleven-year-old Princess Elizabeth had a fourth stepmother, Catherine Parr. Her first stepmother, Jane Seymour, had died giving birth to Elizabeth's half-brother, later Edward VI. The marriage between Henry VIII and her second stepmother, Anne of Cleves, had been declared null and void. Her third stepmother, Catherine Howard, had been executed on the charge of adultery. "Mother, mother, mother," says Hamlet.[23]

Anne Boleyn had risen to the place of queen thanks to Henry VIII's memorable charge that he and Catherine of Aragon were living in adultery and incest and that their marriage therefore ought to be declared null. The charge, which recalls the complexities of the liaison between King Claudius and his sister-in-law Gertrude in Shakespeare's *Hamlet*, was momentous in the English Reformation. Catherine was the widow of Henry VIII's brother Arthur; she was Henry's sister-in-law. Should Henry have married her? Legally, could he? On the one side of this debate stands the law of the levirate, according to which a man must marry the childless widow of a deceased brother.[24] On the other side stands the doctrine of carnal contagion, according to which it is incest to have sexual intercourse with one's sister-in-law.[25] Henry himself took the view that his sexual intercourse with Catherine had been incest.[26] Thus began a series of spe-

8

cifically English charges of incest in the royal family.[27] Such charges are germane to the foundation of the English Reformation, and, like Thomas More's Romish claim that such Brothers or ex-Brothers as Martin Luther — as well as Elizabeth's tutors and mentors John Bale and Bernardino Ochino — commit incest when they marry, they are part of a general Renaissance revaluation of profane and sacred sexual liaisons.[28]

Elizabeth's mother, Anne Boleyn, not only rose to power by a charge of incest (against Catherine) but also fell from power by means of one (against herself): she lost her head when Henry argued that she had been unfaithful. We may consider the full ramifications of the charge by examining how it affected Elizabeth's legal status and hence, of course, the English people's natural concern with problems of succession; they had reason to wonder whether a princess conceived in adultery or incest was legitimate.[29] Elizabeth was deemed a bastard on several counts, five of which are worth pursuing here.[30]

First, Elizabeth's *pater*, Henry VIII, had claimed publicly that she was a bastard and that her uncle Lord Rochford, her mother's brother, was her consanguineous *genitor*. Just as Anne was accused of having had sexual intercourse with her brother Lord Rochford, Elizabeth was declared a bastard by a 1536 Act of Parliament.[31]

Second, Sir Thomas More argued that the union between Henry VIII and Catherine of Aragon was not incestuous and hence that both Henry's divorce of Catherine and his marriage to Anne Boleyn were null. It follows that whether Henry or Rochford was Elizabeth's *genitor*, she was in either event a bastard.

Third, Henry VIII and Anne Boleyn were married less than nine months before Elizabeth's birthday, in suspiciously speedy and secret circumstances. Even if the marriage to Anne was legitimate (which More said it was not) and Henry the *genitor* (which Henry himself said he was not), Elizabeth might at least seem to have been conceived out of wedlock.

A fourth allegation was that Elizabeth's mother was also her sister, or, put otherwise, that Anne Boleyn was not only Henry's loving wife by marriage and sister by carnal contagion but also his daughter by consanguinity.[32] (The ambiguous kinship is suggested in the couplet that the possibly pregnant Anne inscribed on an illumination of the Annunciation in a Book of Hours that she gave to Henry: "Be daly prove you shalle me fynde / to be to you bothe lovyng and kynde"; see Illustration 2. The Annunciation is the intimation to the Virgin Mary — who is not only the wife of God but also, as we shall see, his sister and daughter — of the divine incarnation in her womb.)[33] Though the allegation was false, we ought not to dismiss it as altogether frivolous, for in the context of the Christian religion, children of incestuous unions — including the annunciated God (Jesus) and several saints (Gregory the Great) — come to assume powerful places in both profane and sacred institutions.

Finally, Elizabeth's consanguineous aunt, Mary Cary (*née* Boleyn), had been her father's mistress either before Anne or at about the same time (probably 1527–28); therefore, Thomas Cranmer, Archbishop of Canterbury and Elizabeth's godfather, relied on the doctrine of carnal contagion and the parallel 1536 Act of Parliament — according to both of which it was nominated incest to sleep with the sister of one's mistress ("flesh of my flesh") — to declare both that the marriage between Henry and Anne was incestuous and that Elizabeth was a bastard.[34]

The doctrine of carnal contagion, then, and the charges of incest and bastardy that go along with it affected Elizabeth's sense of identity and help give us some access to what one biographer has called her spiritual "girlhood."[35] The doctrine's

2. *The Annunciation. Illumination in a Book of Hours. The couplet is in
Anne Boleyn's handwriting: "Be daly prove you shalle me fynde /
to be to you bothe lovyng and kynde." King's MS 9, folio 66v. Reproduced
by courtesy of the Trustees of the British Library.*

implementation in law during the 1530s and 1540s affected the very foundations of the new England. Its redefinition of the taboo on incest in the most generalizable terms also helps us define the origin of the English nation-state and its new Anglican institutions.

3. CARNAL CONTAGION

He that comforts my wife is the cherisher of my flesh and blood.
— Shakespeare, *All's Well That Ends Well*

English men and women used the doctrine of carnal contagion to claim that Henry VIII's marriages to Catherine of Aragon and Anne Boleyn were both incestuous. If the king's brother (Arthur) had slept with a woman (Catherine of Aragone), it was argued, then she was the king's kin, and his marriage to her was null and void (any such offspring as Mary Tudor, later Queen Mary I, would be illegitimate).[36] By the same token, if the king had slept with a woman (Mary Boleyn), then that woman's sister (Anne Boleyn) was also the king's kin, and there stood between them a diriment impediment to marriage (any such offspring as Elizabeth Tudor, later Queen Elizabeth I, would be illegitimate). The argument that the siblings of a sexual mate become one's own sibling tended to make Elizabeth both legitimate by nullifying Catherine's marriage with Henry, and illegitimate by nullifying Anne's marriage with Henry.

The doctrine of carnal contagion involves the spread of blood kinship as if it were a disease. As J. H. Fowler summarizes the medieval theologian Rabanus Maurus, "there is something like a communicable disease metaphor involved in early medieval notions of sexuality. If one sleeps with a woman who sleeps with another man who sleeps with another woman who sleeps with me, then whether I will it or not my flesh is inextricably bound up with the flesh of that first man's. A term which con-

13

tinually shows up in these canons and letters to describe fornication is *contagio carnalis* — carnal contagion."[37] Thus the English *Jacob's Well* (c. 1450) states that "whan a man hath medlyd
wyth a womman, or a womman wyth a man, neyther may be
wedded to otheres kyn, into the fyfte degre, ne medle wyth
hem; for if thei don, it is incest." Fornication not only leads to
venereal disease and to incest through illegitimacy; it also leads
to incest through the secret spread of kinship by contagion of
the flesh. This contagion, which involves a general teleology of
all sexual activities, leads to such views as Jonas of Orleans's
strident argument that "all illicit carnal relations are incestuous." Promiscuity gives rise to incest insofar as one becomes
kinsperson to all the kinspersons of one's marital or extramarital partner, and record-keeping becomes all but impossible.[38]

During Elizabeth's time, potentially universalist "figurative"
kinship structures of this sort were replacing "literal" physical
ones. It would seem, especially to one in a position like Elizabeth's, that all sexual liaisons were, or were likely to be, incestuous. This appearance, which appears to inform Elizabethan "sexual nausea," was a fulfillment of earlier Church history.[39]
For example, the archaic doctrine that cousinship even to the
seventh degree makes a sexual liaison incestuous — indeed cousinship to any known and verifiable degree even so far back as
Adam![40] — means that almost all sexual liaisons in a small town
are incestuous, and in a large town without perfect record-
keeping it makes all liaisons potentially incestuous.

In carnal contagion cases, moreover, the diriment impediment to marriage involves keeping the books not only on sexual
unions within wedlock but also on those without. According
to the "great mystery" — or quasi-philosophical dialectic — of
Pauline Christianity, a man "shall be joined unto his wife, and
they two shall be one flesh." The Church, taking marriage to be

the essential *telos* of all sexual intercourse, easily extended the marital union here defined to include also the conjunction of fornicator and fornicatrix. "Know ye not," asked Paul, "that he which is joined to an harlot is one body? for two, saith he, shall be one flesh." Thus sexual intercourse, whether marital or extramarital, spreads kinship by bringing the relatives of each party into the kindred of the other.[41]

The Christian notion of the growth of kinship relations without as well as within marriage casts doubt on the old, or the Old Testament, distinction between legal and illegal sexual relations, between marital and extramarital relations, and between the sexual relations of people who are related "in law" and those who are not. It puts into question the crucial distinctions between incest and endogamy (whether one marries or not is now essentially immaterial) and between endogamy and exogamy.

By conflating extramarital with marital sexual intercourse, the doctrine of carnal contagion undermines and transcends the ordinary notion of kinship, which looks to marriage — as to incest — as a definitive institution. As we shall see, the conflation seems also to allow for the transformation of the Catholic *sponsa Christi*, queenpin of Christian kinship systems: she who is engaged to God in a chaste and incestuous relationship that is at once marital and extramarital. The conflation allows for the transformation of the *sponsa* into such a Virgin Queen as Princess Elizabeth seems already in her eleventh year to comprehend. John Bale writes of Elizabeth's "Glass of the Sinful Soul," the young princess's first public accomplishment, that "such noble beginnings are neither to be reckoned childish nor babyish, though she were a babe in years, that hath here given them."[42] The child is mother to the woman; a full and accomplished childhood can tell much about a life.

4. SPECULATION ON PRINCESS ELIZABETH

Edipus [Oedipus] busy serche did wrap him in most harmes;
   for whan of him selfe he ased as he no Corinthe wez,
but Guest, he met with Laius, who after kild he had,
   and mother his owne in mariage tok, with whom he got kingdom,
with dowary hers, whan than happy he thought he was,
   Again he questioned who he was, whiche whan his wife wold Let
   more earnest he, the old man as gilty he were rebukd;
Omitting no good menes to make bewrayd al that was hid.
   Than whan suspect herof his mynd had moche distract
And old man had skrigd out, "O worthi me whom nide to spoke
   contrains;"
yeat kindeled and vexed with Curiositis stinge made answer,
   "Compeeld to heare, yeat heare I must."
   — Elizabeth I, Englishing of Plutarch, *De curiositate*

The eleven-year-old princess Elizabeth was in the position of Sophocles' Antigone: caught between horror at sexual transgression and pious duty to a family constituted by such transgression.[43] A brilliant and brilliantly educated young woman, blessed or cursed with the knowledge of her origin,[44] what might she have felt about herself and about her consanguineous and national families? Did a perhaps too curious young Elizabeth feel that she herself had, as in some Oedipal drama, "the seed of incest" for which her aunt-mother Anne and uncle-father Lord Rochford had been executed and of which her father Henry VIII himself stood accused?[45]

Many biographers aver that for her aunt-mother, Anne Boleyn, Elizabeth never displayed any posthumous affection. That would be understandable enough in the circumstances. But what about the adage "Like mother, like daughter"? Did Elizabeth see, or fear to see, her mother in herself, as in a *glass*? Is that why she pointedly adopted as her own the badge of the sinful Anne Boleyn with its inscription *Semper Eadem*, "Always the Same" (Illustration 3), and retained it even after becoming queen?

Elizabeth's own familial liaisons were tinged by incest. Her uncle-father Thomas Seymour seduced the thirteen-year-old Elizabeth, or tried to. Thomas was Elizabeth's step-uncle: his sister, Jane Seymour, who had been lady-in-waiting to Catherine of Aragon and Anne Boleyn, had married Henry VIII in 1546 only one day after the execution of Elizabeth's mother. And Thomas was her stepfather: in 1547 he married, in indecent haste (Henry VIII's funeral was barely done with, much as was Old Hamlet's when Gertrude married Claudius: "O, most wicked speed! To post / With such dexterity to incestuous sheets!")[46] dowager queen, Catherine Parr, fourth stepmother to Elizabeth. Sometime after Catherine Parr died, Thomas Seymour tried to marry Elizabeth herself.[47] (In a letter to Edward Seymour, Lord Protector, in 1549, Elizabeth writes, "Master Tyrwhitt and others have told me that there are going rumors abroad, which be greatly both against my honor and honesty . . . that I am in the tower; and with child by my Lord Admiral. My Lord, these are shameful slanders.")[48] Was it a childhood memory about Thomas Seymour that somehow effected the aged Elizabeth's infatuation half a century later with the young Robert Devereux (second Earl of Essex), he whose maternal great-grandmother, Mary Boleyn, was Anne Boleyn's sister?[49] When in 1598, fifty years after John Bale published her "Glass of the Sinful Soul," Elizabeth translated Plutarch's warning against an Oedipal curiosity about familial

3. *Badge of Anne Boleyn, which was resumed by Elizabeth, with Elizabeth's motto, "Semper Eadem" (Always the Same). From Ames,* Mirror of the Sinful Soul.

origins, did she not reflect upon the publicly acknowledged inascertainability of her own paternity and the never entirely suppressed charge, often leveled by recusant Catholics, that she had been conceived in sinful incest? ("Compelled to hear, yet hear I must.")[50]

We might speculate about the young Princess Elizabeth that she attempted to deal with problems involving paternity and incest.[51] Of Elizabeth's interest in incest we may be sure. She chose to translate a book, *Le Miroir de l'âme pécheresse*, about incest—a book written by and probably given to her supposedly incestuous mother by Marguerite of Navarre, an author known for her spiritual libertinism and love for her brother.[52] Marguerite was also known to the princess as one of her potential "mothers" and "aunts": Henry VIII had once entertained the idea of marrying Marguerite, which would have made her one of Elizabeth's stepmothers;[53] and Henry had also tried to arrange a marriage between the thirteen-month-old Princess Elizabeth and Marguerite's nephew, the young Duke of Angoulême, third son of Francis I, which would have made Marguerite one of Elizabeth's aunts.[54]

Moreover, the young Elizabeth did not fail to remark how the general theme of Marguerite's work involves sensuality and incest. The *Miroir* depicts, as Elizabeth puts it in the "Glass," a young woman "having both her feet bound by her concupiscence, and also both her arms through evil use," having a "body ready and prompt to do all evil, not willing other study," and subject to "my enemy, my sensuality (I being in my beastly sleep)."[55] And in the New Year's letter to Catherine Parr that accompanied her translation, Elizabeth notes that the *Miroir* shows how a woman for whom it was once sin to be related to a being as both his daughter and wife can become affined guiltlessly to another Being as "mother, daughter, sister, and wife."[56] In her "Glass," Elizabeth discovers and explores a way to rise above the taboo of ordinary incest, a way that derives partly from the free-thinking and spiritual libertine French tradition in which a kinship by *alliance* supersedes kinship by blood (where some people are brothers and some are others) and which looks to universalist standards of kinship (where all people are equally brothers and others).[57] Such universalist standards make all sexual intercourse equally chaste or unchaste, literally incestuous. They eventually even require the conflation of a libertine whore with the virginal mother. (Shakespeare's Cranmer reminds us of Elizabeth's reputation for virginity when, in *Henry VIII*, he predicts that his godchild Elizabeth, daughter of the whorish libertine Anne, will die "yet a virgin, / A most spotted lily.")[58]

The question of ordinary paternal legitimacy, which dogged Elizabeth throughout her life, may be transcended by taking a Roman or Hellenist "cosmopolitan" or Christian "universalist" view. This view would make every human being equally a child of the earth or of God, say, or essentially an "orphelyn of fadyr and modyr" (Chaucer's *Boethius*).[59] In translating Boethius's *Consolation of Philosophy*, where Christianity prescribes Jesus as the divine Father of everyone in much the same way that Rome prescribed Caesar, Elizabeth may have been consoled by the idea that she was no more or less bastard than anyone else.:

> All humain kind on erthe
> > From like beginninge comes:
> One father is of all,
> > One Only al doth gide [guide]. . . .
> What crake you of your stock
> > Or forfathers old?
> If your first spring and auther
> > God you view,

Speculation on Princess Elizabeth

> No man bastard be,
> > Unles with vice the worst he fede
> > And leveth [leaves] so his birthe.[60]

In the words of the Elizabethan poem called "The Lord's Prayer," "Our Father, which in heaven art, / . . . hast [made] us all one brotherhood."[61] When Adam delved and Eve span, there was no gentleman — or, at least, everyone was equally a gentleman and nongentleman.[62] All are essentially children of the same *genitor*. The Boethian appeal to universally equal kinship suggests that the distinction between illegitimacy and legitimacy is transcendable or irrelevant.

At first blush, such a sentiment might seem able to console one such as Elizabeth: no one should call her a bastard anymore because in God's eyes there are not bastards and legitimate children but only children of God, say, or of the Earth. But on second thought, the sentiment for universal kinship must also have been unsettling to Elizabeth, and to Bale. If it is not our particular family's blood that distinguishes one person from another, one might ask, by what right does any British monarch rule? (Elizabeth and Bale think of Elizabeth as potential monarch.) England was not, after all, an elective or constitutional monarchy (like Hamlet's Denmark) or an empire where adopted or adrogated sons inherit the throne (like the Caesars' Rome). In England, for good or ill, the right to the throne had to be defended in terms of blood.[63] Thus Elizabeth's supporters needed to establish not merely that legitimate British princesses could inherit the throne (a task that Bale, countering the proponents of the Salic law, sets himself in his fine catalogue of women rulers of Britain) but also that Elizabeth was legitimate in terms of blood (a nearly impossible task). Or Elizabeth's supporters needed to take a polar opposite tack, replacing familial blood as the standard for kinship and for political inheritance with some such quality as nobility of spirit (a task that Bale seeks to accomplish in his "Epistle Dedicatory").

Replacement of blood with nobility of spirit would itself be dangerous to any would-be ruler. Rejection of blood as the standard for kinship would bring into disrepute the familial reverence ordinarily due to earthly parents ("Honor thy father and thy mother" says the Old Testament) and, by common analogy, destroy the political reverence due the king ("The king is the father of his people," says the old adage). Transcendence of consanguinity as the standard for kinship would tend to transform the very idea of family and nation, as Bale suggests in his ancillary essays.

5. THE SPONSA CHRISTI

Then God is in us, and all we are in Him, and
He in all men. If we have Him through faith, then
have we a greater treasure than any man can tell.
— Elizabeth, "The Glass of the Sinful Soul"

In physical incest, two people who are consanguineously related to each other act as though they are not. A consanguineous sister, for example, acts as a spouse, and that is called bad, even absolutely profane. In the Holy Family, however, the Virgin Mary is at once the spouse, sibling, child, and mother of God the Father and/or Son, but her obviously incestuous sexual intercourse with Him (or Them) is called "good," even absolutely sacred. The term "taboo" means both "sacred" and "dangerous, forbidden."[64] And the term *sponsa Christi* (spouse of Christ), which defines Mary's relation to God, emphasizes a woman's marriage with Christ in a union at once extramarital (Mary is married to Joseph) and incestuous. Mary is the human female parent of God as Son (she parented the Son); she is the spouse of God; she is the sibling of God (the Son and she are children of the same Father); and she is the child of God (the Father's child). There is no denying that Mary's relationship to God, which is the model for perfection in Roman Christian life, amounts to incest of a kind. ("Is't not a kind of incest, to take life / From thine own sister's shame?" Shakespeare's Isabella demands of Claudio. Isabella, the would-be Sister, is sister to Claudio, and her name, which means something like "consecrated to God," is cognate with *Elizabeth*.)[65] Hence, the Virgin Mary is the archetypal *sponsa Christi*,

23

and her mysterious puzzle has occupied many a Church father and pope from the earliest to the latest periods of Christian theology.[66]

Incest, the centerpiece of political controversy during Elizabeth's girlhood, has long been associated with puzzles, as in the case of the riddle of the Delphic Oracle or the Theban Sphinx, whose terms Oedipus cannot solve but is compelled to enact. Consider the riddling of this late medieval epigraph inscribed in the exact middle of the collegial church of Ecouis, in the cross aisle:

> Here lies the child, here lies the father,
> Here lies the sister, here lies the brother,
> Here lie the wife and the husband,
> Yet there are but two bodies here.[67]

The solution to this riddle involves a local story: "The tradition is that a son of Madame d'Ecouis had by his mother, without knowing her or being recognized by her, a daughter named Cecilia, whom he afterward married in Lorraine, she then being in the service of the Duchess of Bar. Thus Cecilia was at one and the same time her husband's daughter, sister, and wife. They were interred together in the same grave at Ecouis in 1512."[68] The riddle is about how a woman and man are, at one and the same time, wife and husband, sister and brother, and daughter and father. The woman has a relationship to her man like that of Mary to God and of any nun who, as *sponsa Christi*, is likewise related to Christ.

Similar epigraphs appear in other churches in Europe:

> Here lies the son, here lies the mother,
> Here lies the daughter with the father;
> Here lies the sister, here lies the brother,
> Here lies the wife with the husband;
> And there are only three bodies here.[69]

Shakespeare begins *Pericles, Prince of Tyre* with a riddle about a kind of incestuous self-consumption:

> I am no viper, yet I feed
> On mother's flesh which did me breed.
> I sought a husband, in which labour
> I found that kindness in a father.
> He's father, son, and husband mild;
> I mother, wife, and yet his child:
> How they may be, and yet in two,
> As you will live, resolve it you.[70]

Nearly identical puzzles inform such writers as John Gower, Laurence Twine, and the sixteenth-century Navarre-born Spanish poet Julian Medrano.[71] The freethinker Rabelais, in his *Gargantua* and *Pantraguel* (published in the 1530s), writes of people on the Island of Ennasin that "they were so related and intermarried with one another that we found none of them who was a mother, or a father, an uncle, or an aunt, a cousin or a nephew, a son-in-law or a daughter-in-law, a god-father or a god-mother, to any other; except indeed for one tall noseless man whom I heard calling a little girl of three or four, Father, while the little girl called him Daughter."[72]

What else is Elizabeth's "Glass," in this context, except a kinship riddle? Elizabeth herself teases out the matter thus: "I am sister unto Thee, but so naughty a sister that better it is for me to hide such a name."[73] Certainly Elizabeth had incest in mind when she wrote these words. Her father Henry VIII had committed incest with Catherine of Aragon, and her deceased stepmother Catherine Howard had committed adultery with Catherine's cousin Thomas Culpepper. Elizabeth's *genetrix* Anne Boleyn had been accused of being sexually "handled" by Elizabeth's uncle (Rochford) and by Elizabeth's father (Henry

VIII). Elizabeth's uncle-father (Thomas Seymour) was soon to be accused of "handling" Elizabeth herself. To father or Father, to brother or Brother, to son or Son, Elizabeth's narrator calls out in the "Glass": "O my father, what paternity; O my brother, what fraternity; O my child, what delection; O my husband, O what conjunction! Father full of humility, brother having taken our similitude, son engendered through faith and charity, husband loving in all extremity." Lest we miss the extraordinary quality of the poet's love, the speaker asks of her unnamed fourfold kin, "Is there any love that may be compared unto this, but it hath some evil condition?"[74] (see Illustration 4). For it is ultimately Father, and not father, who handles the young girl. And so, to Jesus, she cries out: "Thou dost handle my soul (if so I durst say) as a mother, daughter, sister, and wife. . . . Alas, yea, for Thou hast broken the kindred of my old father, calling me daughter of adoption."[75]

In the end the narrator comes to recognize that on one's own, one can do nothing to overcome the sinful desire for physical incest. Only through the grace of God can profane incest be converted to sacred. The soul must look into herself as into a mirror, and "(beholding and contemplating what she is) . . . perceive how of herself and of her own strength she can do nothing that good is, or prevaileth for her salvation, unless it be through the grace of God, whose mother, daughter, sister, and wife by the scriptures she proveth herself to be."[76]

The "Glass" is about the conversion of a soul from sensual or physical sin to a kind of spiritual incest, or about that logical or psychological and spiritual metamorphosis in which such opposites as incest and chastity become each other. (By the same token the "Glass" is about a conversion from betrayal defined in terms of fourfold kinship to a union in faith.)[77] Bale, in consideration of such conversion, writes in his "Conclusion": "And

*4. Elizabeth's coat of arms. The Order of the Garter: "Honi soit qui mal
y pense" (Evil to him who evil thinks). With "Godly Meditations or
prayers, set foorth after the order of the Alphabet of the Queenes
Maiestes name." From Elizabeth,* Godly Medytacyon, *1568.
BM C.38.c.57. Reproduced by courtesy of the Trustees of
the British Library.*

5. *The Dormition of the Virgin Mary. Jesus the Son holds up the childlike soul of Mary his Mother. Mosaic at La Martorana, Palermo, Sicily. 1143* A.D. *Alinari/Art Resource, New York.*

though the facts be as the purple, yet shall they appear so white as the wool"; from this viewpoint, the "Glass" is in Bale's words "a spiritual exercise of [Princess Elizabeth's] inner soul with God."[78] And the figure of fourfold kinship, far from being a mere "oddity" in the poem, is central to it.[79] For in this exercise it is not Elizabeth or her immediate family members who occupy center stage as "sexually abused persons" or as "sexual abusers." It is God who is "familiarly commoned with," writes Bale.[80] God is treated as though he were a human being (which Jesus partly was) and a family member (which Jesus is to the *sponsa Christi*; see Illustration 5).[81] God is kind and kin.

6. QUEEN MARGUERITE OF NAVARRE

Elizabeth's life was a continuation and fulfillment
of the promise of Margaret's.
— Percy W. Ames

The title page of the 1533 edition of Marguerite's poem states that its central theme is the place of God as spouse: "Le miroir de lame pecheresse: auquel / elle recongnoist ses faultes et pechez. aussy / les graces et benefices a elle faictz par Jesus Christ son espoux" (the mirror of the sinful soul, where she [the soul] recognizes her faults and sins, as well as the graces and benefits made to her by Jesus Christ her spouse). And, indeed, the central issue of Elizabeth's translation is the transmutation by the sinner of her profane desire for, or fear of, ordinary physical incest into a sacred desire for, and love of, that extraordinary incest which informs the Holy Family. As the subtitle goes on to say, the *Miroir* is about "the discord being in humankind by the contrariness of spirit and flesh and its peace through spiritual life."

The same issue is present in some of Marguerite's other works.[82] The central story in the *Heptameron*, for example, concerns a young man who unknowingly has sexual intercourse with his mother and then marries the offspring of this union — his sister, daughter, and spouse. His mother had chosen as this young son's tutor "a schoolmaster, a man of holy life"; but "Nature, who is a very secret schoolmaster, taught him a very different lesson to any he had learned from his tutor." The son and daughter never learn of their blood kinship, and for them (if not for their knowingly incestuous mother) the tale ends happily: "And they [the son and daughter] loved each other so much that never were there husband and wife more loving, nor yet more resembling each other; for she was his daughter, his sister and his wife, while he was her father, her brother and her husband."[83]

In Marguerite's *Miroir*, the sin of earthly incest reappears as the blessing of heavenly incest.[84] The work as a whole is informed almost entirely by the *topos* that a woman mystically in love with God is involved with him in a fourfold incestuous relationship and that this relationship, by virtue of its being spiritual, is not only bereft of its horrid and profane quality but actually made sacred. The *Miroir* and the *Heptameron* are thus polar opposites, containing both thematic parallels (the former focuses on spiritual incest, the latter on physical incest) and verbal parallels ("mother, sister, daugher, and wife").

The protagonist in the *Miroir* is a woman who compares herself with the Virgin Mary — the mother and sister of God the Son, and the daughter and spouse of God the Father. She acknowledges that her wicked desire for physical sex, even incest, can be overcome only by a liberating, graceful raising of the physical into the spiritual. Without God, fleshly desire will turn to naughty action. Marguerite's *Heptameron* says of the woman who knowingly slept with her son that "she must have been some self-sufficient fool, who, in her friarlike dreaming, deemed herself so saintly as to be incapable of sin, just as many of the Friars would have us believe that we can become, merely by our own efforts, which is an exceedingly great error." The woman's presumption was trusting to her individual power to overcome lust "instead of humbling herself and recognizing the powerlessness of our flesh, without God's assistance, to work anything but sin."[85] It is for Marguerite of Navarre as it is in

Shakespeare's Navarre in *Love's Labour's Lost*, where the members of the "little academe" are unsuccessful in their attempt to live a life like that of celibacy because "every man with his affects is born, / Not by might master'd, but by special grace."[86] The *Heptameron* suggests that it is in the nature of men to commit incest; incest of one kind or another is inevitable because without grace, repression of incestuous desire is bound to be unsuccessful.[87]

Marguerite's reformist and spiritualist work involved her conflicts with the traditional Catholic and Protestant movements. That the *Miroir* itself contains no mention of male or female saints, merits, or any purgatory other than the blood of Jesus was noted as a dangerous theoretical tendency, and students of the College of Navarre acted a comedy in which Marguerite was represented as a Fury of Hell.[88] Her biblical commentaries, moreover, were condemned by the censors at the Sorbonne, who ordered her books to be burned. (They were saved by express order of King Francis, her beloved brother.)[89] Marguerite's intermittent support of the antinomian and pantheistic spiritual libertines was attacked by Calvin in his strident pamphlet "Against the . . . Libertines" (1545).[90] Many libertines believed that everything is a manifestation of the Spirit of God; for them, this meant undoing the distinction between "good" and "evil" acts, since nothing could be truly outside God. And they laid out in almost anthropological terms how both a spiritual libertine and a traditional nun, in imitating the Virgin Mary, ought to make of God a father, husband, brother, and son.

> We see, then, that these savages have an unusually great
> horror of incest or are sensitive on the subject to an unusual degree,
> and that they combine this with a peculiarity which remains
> obscure to us of replacing real blood-relationship by totem kinship.
> This latter contrast must not, however, be too much exaggerated,
> and we must remember that the totem prohibitions include
> that against real incest as a special case.
> — Sigmund Freud, *Totem and Taboo*

Totemic tribes that enjoin exogamy (marriage outside the tribe) and allow for the existence of other totemic tribes can thereby avoid incest. But a tribe that believes its totem to be universal and all other human beings to be part of itself — or, teleologically speaking, potential converts to its universalist doctrine — makes exogamy impossible and all intercourse incestuous. Christianity calls for the establishment of such a tribe in its motif of the universal brotherhood of man — ("All ye are brethren"),[91] and in its proselytizing character it claims to think of, and treat as, brothers even those who believe themselves to be non-Christians.

"All ye are brethren" — the question may arise here as to whether Jesus really meant what he said when he said this. For the implication of universal incest or universal annihilation — either to love one another equally or to die out — is a heavy burden. Some theologians, therefore, claim that Jesus did not really mean what he said — or did not really mean it for every-

33

one. They fall off from the words of the New Testament and claim that not all people were meant to become "perfect." To be celibate, they say, is merely a "counsel" — which is "one of the advisory declarations of Christ and the apostles, in medieval theology reckoned as twelve, which are considered not to be universally binding, but to be given as a means of attaining greater moral perfection."[92] Thomas Vautrollier in his *Luther's Commentarie ypon the Epistle to the Galatians* (1575), following out the tendency of such ideas about "perfection" as those of Bale in his 1548 "Epistle Dedicatory" and "Conclusion" to Elizabeth's "Glass," dismissed the controversy as to whether all people should treat all others as siblings: "The Papists divide the gospel into precepts and counsels. To the precepts men are bound (say they) but not the counsels."[93] A few English Renaissance thinkers, however, take Jesus to mean what he says in the New Testament and argue that *Perfection*, by which they mean "the austerity of monastic life, monastic discipline," was the only nondegenerative form of life: Archbishop John Hamilton in his *Catechism* (1552) writes that "matrimonye was degenerat fra the first perfectioun."[94]

Whether or not Jesus meant people to be perfect, the Christian monachal and libertine sects are microcosms of a perfect and potentially cosmic universal siblinghood in which everyone is a Brother or Sister in Christ. Freud remarks that terms like "Sisters in Christ" have analogues in societies where kinship terms "do not necessarily indicate any consanguinity, as ours would do: they represent social rather than physical relationships."[95] But the monachal use of such terms assumes more than this replacement of "physical" relationships by social ones: it assumes the conflation of all social and theological relationships with biological relationships, whereby a Sister or nun who violates the taboo on incest by marrying the Son of her Father is both sacred and taboo.[96]

The Old Way — siblings Becoming Siblings

The rule of the Old Testament is that a man or woman must leave his mother and father and marry in order to fulfill the ancient commandment to be fruitful and multiply. The New says, on the contrary, that a man or woman must give up entirely the old kinship ties — even hate his or her mother and father — in order to replace those ties not with new human ones (to replace a father with a husband) but with divine ones (to replace an entire family with Christ).[97] These divine ties would make every human being a child of adoption to God. Who then are my family? "Ceux qui feront le vouloir de mon Père / Mes frères sont, et ma soeur, et ma mère" (they who do the will of my father, they are my brothers, and my sister, and my mother).[98] For such a child of adoption to God, *all* physical sexuality is as incestuous as it would be for consanguineous brothers and sisters to sleep together. Thus Sisters (nuns) and Brothers (friars and monks) are barred from having sexual intercourse with any human being by rules against not only fornication but also incest, as in Sir Thomas More's traditional attack in 1528 on the monk Luther, who had married a nun, as an incestuous fornicator.[99]

In theory, the love of blood relatives might combine with the fear of earthly incest and make for an individual's decision to join a monastic order or even to found one.[100] Historically, earthly sibling love and heavenly Sibling love have often been joined in the same persons. In the sororal families, or nunneries, of Europe, women gave up all consanguineous ties (for them, he who had been a consanguineous brother was now essentially the same as any other man) and modeled their new family on Mary's relations with God, who was to her as brother, husband, son, and father alike. For women who adopted this sacred fourfold relationship to God, it was an "absolutely profane" act to have sexual intercourse with any person at all. Having become no longer consanguineous sisters to any person and forevermore Sisters to all persons equally, they regarded sexual intercourse with a man who had been a consanguineous brother now no better or worse than sexual intercourse with any other man.

Sigmund Freud, in his discussion of how some people "find happiness . . . along the path of love . . . by directing their love, not to single objects, but to all men alike," calls Saint Francis of Assisi the man who "went furthest in exploiting love for the benefit of an inner feeling of happiness." Franciscan "readiness for universal love of mankind," says Freud, is, "according to one ethical view, . . . the highest standpoint which men can achieve.[101] Yet Francis's love for every being universally seems inextricably linked with love for one Sister in particular, as his remarkable poem "Brother Sun and Sister Moon," suggests.[102] What Francis and Clare could never permit in physical relations becomes a blessing in spiritual relations. (In *The Soul's Journey into God*, the great Franciscan thinker Bonaventure likewise put the balance of all the soul's relationships into its one supposedly whole relationship with God as Christ—a spiritually incestuous relationship, since the soul becomes the daughter, spouse, and sister of God.)[103]

In Christian hagiography generally, a saintly person's intense earthly sibling love is often followed by an extraordinary Sibling love of all human beings, just as if each and every human being had become a brother or sister. The *Acta sanctorum* (Acts of the saints) includes more than 150 men and women who were brother and sister as well as Brother and Sister.[104] Sibling celibates appear from the very beginning of Christian monachism: Saint Anthony, traditionally the first Christian monk, placed his sister in a nunnery when he left the world for the ascetic life. More strikingly, brother-sister liaisons played an important role in the historical beginnings of the Christian orders, for the sister of each of the three great cenobitical founders, Saint Pachomius, Saint Basil, and Saint Benedict, helped to preside over a community of nuns that followed an adaptation of her brother's rules for monks.[105]

Examples of earthly sibling and Christian Sibling love in the lives of great saints whose doctrines were influential in pre-Dissolution England may be useful. Saint Benedict, founder of the order in which Thomas More was educated, visited his sister, Saint Scholastica, once a year. On the last of these visits, according to Gregory the Great, Scholastica entreated Benedict to stay the night. When he adamantly refused, she fell to prayer until a sudden storm arose, so that she had her way. The consummation of that night, spent all in spiritual conversation, may be seen as the incorporation and transcendence of any earthly attraction, physical or otherwise, between the brother and sister.[106]

Legends about Gregory the Great's own life involve incest and its atonement. As Hartmann von Aue tells the story, Saint Gregory was the child of a brother-sister union and unknowingly married his own mother. When he became pope, he forgave his mother's incest and his own, restored Benedictine discipline, and enforced the rule of celibacy for the clergy.[107] This Christian solution — repentence and atonement — to the Oedipal situation suggests that the Catholic orders made possible an atonement for the desire for incest or unchastity, even when the actual act was not in question. The Holy Family atones for the earthly one by making all even.

Some brother and sister saints voiced explicit concern for their siblings' sexuality in terms that border on identification and possessiveness. Saint Leander exhorted his sister Florentina to marry the Son and enter the religious life: "Ah, well-beloved sister, understand the ardent desire which inspires the heart of thy brother to see thee with Christ. . . . Thou art the better part of myself. Woe to me if another take thy crown."[108] And he identifies the virginity of his sister as Sister with the goal of the entire Church: "Christ is already thy spouse, thy father, thine inheritance, thy ransom, thy Lord, thy God."[109] Florentina's earthly crown will be Leander's as much as any man's. Saint Damasus, in an epitaph composed for the tombstone of his sister, Saint Irene, expressed a similar proprietary interest: "A witness of our love (our mother) / Upon leaving the world, / Had given thee, my blood sister, to me as a pure pledge."[110]

Bernard of Clairvaux provides yet another example. After he left home with his brother Andrew to enter the austere monastery of Citeaux, his sister Humberlina came, richly dressed, to visit them. Andrew greeted her, "Why so much solicitude to embellish a body destined for worms and rottenness, while the soul, that now animates it, is burning in everlasting flames?" Humberlina answered, "If my brother Bernard, who is the servant of God, despises my body, let him at least have pity on my soul. Let him come, let him command; and whatsoever he thinks proper to enjoin I am prepared to carry out."[111] Some time thereafter she entered a convent. In Bernard's famous sermons on the Song of Songs, in which some theorists say he demonstrates the "ultimate liberation of the soul," sisterly virginity and the theme "my sister as my wife" (*soror mea sponsa*) are sexualized in a manner familiar from the lives of other sibling saints.[112] Curtius remarks that it is not far from "the mystical love of the Madonna" of Bernard, who "spiritualized love into a divine love," to such cynical descriptions of erotic orgies at convents as the Latin poem "The Council of Love at Remiremont" (c. 1150).[113]

Almost an exact contemporary of Elizabeth, Saint Teresa of Avila ran away from home with one of her nine brothers, Rodrigo, at the age of seven, and with another, Antonio, at the age of twenty, to a Carmelite convent (1534).[114] Originally, Teresa had wanted Antonio to become a Brother and herself a Sister, but in her *Life* she seems to forget Antonio as brother from the moment she enters the Sisterhood.[115] In her *Meditations on the Song of Songs* (1566), she seeks to replace the fraternal love she once had for Antonio by a "spiritual marriage" and rebirth into a family where earthly kinship distinctions do not exist. Just such a transcendence of consanguinity was Teresa's essential goal for the discalced Carmelite order that she helped to found: "For the love of the Lord refrain from making individual friendships, however holy, for even among brothers and sisters such things are apt to be poisonous."[116] Reminding her Sisters to "think of the brotherhood which you share with this great God" as "children of this God," she exhorts them, and all Christians, "to make our actions conform to our words—in short, to be like children of such a Father and the brethren of such a Brother."[117] Saint John of the Cross, an ideological mainstay of Teresa's order, wrote in his *Precautions*, "You should have an equal love for or an equal forgetfulness of all persons, whether relatives or not, and withdraw your heart from relatives as much as from others."[118] In precisely this way Teresa erased and raised herself above differences between family and nonfamily. The saintly Teresa, who verges in her *Life* on confessing to spiritual incest (a biographer, pressing too hard, might conclude that she made love with a certain Dominican Brother), came to accept the ordinary taboo on sexual intercourse with a brother only when she accepted the extraordinary taboo on sexual intercourse with any human being.[119]

Widespread, therefore, was the monachal attempt to transform sibling love into Sibling love—and to test that transformation. A few Catholic orders allowed close physical communication between siblings or Siblings in "double cloisters": monasteries and nunneries standing side by side. Among the Faremoutiers, who developed double cloisters in the seventh century, Saint Cagnoald ruled the monks in one wing, and his sister, Saint Burgundofara, ruled the nuns in the other.[120] The Order of Fontevrault encouraged nuns and monks to sleep together in the same bed[121]—their doing so for the "mortification of the flesh" is the basis of one of Marguerite of Navarre's tales.[122] The Brigittines adopted the same organization, and the order of Saint Gilbert of Sempringham (the only order founded in England) was a double cloister of cohabiting Brothers and Sisters.[123]

In all these examples we see that the attempt to flee from the family to the Sisterhood or Brotherhood, from mother and father to Mother Superior and Pope, relocates the problem of incest from the consanguineous family to the Christian family. Consanguineous *siblings* (brothers or sisters) who become religious *Siblings* (Brothers or Sisters) avoid incest either because they thereby adopt chasteness or because the distinction between chastity and incest is thereby erased.

The New Way—Siblings Becoming spouses

The orders and the siblings or Siblings we have so far considered attempted to transcend the desire for incest through chastity, to solve the problem of the desire for incest by getting over it, rising above earthly sex and incest by lifting it from earth to heaven: "We ourselves groan within ourselves, waiting for the adoption, to wit, the redemption of the body."[124] But other orders, ultimately more influential in shaping our present world's emphasis on *fraternité* and *liberté*, tried to solve the problem in the obverse way: they adapted to earth the universalist love that the traditional orders had reserved only for heaven. For them there was a corporeal redemption that did not so much spiritualize the body for the "perfect" as liberate it even for the "imperfect."

As at the origin of Catholicism there are siblings who become Siblings (that is, brothers and sisters who become Brothers and Sisters), so at the origin of Protestantism there are Catholic Siblings who become spouses (that is, Brothers and Sisters who become husbands and wives). In the context of the English Reformation, this kind of incestuous marriage constitutes psychologically the decisive characteristic in the life of Elizabeth and sociologically the decisive moment in the history of Renaissance sexuality.

Among Brothers who became husbands were monks who directly influenced the education of Princess Elizabeth. One was Bernardino Ochino, whom Elizabeth knew and whose *Sermo de Christo* she translated for her half-brother Edward in 1547. (Ochino was driven from England during the Catholic Mary Tudor's accession to the throne in 1553.)[125] Another was John Bale, who, having argued for the impossibility of absolute temperance, forsook his monastic habit and got married almost as an act of religion. (In Bale's play *The Three Laws of Nature* [1538, 1562], the allegorical figure "Sodomy" appears dressed as a monk.)[126] In the material he attached to Elizabeth's "Glass," Bale attacks the false doctrine of kinship that inheres in Catholicism; and in *The Image of Both Churches* he insists that neither popish orders nor gossipry (godparenting) bring with them any diriment impediment to marriage: "No more shall that free state of living be bound under the yoke of thy damnable dreams, either for vows unadvised, nor for popish orders, nor yet for any gossipry, but be at full liberty."[127]

There are other precedents for Sibling marriage: for example, Leo Judae, a disciple of Zwingli, married a Beguine in 1523; and the Franciscan monk François Lambert proposed in 1528 that his monastery might become a school of marriage! (Consider also the remarkable papal legitimatization of Brother Rabelais's bastard children.)[128] None of these Sister-Brother marriages, however, is as important as Brother Martin Luther's 1525 marriage to the Cistercian Sister Catherine von Bora. Luther's doctrine of justification by faith instead of by acts, and his corresponding view of the relationship between intent and act, sparked the Reformation. An Augustinian eremite who thought that his unfulfilled desires made him prey for the devil, Luther argued that few if any men were "perfect" enough to be celibate.[129] Thus he denounced both monastic vows and distinctive dress for the clergy.[130]

Any Catholic in England knew that such a marriage as Luther's to Catherine was incestuous. Friars and monks — spiritual or "ghostly" fathers, Bale calls them — were regarded much like biological fathers. Thus we read in the thirteenth century, "Incest, thet is, bituhe sibbe, fleschliche oðer gasteliche";[131] and in the fifteenth century, "Inceste . . . is bitwene sibbe fleshli or gasteli."[132] The late fifteenth-century *Treatise on the Ten Commandments* includes the rule that "incestus is he þat delith with nonne, with kosyn, or with a maydon, þe wich is called defloracio."[133] And in Lydgate's *Fall of Princes* it is written that "incestus is . . . trespassyng with kyn or with blood, Or froward medlyng with hir that is a nunne."[134] Similarly, it was considered incest for anyone to have sexual relations with a godparent. Chaucer had written: "For right so as he that en-gendreth a child is his fleshly fader, right so is his godfader his fader espiritueel. For which a womman may in no lasse synne assemblen with hire godsib than with hire owene flesshly brother."[135]

It was in this tradition that Sir Thomas More, author of the great *Utopia* (1516) — which exhibits a Stoic cosmopolitanism and propertal communism reflecting aspects of the Benedictine order[136] — accused Martin Luther in 1528 of committing incest when he married Sister Catherine. Any human being who be-comes a nun or friar, More argued, commits incest when she or he has sexual intercourse with anyone, whether with a con-sanguineous kinsperson or not; therefore, clerical marriage "defileth the priest more than double or trebel whoredom."[137] In his *Confutaycon with Tindale*, More makes clear his view of Luther and his wife, "the frere and the nunne":

> Let not therefore Tyndall (good reder) wyth his gay gloryouse wordes carye you so fast & so far away, but that ye remembre to pull hym bakke by the sleue a lytle, and aske hym whyther his owne hyghe spirytuall doctour mayster Martyne Luther hym selfe, beynge specyally borne agayne & new created of the spyr-yte, whom god in many places of holy scrypture hath com-maunded to kepe his vowe made of chastyte when he then so far contrarye there vnto toke out of relygyon a spouse of Cryste, wedded her hym selfe in reproche of wedloke, called her his wyfe, and made her his harlot, and in doble despyte of maryage and relygyon both, lyueth wyth her openly and lyeth wyth her nyghtly, in shamefull *inceste* and abominable lycherye.[138]

Incest of a kind, then, was the charge not only against such secular notables as Anne Boleyn, Elizabeth's earthly mother, but also against such religious notables as Bernardino Ochino and John Bale, Elizabeth's spiritual fathers.

8. LIBERTINISM AND LIBERTY

Thou'rt my Mother from the Womb,
Wife, Sister, Daughter, to the Tomb.
— William Blake, *For the Sexes*:
The Gates of Paradise

I f sex is what most men and women want, whether they
know it or not, and if "all ye are brethren," as Jesus says,[139]
then all men and women want incest. If, in this context,
grace means doing what one wants guiltlessly, then Christian
liberty allows for — and even mandates — a libertinism of the
body. Liberty, or libertinism, amounts to universal incest en-
acted without guilt.

The idea that guiltless incest is a sign of grace appears even at
the historical origin of Christianity. For example, the Corinth-
ian sect's acts of incest — which Paul calls "such fornication as is
not so much as named among the Gentiles, that one should
have his father's wife"[140] — may have been not "deed[s] done
secretly out of weakness but . . . ideological act[s] done openly
with the approval of at least an influential sector of the community."[141] In fact, the sect had actually taken Paul's own words
about freedom from the law ("All things are lawful for me") to
indicate, among other things, freedom from such Old Testament rules as those concerning incest ("The nakedness of thy
father's wife shalt thou not uncover").[142] The sect of the Es-
senes potentially offers much the same endorsement of incest,
as Rabelais's parody of it suggests.

In the medieval period the endorsement of guiltless incest

6. *Illustration from William Blake's* For Children *(1793), later issued as* For the Sexes: The Gates of Paradise. *Blake's caption reads,* "I have said to the Worm: / Thou art my mother & my sister." *Reproduced by courtesy of the Beinecke Rare Books and Manuscripts Library, Yale University.*

45

was crucial to the lay order called the Brethren of the Free Spirit, which had throughout Europe perhaps hundreds of thousands of adherents between the thirteenth and seventeenth centuries.[143] For the Brethren, the spiritually incestuous relations of the Virgin Mary to God were to be reproduced in the Edenic or paradisiacal state of grace. Their motto was the Pauline rule *Ubi spiritus, ibi libertas*: when the spirit of the Lord is in one, then the law is erased, and one is raised above the law.[144]

The similarity between the so-called heretical sect of the Brethren and traditional Christian orders, for whom incest is anathema, should not be overlooked. Similar motivations and appeals to grace are involved (1) when a religious celibate in the traditional orders overcomes sexual desire and loves everyone equally as universal siblings and (2) when a religious libertine in the Brethren of the Free Spirit overcomes the restrictions of law or conscience and loves everyone equally, including siblings. Both the celibate of the traditional orders and the libertine of the Brethren hypothesizes a universal siblinghood in which sleeping with a brother is no worse than sleeping with any other man. The religious celibate seeks liberty from physical desire; the libertine seeks liberty from rules that restrict physical intercourse. But for both, in the words of Saint Paul, "where the Spirit of the Lord is, there is liberty."[145]

The key spokesperson for the sect, Marguerite Porete, though she was burned at the stake by the official Church, remains our most trustworthy source about the early Brethren; most other sources are obviously hostile.[146] Her remarkable *Miroir des simple âmes* (Mirror of simple souls) stands as an important document in the history of Christian thought, with links to the "libertine" Marguerite of Navarre's *Miroir de l'âme pécheresse* (Mirror of the sinful soul)[147] — which Calvin attacked as antinomian in *Against the Fantastic Sect of the Libertines*[148] —

and to the doctrine of "liberty, equality, and fraternity" of the French Revolution.[149]

The *Miroir* of Marguerite Porete was influential in England (as well as elsewhere in Europe).[150] In the sixteenth century, several Middle English translations circulated, just when John Champneys was arguing that God condones for his chosen people such "bodily necessities" as "fornication, adultery, . . . or any other sin."[151] The Free Spirit directly affected the doctrines of the Elizabethan "Family of Love" and its communal sexual practices. And it influenced the seventeenth-century Ranters and Levelers, whose attempts to transcend ordinary norms of "right" and "wrong," or chasteness and incestuousness,[152] eventually involved both the doctrine of liberty and fraternity of the French Revolution and the quasi-medieval ideologies of other nineteenth-century utopian projects. John Noyes's incest-practicing Perfectionists in Oneida, New York, for example, looked to the Diggers and Levelers of Commonwealth times as well as to the Brethren as their precursors.[153] The American hippie movement of the 1960s, especially the San Francisco Diggers, seemed similarly influenced by the Free Spirit.[154]

England of the sixteenth century was rife with antinomian, Anabaptist, and Wycliffite Lollard trends.[155] Anabaptists in London asserted "that a man regenerate could not sin; that though the outward man sinned, the inward man sinned not."[156] And they insisted, probably in response to juridical questions about incest in the Holy Family, that Jesus did not take flesh from his mother.[157] Bale takes up the cause of the martyred antinomian Anne Askew in his "Conclusion" to the "Glass," and in booklets published in November 1546 and January 1547 he similarly defends Askew's heterodox views regarding transubstantiation (see Illustration 7).[158] He published these, as well as Elizabeth's "Glass" (*Godly Medytacyon*, 1548),

47

in Reformation Germany, where the Anabaptists of Münster practiced a kind of polygamy that did not allow for the sort of distinction between "mother" and "aunt" on which traditional society, as well as such typical Elizabethan works as *Hamlet*, rely.[159] Catherine Parr was herself suspected of favoring Anne Askew.[160] Joan Boucher, Askew's colleague and a member of an English Anabaptist community in England, was martyred in 1550 for her heretical views concerning the Virgin Mary as spiritual and fleshly mother — and as the daughter, sister, and wife of God. The English Anabaptists, like their European counterparts, tried thus to erase and rise above the old distinctions between good and evil, even chastity and incest, and in the spirit of the Free Spirit they asserted publicly that "when the spirit of the lord is in one, one can do no sin."

The doctrine of the Free Spirit is largely defined by this attempt to return to prelapsarian innocence and "perfect" liberty. The Second Clementine Decree, promulgated at the Council of Vienne in 1311, announced of the Siblings of the Free Spirit that "those who have achieved this state of perfection and absolute freedom are no longer subject to obedience and law or obligated to follow ecclesiastical regulations, for where divine spirit rules, there is liberty."[161] For at least one Brother of the Free Spirit, John Hartmann of Achmansteten, spiritual liberty meant "the complete cessation of remorse and the attainment of a state of sinlessness."[162] This entailed total transcendence of the post-Edenic taboo against incest:

> The free man could do as he wished, including fornicate with his sister or his mother, and anywhere he wished, including at the altar. He [Hartmann] added that it was more natural with his sister than any other woman because of their consanguinity. His justification lay in being perfectly free and bound by no law or ecclesiastical statutes and precepts; such a man was a Free

The first examinacy=
on of Anne Askewe, latelye mar
tyred in Smythfelde, by the Ro=
mysh popes vpholders, with
the Elucydacyon of
Johan Bale.

The veryte of the lorde endureth foreuer.

Psalme 116.

BIB
LIA

Anne Askewe stode fast by thys veryte of
God to the ende.

Fauoure is disceytfull/ and bewtye is a vay
ne thynge. But a woman that feareth the
lorde/ is worthye to be praysed. She ope-
neth her mouthe to wysdome/ and in her lan
guage is the lawe of grace. Prouerb. xxxj.

7. *Anne Askew confronting the papal dragon. Woodcut in Askew,*
The First Examinacyon *(1546). Reproduced by permission
of the Folger Shakespeare Library.*

Spirit in contradistinction to the gross ones who were subject to existing authority of the church. His sister, far from losing her chastity, increased it as a result of their intercourse.[163]

The same view appears in the testimony of Conrad Kannler, who said that he was "at liberty to have sexual intercourse with mother and sister, although he did not believe God would permit it for the imperfect."[164]

In her *Mirror*, Marguerite Porete writes, "Friends, love and do what you want."[165] In the state of spiritual liberty she experiences "that love [that] maketh of the innocents that thei don nothing . . . but if it please them."[166] In such a state, says Marguerite, "the soul taketh leeve of vertues";[167] "the soul . . . giveth to nature al that he askith withoute grucchynge of conscience."[168] It is as if one were restored to a state of Edenic or paradisiacal simplicity, a state where the ability to commit incest without feeling guilty is itself a sign of grace, as it was for certain English Ranters.[169] When the spirit of God is in me, "I belong to the liberty of nature, and all that my nature desires I satisfy. I am a natural man." According to one adept, "the Spirit of Freedom or the Free Spirit is attained when one is wholly transformed into God."[170] "Then is God in us, and all we are in Him, and He in all men," wrote Princess Elizabeth.[171] A person's guiding principle must be "Do what you want" — the single rule of Rabelais's anti-abbey of Thélème.[172] Not to enact what one desires to enact would be in itself a sign of disunion with God.

Involved in this appeal to freedom was Marguerite of Porete's radical heresy: that perfect and free souls are fourfold kin with God. Perfect souls, she writes, have transcended regular kinship and become "daughters, sisters, and spouses of kings," and as such they attain the state of pure liberty.[173] Marguerite of Navarre and Princess Elizabeth suggest much the same: "O what union is this, since (through faith) I am sure of Thee. And now I may call Thee son, father, spouse, and brother. Father, brother, son, husband. . . .[174] (Marguerite Porete was heretical in other ways as well. She translated the Bible into the vernacular,[175] insisted that becoming one in Christ raises men and women above gender differences,[176] and claimed that one could be saved by faith, without "good" works.)[177]

The Brethren's liberty was often misinterpreted as empty libertinage or mocked as pagan sexual communism. This charge the Middle English translator tried to refute when he wrote: "Now God forbeede that eny be so fleischli to thenke that it schulde mene to give to nature eny lust that drawith to fleischli synne, for God knowith wel it is not so ymened."[178] In any case, such labels do not go to the heart of the issue. What characterizes a celibate fraternal order (such as the Franciscans) is its liberty *from* flesh or its razing the desires of the flesh and raising them to heaven. What characterizes a libertine order such as the Brethren of the Free Spirit is its graceful liberty *of* flesh: "Now libertines are named after the liberty of the flesh, which their doctrine seems to allow."[179] Although it might at first seem that between the two kinds of sexual freedom there is all the difference in the world, religious celibacy and religious libertinism are significantly linked, and both sides resonate with the larger antinomian and Manichaean debates of the sixteenth century.[180]

9. FRATERNAL LOVE VERSUS RESPECT FOR PARENTS

> To endow parents with the authority of wisdom,
> it is first of all necessary to look upon them as nonsexual
> beings, i.e., as non-possible objects of sexual desire. The
> prohibition against incest embodies this reverence.
> — Seth Benardete, on Thomas Aquinas

> *Tous de goneis tima* (Honour thy parents).
> — Elizabeth, trans. John Bale

Teleologically, incest dissolves the *pater* (father) in the *liber* (son) and replaces the patriarchy with a radical egalitarian liberty.[181] Sexual liberty would restructure kinship relations by destroying the crucial distinction between generations. In 1544 Thomas Elyot and George Chapman thus use the term *libertine* to mean "any man of bonde ancestour" and "an urban freeman."[182] The tension here between the tendency toward liberty in religion and "parentarchy" in politics is inevitable because the practice of incest, whether of the ordinary sort, (as by libertines) or the extraordinary sort (as by religious celibates as members of the Holy Family), which true liberty would seem to entail, shows a politically consequential disrespect of one's parents and hence to parentarchal political order. The Roman *respectus parentelae*, the reverence due to near kin, is the most frequent argument against incest advanced in Western culture.

In England of the sixteenth century, the Family of Love, a radical libertine religious sect, claimed that all its member were "one Being" with the "Godded man: and so bee all named Gods and Children of the most highest."[183] They assumed that all "are equal in degree among themselves; all Kings, and a kingdome of kings" and announced a communist society where a new brother's "goodes shal be in common amongst the rest of his berth."[184] With this subversive aspect, the Family of Love was savagely parodied on the more politically conservative English stage.[185]

Like libertinism, traditional monachism had a subversive aspect. Originally or ideally, monachism was an essentially revolutionary "sibling" movement against more conservative "parentarchal" authority.[186] Even before the formal establishment of eremitic communities in the early Church, ascetics joined together in single residences in familylike sibling relationships that excluded intergenerational hierarchies. The fourth-century pseudo-Clementian epistle "To Virgins," for example, refers to such ascetics as were living in "spiritual marriage" as brothers and sisters, and it emphasizes Jesus' injunction to "call no man *father*."[187] Patriarchal ecclesiastical critics such as Eusebius of Emesa viewed these practices with alarm because they furthered "either radical asceticism or radical libertinism."[188] They feared not only a communal libertinism but a corresponding radical propertal communism and even a propertyless condition. Saint Jerome writes, "Since you have been consecrated to perpetual virginity, your possessions are not your possessions [*tua non tua sunt*], because they now belong to Christ"; and Saint Gregory of Nyssa praised his sister, Sister Macrina, because she "found delight in temperance" and at the same time "thought it affluence to own nothing."[189] Saint John Chrysostom says, in his essay on virginity, "Now is not the time for matrimony and possessions; rather it is the time for penury and for that unusual way of life that will be of value to us in the time to come."[190] In this spirit, certain Catholic orders do not merely endorse poverty; they raze all property relations just as they raze all sexual relations. John Chrysostom succinctly expresses the politically threatening aspect of this rejection of possessions by calling virginity *isaggelos polité*, an extreme homogenization at once communist and incestuous.

In its essential form, then, monachal fraternity militates against any and all propertal and sexual ownership, making monachism in and of itself a cause of political conflict. Many Elizabethans feared the political dissolution that is implicit in the rejection of ordinary kinship structures (the parentarchy) and ordinary economic structures (property).

During the Tudor Renaissance, as throughout the history of the Christian West, a political ruler was viewed generally as a parent and the people as her or his children.[191] For a child to beat his father was thus, according to the Elizabethan Thomas Nashe, tantamount to upsetting the natural and political order: "It is no maruaille if euery Alehouse vaunt the table of the world vpside downe, since the child beateth his father."[192] And they understood the link between political dissolution and the sexual liberty that would destroy respect for the parent.[193] Bishop Stephen Gardiner thus compares the radical libertine position "all is for the flesh, women and meat with liberty of hand and tongue" to the political "dissolution and dissipation of all estates."[194] Moreover, few persons in Elizabethan England could overlook the connection between the monastic orders and a more specific threat of political chaos — revolt. The orders had been prominent among the opponents of Henry VIII, and one of the reasons he gave for his notorious Dissolution of the Monasteries was a fear that monks would incite the commons to rebel.[195] During Elizabeth's reign about two hundred Catholic priests were executed, and monks had figured in such anti-Tudor plots as the Northern Rebellion and the Archpriest Controversy.[196]

Fraternal Love versus Respect for Parents

By the early seventeenth century, the challenge by proponents of Brotherhood and Sisterhood to religious and political parentarchy was growing into modern liberalism. In that
century the defenders of absolute monarchy had such spokes-
persons as King James I of England, who in his *Trew Law*
(1598) stressed the identity between the duty of a subject and
that of a child;[197] and Robert Filmer, who in his *Patriarcha*
provided both sides of the debate with a major rallying point.
John Locke, among others, came to be the political spokesperson for the advocates of liberalism. Locke criticized Filmer's
conceptual reliance on a "strange kind of domineering phantom, called 'the fatherhood' " and opposed to it his own idea of
all men free and equal in the state of nature.[198] For Locke, as
Norman O. Brown puts it, "liberty . . . means equality among
brothers (sons)."[199] The *liberi*, or free sons, of the French Revolution — and to a lesser extent the English Revolution — sought
to turn the world upside down by killing the king who heads the
family.

Whether or not monachal resistance to the parentarchal English monarch in the sixteenth century can be explained as a
speculative extension of monachal fraternalism as well as by the
specific historical circumstances surrounding the Dissolution,
there is little doubt that in these times such rulers as Henry
VIII himself feared in certain religious and lay movements a
tendency toward liberty. They believed that the public needs to
believe — or they wanted the public to believe — in the "strange
kind of domineering phantom" of the father. The absolutist
king and his apologists were right in one sense: the struggle
between liberty and absolute monarchy did involve the break-
down of the old family order and the development of a new
political one. Lawrence Stone contends, in *Crisis of the Aris-
tocracy*, that in the sixteenth and seventeenth centuries "the

55

most remarkable change inside the family was the shift away from paternal authority"; further, "it was slowly recognized that limits should be set not merely to the powers of kings . . . but also [to] those of parents and husbands."[200] And libertine religious groups, arguing that "where liberty is, there is the spirit of God," eventually provided the liberal revolutions of England and France with their most extreme ideologies. The Marquis de Sade was emphatic in arguing, in his proposals for the French Revolution, that France would become a real republic only when men could call their sisters Mother.[201]

In the Renaissance tug-of-war between spiritual liberty and political parentarchy, Princess Elizabeth in her "Glass" and Queen Elizabeth in her reign toed the line between spiritual libertinism's claim that consanguinity and the particular family do not count and parentarchy's claim that they do. There was, for example, the old debate about the real substance of nobility, and hence about the right to rule of a bastard child whose parents hardly deserved (full) respect. Here Bale helps Elizabeth to establish a notion of kinship that would serve her as Virgin Queen and enable her to develop an ideology of family and nation that would endure for centuries.

In his "Epistle Dedicatory" and "Conclusion" Bale introduces the following propositions:

(1) Elizabeth is of noble blood, whether she is legitimate or illegitimate: "Nobility . . . she hath gotten of blood in the high degree, having a most victorious king to her father, and a most virtuous and learned king again to her brother."[202]

(2) Noble blood does not confer true nobility. Nobility resides neither in "renowned birth or succession of blood" nor in "worthiness of progeny." It is not by blood but by plain virtue that one becomes God's child of adoption:

"Of the most excellent kind of nobility is he sure (most virtuous and learned lady) which truly believeth and seeketh to do the will of the eternal father, for thereby is he brought forward and promoted into that heavenly kindred. By that means becometh he the dear brother, sister, and mother of Christ, a citizen of heaven with the apostles and prophets, yea the child of adoption and heir together with Christ in the heavenly inheritance. No such children left Socrates behind him, neither yet Demosthenes, Plato, nor Cicero with all their pleasant wisdom and eloquence. No such heritage could great Alexander the Macedonian bequeath to his posterity, neither yet Charles, Arthur, nor David."[203]

(3) Elizabeth's production of the "Glass" itself proves that she has in abundance true nobility as virtue. "Of this nobility I have no doubt (Lady most faithfully studious) but that you are, with many other noble women and maidens more in this blessed age." As evidence, Bale points to Elizabeth's book as a "spiritual exercise of her inner soul with God," and to her allowing the book to be published: "By your godly fruits" you shall be known, he reminds us.[204]

(4) Whether consanguinity counts (in which case Elizabeth has it) or doesn't count (in which case Elizabeth does not need it), Elizabeth does not hate, or even regard indifferently, her consanguineous parents. The liberal Jesus of the New Testament is sometimes interpreted as encouraging his followers and all God's children to hate their parents: "If any man come to me, and hate not his father, and mother, and wife, and children, and brethren, and sisters . . . he cannot be my disciple."[205]

(5) Elizabeth, on the contrary, follows the rules of the Roman *respectus parentelae* and the Hebraic Ten Commandments. Bale

draws our attention to Elizabeth's Greek phrase *tous de goneis tima* to prove her respect for parental authority: "Your . . . clause in the Greek inciteth us to the right worshipping of God in spirit and verity, to honoring of our parents in the seemly offices of natural children, and to the reverent using of our Christian equals in the due ministrations of love. Neither Benedict nor Bruno, Dominick nor Francis (which have of long years been boasted for the principal patrons of religion) ever gave to their superstitious brethren so pure precepts of sincere Christianity."[206]

In the old debate about whence nobility comes, bastardy and incest generally play major roles, as reflected in Shakespeare's *All's Well That Ends Well.*[207] But Bale and Elizabeth manage to walk the line between rejecting and reverencing consanguineous familial and national parenthood, between the spiritual mysticism wherein all are one in God and the political fact whereby someone lords it over others.

The central motif of Elizabeth's "Glass" — the spiritually incestuous relationship to one's Lord — was important not only in the Christian devotional and monachal institutions of Roman Christianity but also in the political and religious institutions of the ancient Roman Empire, where Roman Christianity first took hold on the political life of Europe. Indeed, Roman Christendom seems to have incorporated both the political and religious institutions of the Roman Empire concerning spiritual and physical "fourfold kinship." In the political sphere, for example, the Roman Empress Livia (wife of Augustus Caesar, who vied with Jesus for the title of Lord God) stood in multifold kinship relations to Caesar. And Agrippina (wife of that Claudius who first subjugated Britain in Rome's name) stood precisely in a fourfold relationship to Rome's God. Tacitus, the historian, remarks of the incestuous Agrippina that her kind of distinction was "traditionally reserved for priests and sacred objects," since she was remarkable as "the *daughter* of a great commander and the *sister, wife,* and *mother* of emperors."[208] And in the religious sphere, the figure of fourfold kinship informed the Roman Empire's institutions of adrogation (adoption) and the Vestal Virgins; the nunneries of Christendom were the Roman Christian end of both institutions.[209]

The incorporation and supposed transcendence by Roman Christianity of such Roman imperial institutions as the Empress and the Vestal involved the eventual transformation of the Vestals' Palladia — the archaic idols symbolic of an older matriarchy, probably Trojan, to which the Vestals were devoted — into the Christian Sisterhood's spiritually incestuous Virgin Mary. The transformation meant a certain power, or at least ideal autonomy, for the Sisters. Incest, which Empress Agrippina practiced on the physical plane and which the Roman Vestals raised to a spiritual plane, helped provide some women of imperial Rome and Roman Christendom with a certain independence. As a violation of propertal (economic) as well as sexual "norms," this incest provided a potential refuge for those who refused to traffic — or to be trafficked in. Having rejected their consanguineous families, the Vestals were exempt, for example, from the *patria potestas*: no human had the *patria potestas* over the Vestal — only the divine *pontifex maximus*, the Vestal's religious father (*pater*). (For example, the Vestal could free any prisoner she happened to run across on the way to execution and, more important in the present context, she could dispose of her property at will.) The nunneries of Christendom, whose family ties inform the work of two reform-minded queens of almost imperial power (Elizabeth and Marguerite), had much the same liberating and economic effect on their inmates: "A convent was . . . the only place where a girl could escape her father's absolute authority."[210] And an ideal Mother Superior transformed to the political world would make for a real Empress.

In preparing the stage for the supposedly illegitimate and incestuously conceived Elizabeth to assume a new political place in the English nation, the reformer John Bale sought to define in British terms the matriarchy underlying Roman institutions. Imperial Rome's original institutions, suggests Bale, were the Trojan matriarchal ones. Aeneas's ancestors ruled in Britain no less than in Rome, says Bale, relying on the old British tradition, memorialized in Geoffrey of Monmouth and elsewhere, that the British and Trojan nations are one and the same. And in this same vein Bale recalls the old view that "in the reign of Belinus [among the first British kings] the Trojan and British custom was succession by primogeniture."[211]

That British monarchs should succeed to the throne in the supposedly Trojan fashion, by simple primogeniture regardless of gender, was no small point. And Bale's pro-British attack on Roman Catholicism involves centrally his myth of the British *domina* — an empress or *regina* who holds the throne by her own right of inheritance.[212] Women who inherited the throne were not common in Christendom.[213] Marguerite of Navarre, certainly, knew the traditional "Salic law," which supposedly kept women from doing so.[214] The Salic law, known to readers of Shakespeare's *Henry V,* insisted that a royal or aristocratic woman was a kind of property and could not herself inherit property.[215] Though she might rule as coheir or regent — as did Catherine de Medici, who became queen of France in 1547[216] — she could not inherit the throne. Bale, understanding how the idealization of woman in Christian institutions had "disempowered" her in the political sphere, wanted to prepare the way for Elizabeth to inherit the kingdom in uncommon fashion.

Among early defenses of women (Bale lists Boccaccio's and Plutarch's), Bale's catalogues of famous women are unique in their praise of women's political and military as well as religious accomplishments,[217] and their direct attack on the prevailing derogatory view of women.[218] And they generally involve positions against a supposedly perverted Rome, positions that are both antiimperialist (since British nationalists would take the cause of Boudicca, or Boadicea, and other great British queens against the Roman Emperor Claudius and his successors) and anti-Catholic (since nationalists would take the cause of the early Celtic church and Wycliffe against that of the Roman popes).[219]

In a nationalist and matriarchal spirit, then, Bale culls from histories and legends of Britain the names of great queens who ruled by might or right: Boudicca, who fought the Romans; Helena, who inherited the throne like a man; and Gwendolyn, Cordelia, Marcia, and others.[220] Among British women who ruled by reason of inheritance (*iure hereditario*) were Sexburth, who succeeded in 672 to the royal throne of the Kingdom of Wessex, and Elfleda, the widow of King Ethelred and the daughter of King Alfred, who ruled as *domina* from 912 to 918. And there was the famous Empress Matilda, who ruled with her husband as a kind of "imperial jointress to this . . . state"—like Gertrude in Shakespeare's *Hamlet*.[221] The Empress Matilda's political status as *domina* was controversial (as is Gertrude's) since it was not clear how far she "was to reign independently of her second husband [Geoffrey Plantagenet], married 1128, a few months after Henry [I] had imposed her as his heir."[222] Edelradus in Saxo Grammaticus's twelfth-century *Historiae Danicae*—a source for *Hamlet*—may well have said "aliquanto speciosius mares quam feminas regni usum decere nouerat."[223] But British women ruled and, in Elizabethan times, ruled well.

The position that a woman should have a hereditary right to rule independently of her husband was, in the context of the British Reformation, a Protestant and nationalist turn by which Bale was able to steer an ideologically effective course between native British and alien Roman custom. It was a course that would help transform the cultic figure of the Roman Vestal Virgin or Catholic Virgin Mary, which placed women on an ideal pedestal (already manipulated to Reformist purposes in Marguerite's *Miroir*), not only into the image of a martyred Protestant saint—like the anti–Roman Catholic Anne Askew in the sixteenth century and the anti–Roman Empire Saint Blandina in the second century[224]—but also (back) into the supposedly original Trojan figure of propertied matriarchal and victorious empress who plays, in the real sphere of politics, the role of Mother Superior in a national siblinghood.

Englande: Thes vyle popych swyne hath clene exyled my hos-
             band.
King Johan: Who ys thy husbond? Tel me, good gentyll Yngland.
Englande: For soth, God hym-selfe, the spowse of every sort
             That seke hym in fayth to ther sowlys helth and com-
             fort.
             —John Bale, *King Johan*

In the intellectual development of the orphan princess and in the ideological life of the nation during the period of the English Reformation, Elizabeth's "Glass" represents a complex and politically fruitful vacillation between physical and spiritual incest. It is a vacillation that suggests how a nation, reeling from the conjunction of English and French identities that began in 1066, would now be informed by a new ideology of siblinghood and reformed by a great queen.

Bale's additions to the "Glass" prepare Elizabeth and the English people for her monarchy; even her gender, he says, is sufficient to make her "king."[225] He imagines that the princess will become in time a kind of Protestant spouse of Christ: "If such fruits come forward in childhood, what will follow and appear when discretion and years shall be more ripe and ancient?"[226] But Elizabeth actually became neither an ordinary monarch nor a Protestant nun — despite some public identification by herself with Saint Elizabeth and with the heavenly Mary as Virgin Queen.[227] She became instead the *sponsa Angliae*. As the mature leader of Britain, she participated in making a nation-state in ways Machiavelli did not foresee and in providing that nation with liberty and sovereignty.

Elizabeth participated, for example, in bringing to political fruition an ideology of spousal political economy. Two thousand years earlier, Aristotle had written in his *Politics*:

> Since there are three parts of expertise in household management (*oikonomia*) — expertise in mastery, which was spoken of earlier, expertise in paternal [rule], and expertise in marital [rule] — [the latter two must now be taken up. These differ fundamentally from the former, since one ought] to rule a wife and children as free persons, though it is not the same mode of rule in each case, the wife being ruled in political, the children in kingly fashion.[228]

As Thomas Aquinas underscores, the difference that Aristotle remarks between a parent as ruler and a spouse as ruler marks one distinction between a mere "monarchy" and a genuine "polis."[229]

In the early medieval period a prevalent notion was that the ruler was a monarchal *pater* or *papa* to his people. The subsequent metaphor of the Christian ruler marrying the body politic was based mainly on the way a bishop at his ordination became the spouse of his church.[230] But in the sixteenth century, jurist Lucas de Pennas published his influential comparison of the ruler with a spouse (1544), and Charles de Grassaille called King Francis I — Marguerite of Navarre's brother — the king *maritus reipublicae* (1538–45).[231] Other French political thinkers (including François Hotman, Pierre Grégoire, and Jean Bodin) similarly chronicled and encouraged a politically crucial transformation of a bishop's marriage with the *corpus mysticum* (the Church) into the monarch's marriage with the *corpus politicum* — or with the *corps politique et mystique*, as the jurist Guy Coquille put it.[232] In earlier times, the ring that the prince received at his coronation had been interpreted as a *signaculum fidei*, not as a mark of marriage.[233] But now the coronation ring was understood as a "marque de ceste reciproque conjonction" between royal ruler and kingdom": at the coronation of Henry II of France in 1547, the king thus married the realm itself: "Le roy espousa solemnellement le royaume."[234] And throughout the century such theorists as René Choppin were declaring, "Rex curator *Reipubliciae* ac *mysticus* . . . ipsius *coniunx*" (the king is the mystical spouse of the *res publica*).[235]

In England, too, jurists were interpreting the "mystical body" of the realm as a royal spouse.[236] There was a gradual ideological movement away from an ideology of the ruler as an intergenerational parent toward an ideology of the ruler as an intragenerational spouse in a new siblinghood.[237] At her accession in 1558, Elizabeth, educated in the wake of these events in France, showed the Commons her coronation ring and reminded them not only that the English were her "children and relations" but also that England was her "husband."[238]

But Queen Elizabeth, beyond insisting that the monarch was both parent and spouse, moved toward ending or transcending all kinship. Just as the young Elizabeth meditated in the "Glass" on the significance of the collapse of kinship distinctions for spiritual libertines (Marguerite of Navarre), for nuns or Sisters (those whose houses Henry VIII dissolved), and for physically incestuous persons (Anne Boleyn), so the mature Elizabeth institutionalized that collapse on a national plane at once secular and chaste. The breaking of kindred to which the young Elizabeth first refers in the "Glass" in 1544—"Thou hast broken the kindred of my old father"[239]—was the first step in establishing the new (kind of) state. "You know a kingdom knows no kindred," Elizabeth wrote to Henry Sidney in 1565, a few years after her coronation.[240] "I love and yet am forced to seem to hate," Elizabeth wrote about a suitor.[241]

Elizabeth's second step in establishing the new kind of state was to institutionalize the Head of England — or its Church — in multiple national roles both parentarchal and liberal. In her government speeches and private literary writings, she emphasized that all men are equal in terms of consanguinity. All are brothers and sisters, including Elizabeth herself. (In 1579 she embroidered the words *C[o]elum Patria* — "Heaven [is my] Fatherland" — on the covers of Laurence Tomson's New Testament; see Illustration 8.) Spiritualizing and secularizing the idea of incest, moreover, Elizabeth as queen established herself as the virginal mother and wife of the English people. In her accession speech, when she had succeeded "Bloody Mary" to the throne and John Bale had returned from exile, she put things this way:

> I have long since made choice of a husband, the kingdom of England. And here [showing the coronation ring] is the pledge and emblem of my marriage contract, which I wonder you should so soon have forgot. I beseech you, gentlemen, charge me not with the want of children, forasmuch as every one of you, and every Englishman besides, are my children and relations.[242]

In the ideology of the sixteenth century, it was not merely that Elizabeth became a kind of Virgin Mary transformed to Protestant ends[243] — as though, in John Dowland's words, an "Ave Mari!" could simply become a "Vivat Eliza!"[244] It was mainly that Elizabeth adjusted a specific ideological commonplace — that the Virgin Mary is at once the parent and spouse of God — to the general political requirements of her monarchal maturity.

Perhaps this adjustment served a psychological requirement

8. *Aphoristic texts and mottos embroidered, apparently by Elizabeth herself, on the black cloth covers of a tiny sextodecimo volume containing part of Laurence Tomson's New Testament (1578). Bodl. MS e. Mus. 242. Reproduced by permission of the Bodleian Library.*

as well. The fact that Elizabeth never married has puzzled her biographers for centuries. Adduced to explain the fact are domestic political situations, religious differences between herself and her suitors, desire to make use of courtships in international politics, fear of childbirth, recognition of infertility, unhappy love affairs, and so on. And truly, Elizabeth did have a real aversion to marriage; the French diplomat Salignac reported that she said to the French ambassador, "When I think of marriage it is as though my heart were being dragged out of my vitals, so much am I opposed to marriage by nature."[245] But aversion or no, the psychological requirements of her girlhood (linked, no doubt, to her remarkable education in the ways of marriage and incest in the 1530s and 1540s) together with the political requirements of a nation where Brothers and Sisters no longer played their old roles and the Roman pope, or *papa*, was a mere father figure, demanded that Elizabeth explore anew the interactions between family and politics. Both as traumatized princess and as brilliant statesperson, marriage for her as secular ruler, like marriage for the clergy, was almost completely out of the question. (She strongly disapproved of clerical marriage, but did not make a legal issue of it.)[246] For Elizabeth, marriage — that "earthly paradise of happiness"[247] — seemed possible neither as an earthly wife nor as a paradisiacal nun but only as the royal mother/wife of England. The great queen of England was so successful at establishing herself as this spiritual *mama* — in contradistinction to the Romish spiritual *papa* — that Pope Sixtus V, in the late 1580s, "allowed his mind to dwell on the fantasy of a papal union with the English crown; what a wife she would make for him, he joked, what brilliant children they would have."[248]

In relation to the monarchs of Europe, then, Elizabeth portrayed herself in multiple kinship roles reminiscent of those of the *sponsa Christi*. In letters of the 1580s to her godson, James VI of Scotland, for example, she not only employs the normal kinship terms used by European monarchs — thus frequently calling her royal Scottish godson "my dear Brother and Cousin" and saying that she "mean[s] to deal like an affectionate sister with [him]"[249] — but also extends that employment beyond the norm. In a letter of 1593, for example, Elizabeth writes ambiguously to James as if she were not only godmother, cousin, and sister but also a mother at once consanguineous and virginal: "You know, my dear Brother, that, since you first grieved, I regarded always to conserve it as my womb it had been you bear."[250]

In domestic politics Elizabeth became, in these terms, the comere or cummer (godmother, commother) of England, ruling her people not only as mother and wife but also as godmother (indeed, with no natural children of her own, she became the controversial godmother, or spiritual mother and sponsor, of more than a hundred English subjects).[251] She said often that her subjects should never have "a more natural mother than I meant to be unto all."[252] And John Harington wrote of her as "oure deare Queene, my royale god-mother, and this state's natural mother."[253] John Bale, in the essays he attached to Elizabeth's "Glass," forcefully criticized the institution of "gossipry" as practiced by Roman Catholics because it entailed a diriment impediment to marriage.[254] But Elizabeth adapted the institution to her own ends, replacing the role of the human godparent in the family with that of the divine monarch in the nation.

How Elizabeth replaced "biological" kinship with national gossipred is hinted at in Shakespeare's *Henry VIII*. Here we learn that the possibly illegitimate babe is in some ways less akin to her *pater* Henry VIII than to her paternal *sponsor*, or godfather, Thomas Cranmer. Cranmer, without consulting Henry, names the child "Elizabeth"—which means something like *sponsa Christi*.[255] In Shakespeare's *Richard III*, the curse that Margaret (widow of Henry VI) pronounces on another Elizabeth (wife of Edward IV and one of Elizabeth I's namesakes) depends for its effectiveness on denying to Margaret, in her relation to the rulers of England, what God has granted the Virgin Mary in her relation to God: "Die neither mother, wife, nor England's Queen."[256] Queen Elizabeth I, the wife of no man, was the *sponsa Angliae*, England's regal mother and wife.[257]

Elizabeth was concerned to transform physical incest (of the sort that she had reason to fear in her childhood) and libertine spiritual incest (of the sort that she represented in the "Glass") into a kind of political incest based in the unity of the English people as a single family. If the fear of incest, or of a desire for incest, can help spur a woman to contemplate being truly *elishabet* (in Hebrew, literally "consecrated to God," like a *sponsa Christi*), that fear and its concomitant political aspects also help to explain how Elizabeth defied nature's injunction to reproduce and became England's king of kings. Bale had hoped that she would become an English Reform "nourish-mother," like the Virgin Mary[258]—less a Catholic "Mother Superior" such as Bale feared in Mary Stuart than a Hebraic "nursing father" like Moses.[259] But Elizabeth became instead a secular version of the religious Mary she delineates in her "Glass." She became a national institution. In the iconography and visual representations of her reign, she appears less as the Virgin Queen, which is how some modern-day critics would have it, than as the *sponsa Angliae*.

Elizabeth's reign helped to transform the ideology of British monarchy.[260] In forging a national siblinghood, she helped to make England a "nation" state. Later rulers followed suit. The pattern of unchastity and (over)compensation in (public) virginity, or of tension between a feared libertinism and the celibacy believed to inhere in the "good" monachal or national institution, informs the reigns of later monarchs. A preeminent example is Elizabeth's godson King James VI of Scotland, who, as James I of England, succeeded her. James's concern about the fornication and bastardizing of his ancestors makes him her counterpart; and just as Princess Elizabeth, the supposedly illegitimate daughter of the adulterous and incestuous Anne Boleyn, made a claim to chastity, so James, the grandson of the notoriously libertine and bastardizing James V and the son of the purportedly adulterous Mary (she had married her cousin, to whom she was supposedly unfaithful), made a claim to chastity.[261] Like Elizabeth, James reacted against his family's past; despite a penchant for boys, he became as famous for chastity as his predecessor. Richard Baker writes that "of all the Morall vertues, [James] was eminent for chastity" and claims that he challenged comparison with Queen Elizabeth in this regard.[262] Beginning in 1603 with his first address to the English Parliament, moreover, James adopted Elizabeth's rhetoric of reincarnating the Holy Family on earth in a secularist guise. Bale had called Elizabeth both a spouse and a "nourish-mother"; James claims similarly that he is both the spouse of England — "I am the Husband, all the whole Isles my lawful Wife" — and its "loving nourish-father."[263] Sovereigns would seem to represent in this view the middle term between a parent, who lords it over children, and a spouse, who is an equal-in-law with them.

The main aspect of these ideological means of maintaining the Elizabethan regime was carried over for centuries, well beyond the purview of this book. Eventually, however, there exploded the contradiction between *liber* and *mater* that gives the Elizabethan slant on family and nation its full power. In France, where Margaret Porete and Marguerite of Navarre had lived, a more powerful and idealized form of reform took hold, at least for a while. Intellectual descendants of the libertines, if not of the English regicides,[264] French revolutionaries attempted brilliantly to bring "liberty, equality, and fraternity" to a nation of free children. For a time it seemed that the libertine view of the Brethren of the Free Spirit — *Ubi spiritus, ibi libertas* (Where the Spirit is, there is Liberty) — would win out.

Yet something fell short in the transition from God to Earth. The new American patriotism appropriated for its motto James Otis's sentence *Ubi libertas, ibi patria* (Where Liberty is, there is Fatherland).[265] And indeed the old liberalism met its match again. America had its "Sons of Liberty" and "Daughters of the American Revolution," but liberty in romantic America, and elsewhere in the nineteenth century, really came to mean something like "my parents' place." We are warned (in Genesis) that young men and women "gotta get out of [that] place if it's the last thing [they] ever do."[266] We must leave the heterogeneous family, whether nuclear or tribal, in order to become (as if we could) no more sons of a Fatherland or daughters in a Motherland but — like the sinful soul redeemed, ideally only, in Elizabeth's "Glass" — siblings in the Promised Land of freedom.

John Bale (1548)

Truly, ye come of The Blood.
— Rudyard Kipling, "England's Answer"

John Bale's "Epistle Dedicatory" and "Conclusion" to Elizabeth's "Glass" participate in a general Henrican and Elizabethan redefinition of the British nation in terms of its
blood and religion. One aspect of this definition concerns the
question of whether the British race — its generation — was essentially Trojan or Teutonic. Did the basic genetic blood lineage of Britain start with the Trojan Aeneas and Brutus (after the
fall of Troy) or with the Teutonic Hengist and Horsa (in the
fifth century)?[1]

In the debate about who the Britons really were, those who
said they were Trojan were backed up by traditional authority
and royal self-interest. Geoffrey of Monmouth's *History of the
Kings of Britain*, "the most famous work of [British] nationalistic
historiography in the Middle Ages,"[2] had reported that Julius
Caesar said, "Those Britons come from the same race as we do,
for we Romans too are descended from Trojan stock."[3] Generally speaking, the dogma that the British were essentially Trojan was the official view. William Caxton's first publication,
after all, had been Raoul Le Fèvre's *Recuyell of the Historyes of
Troye*. Henry VII's historian Bernardus Andreas, remembering
the prophecy of Merlin to King Vortigern of the coming of a
British Messiah, traced Henry VII's lineage to the seventh-
century Romano-Welshman Cadwalader;[4] one plan for Henry

VII's coronation included lines about him as the "Fulfiller of the Profesye."[5] "Cadwalader Blodde lynyally descending," went the script, "long hathe bee towlde of such a Prince comyng."[6] It was in the same messianic spirit that Henry VII gave his first son the name of Arthur (after the protohistorical "once and future king"). Henry VIII, Arthur's brother, used the imperial Trojan-Roman myth to prop up his claim of equal standing with the Roman Pope. His representative told a French ambassador that the British King Brennius had conquered Rome, that the Roman Emperor Constantine (the first Christian emperor) had reigned in England, and that King Arthur had been emperor not only of Britain but also of Gaul and Germany.[7] And in 1533, when Princess Elizabeth was born, Henry VIII's "Act in Restraint of Appeals" asserted that England was an empire like Rome and that it was "governed by one Supreme Head and King having dignity and royal estate of the imperial crown." His assertions were part of the tradition that British kings were descended from the Emperor Constantine the Great, who, thanks to his mother (Helena), was half British. Constantine, after all, "had united British kinship with Roman emperorship."[8]

Linked with the debate about British race and blood lineage was the controversy about whether British Christianity began essentially in the first two centuries or in the sixth century. Did it begin with Joseph of Arimathea and his Holy Grail (often etymologized as *sang real*, or "real (royal) blood")[9] or with the British King Lucius, whose conversion people supposed to have made Britain the first Christian nation in the world? If so, that would justify some of Britain's non-Romish religious dogmas and rituals and would support the Protestant view that British Christendom was essentially independent of Rome.[10] Or did essential British Christianity begin later, with the sixth-century proselytizing of the Roman churchman St. Augustine?[11] If so, that would justify the claims of Roman Catholicism.

The nationalist Bale at the age of twelve had been associated with the Carmelite order — to many of whose Brothers he refers in his "Epistle Dedicatory" and "Conclusion." (These include John Stanbury, Walter Hunt, Richard Maidstone, Thomas Netter, John Milverton, and the White Friars to whose abbey at Hulne near Alnwick he himself had one removed.) But Bale converted to Protestantism in 1533, the year of Elizabeth's birth, and he was especially interested in the primordial, pre-Roman British church. An indefatigable collector of books and manuscripts in the wake of Henry VIII's Dissolution of the Monasteries in the mid-1530s, Bale's work, and the work of such cohorts as John Leland and John Foxe, defined Britishness through Anglo-Saxon studies (the academic "field" of Anglo-Saxon studies retained for centuries its telling focus on race and religion).[12] Bale, in his *Image of Both Churches*, emphasized that the English Church was founded with Joseph of Arimathea; and in his works on the Protestant martyr Askew, he claimed that the British church "never had the authority of the Romish pope."[13] Leland planned a fifty-volume history of England to be titled *De nobilitate Britannica*, and Foxe produced his influential *Book of Martyrs*. Matthew Parker, the first Elizabethan Archbishop of Canterbury, used Saxon documents culled from Bale's collections to publish such texts as the sixth-century British monk Gildas's *De excidio et conquestu Britanniae*.[14] The publication of these works was a polemical weapon against the Roman Church. Apparently demonstrating that the Anglican Church represented a return to old English practices, they helped to steer a course between Catholicism and Puritanism.

The final break with the "Trojan origin" tradition began

79

during the reign of Henry VII with the work of his court historian, the Italian Polydore Vergil. (Vergil's controversial work was completed in 1513, but it was not published until the reign of Henry VIII, in 1534.)[15] His *Anglicana historia* presented the view that the Brutus story was a fiction; at the same time, it tried to factor in Germanic immigration—including Danish and Norman or Norwegian influences.[16] One gist was that the British race was neither Trojan-Roman nor Welsh but Teutonic. Many agreed. The Catholic Thomas More's brother-in-law John Rastell, for example, commented in 1529 that for most people the idea that Brutus was the ur-ancestor of the British, which once seemed to give the British monarchy equal footing with the Roman pontiff, was ridiculous.[17] Leland and Bale attacked Vergil's work directly, Leland's well-known critique appearing in 1544.[18]

Bale, although at this period no proponent of the Teutonic view, had taken refuge in Germany and recognized the appeal of Tacitus's praise in his *Germania* for the Teutonic race as unsullied and pure.[19] Bale was aware, moreover, that Polydore Vergil's claims for Hengist and Horsa and their ilk were not without scholarly merit.[20] And he knew Luther's nationalist "Appeal to the Ruling Class of German Nationality": "We have the title of empire, but the pope has our goods, our honor, our bodies, lives, souls, and all we possess; that is the way to cheat the Germans, and because they are Germans, to go on cheating them."[21]

Bale's own nationalist ideology, however, did not include Teutonic blood as a primary component. On the one hand, he thought the traditional ideology of Trojan blood would give the Britons a better footing in opposing Rome. (The city of London, which Geoffrey of Monmouth called Troia Nova, was for many Britishers in the 1540s still the true Rome.) On the other hand, as we have seen, Bale emphasized the importance of spiritual lineage and deemphasized that of blood lineage — albeit without imprudently belittling that royal blood, or *sang real*, which British monarchs claimed gave them the right to rule. This emphasis would further the political opportunities of the princess by whom Bale set so much store. For Elizabeth, as Bale knew, was a bastard — or so said her father, Henry VIII — and, as such, could play a role in England, perhaps all Europe, like that of the purported bastards King Arthur of Britain and Emperor Constantine of Rome.[22] She might intermediate between Trojan and Teutonic generation and, more important, personify a Boethean transcendence of blood in the name of what Leland would call a true "nobility."

For the likes of Bale, moreover, the British proponents of the Teutonic connection were much too concerned with the ideology of "manliness" as the quintessential characteristic of human being. The Teutonic theorists were notoriously mysogynistic. For example, the German satirist Ulrich von Hutten, a friend of Martin Luther and, like Luther, an ex-Brother, contrasted the "womanly Romano-Welsche" with the manly Germans: "A woman race . . . these are the people who rule us!"[23] And in later years the English antiquarian John Speed, in his *History of Great Britain*, likewise praised the "Manhood" of the English Saxons as a band of Teutonic brethren.[24] Bale, by contrast, was a supporter of women martyrs such as Askew and a prophet for women politicians such as Elizabeth. In his "Epistle Dedicatory" and "Conclusion," therefore, he focuses on the important role in European history of such British women as Agasia, Eleanor, Anna, Athildis, Boudicca, Cambra, Claudia Rufina, Constantia, Cordelia, Elizabeth (daughter of Richard Woodville), Emerita, Gwendolyn, Helena, Hilda, Marcia, Margaret of Navarre, Margaret Beaufort, and Ursula. He wanted thus to prepare the stage for a mythic if not an actual role for women in future British political life. Queens as "joiners" of the state were now to be treated as kings once again.[25] That is what Bale in 1548 hoped for Princess Elizabeth. When he was made prebendary of Canterbury upon Elizabeth's succession in 1558, "Bilious" Bale, as he was sometimes called, had reason to think that his messianic plan for England would soon be realized. He died five years later.[26]

To the right virtuous and Christianly learned young
Lady Elizabeth, the noble daughter of our late
sovereign King Henry the Eighth, John Bale wisheth
health with daily increase of godly knowledge.

Diverse and many (most gracious lady) have the opinions been among the profane philosophers and Christian divines concerning right nobility and no fewer strifes and contentions for the same. Some authors have vainly boasted it to take original of the old gods of the Gentiles, as every land hath had its peculiar Saturn, Jupiter, and Hercules, yea, our England here and all. Some have derived it from the four general monarchies of the Assyrians, Persians, Greeks, and Romans. Some have attributed it to the bold battles and bloodsheddings, in Ninus of Babylon, the first inventor of policies in war; in our great Albion the Chamesene, which first in this region [2v] suppressed the posterity of Japhet, usurping therein the first monarchy; in Brutus that more than six hundred years after defaced his tyrannous issue; in Ebranck and Dunwallo; in Brenne and Beline; in great Constantine, Arthur, Cadwalder, Hengist, Egbert, Alfred, William Conqueror, and such other, for like conquests of the Romans, Greeks, Gauls, Picts, Britons, Saxons, Danes, Irishmen, and Englishmen.

The haughty Romans set not yet a little by themselves that they have risen of Aeneas and Romulus, of whom the one most shamefully betrayed his own native kindred and country and the other most unnaturally slew his own brother for worldly dominion. Like as our Welshmen here in England, advancing their succession or progeny above the English, will needs come of Dardanus and Brutus, a foundation not all unlike to the other. These glorious champions for this far-fetched ground of their nobility account all other nations and peoples ignoble, profane, and barbarous, as is to be seen in the monuments of their writers. But in the mean season they are not aware that [3r] they undiscreetly prefer cursed Cham to blessed Japhet, by whose posterity the Iles of the Gentiles were first sorted out into speeches, kindreds, and nations (Gen. 10), and not by Cham's offspring, of whom the Trojans and Romans had their noble beginning. That which the Chamesenes had in those Iles was by cruel usurpation and tyranny, as testifieth Berosus the Chaldean, and therefore that ground of nobility is not all the best. Over and besides all this, some have applied it to renowned birth or succession of blood, some to the abundance of pleasures worldly, some to the maintenance of great families, some to the sumptuousness of notable buildings, some to the high stomach and stature of person, some to valiantness in martial feats, some to seemly manners of courtesy, some to liberality of rewards and gifts, some to the ancientness of long continuance, some to wisdom, learning, and study for a commonwealth, with such like. And these are not all to be disallowed, for we find them in Abraham and David with other just fathers.

But now followeth a monstrous, or whether ye will, a prestigious nobility. [3v] The Romish clergy, imagining to exalt themselves above the lewd laity (as they shame not yet to call the worldly powers), have given it in a far other kind to miters, masses, cardinal hats, crosiers, caps, shaven crowns, oiled thumbs, side gowns, furred amices, monks' cowls, and friars' lousey coats, becoming thereby pontifical lords, spiritual sirs and ghostly fathers. This kind of nobility digged out of the dunghill have I seen gorgeously garnished with the rhetorics of Porphyry, Aristotle, Duns, and Raimundus decretals, in the books of John Stanbery, bishop of Hereford, *De superioritate ecclesiastica, De discrimine iurisdictionum,* and *De potestate pontificia.* In the books also of Walter Hunt, an ordinary reader sometime in Oxford, *De precellentia Petri* and *De autoritate ecclesie.* Yea, and among themselves they have much contended both by disputation and writings which of their sects might other excel in the nobleness of Christian perfection. The monks in public schools, by a distinction of the active and contemplative life, have advanced their idle monkery above the [4r] office of a bishop and the friars their scald craving beggary above the degrees of them both, as is largely seen in the brawling works of Richard Maydeston, Thomas Walden, William Byntre, and others which have written *Contra Wiclefistas* and *Pro mendicatione fratrum.*

In the days of King Edward the Fourth, John Milverton, provincial of the Carmelites, was full three years a prisoner in the castle of Angel at Rome at the suit of the bishops of England for the same, and lost so the bishopric of Saint David's whereunto he was a little before elected. This matter have I heard under the title of Evangelic Perfection, most deeply reasoned in their ordinary disputations at their concourses, convocations, and chapters (as they then called them), yea, by those whom I knew most corrupt livers. Hereunto for furnishing out the same, the Grayfriars added St. Francis's painted wounds, the Blackfriars St. Dominick's bold disputing with heretics, the Whitefriars our Lady's fraternity, and the Augustine Friars the great doctrine of their patron. In the universities after much [4v] to and fro hath it been concluded that the order of a priest hath far excelled in dignity the order of a bishop. And this have

they left behind them for a most grave and deep reason there-
upon. Mark their more than Luciferian presumption therein.
Such power hath a priest (say they) as hath neither angel, nor
yet man, be he of never so great authority, science, or virtue; for
a priest by word may make Him again that by word made
heaven and earth. A priest may every day both beget Him and
bear Him, whereas his mother Mary begat Him (bore Him
they would say) but once. These are their very words in a book
entitled *De origine nobilitas*, cap.5, with much more circum-
stance of matter. O blasphemous belly-beasts and most idle-
witted sorcerers! How idolatrously exalt they themselves above
the eternal living God and His Christ!

John Chrisostomos, a man taught and brought up in the
Christian philosophy, defineth the true nobility after a far other
sort than did the profane writers. He calleth it not with Aristotle a worthiness of progeny, neither yet with [5r] Varro an
opulence of riches, but a famous renown obtained by long ex-
ercised virtue. He is puissant, high, and valiant (saith he) and
hath nobility in right course that disdaineth to give place to
vices and abhorreth to be overcome of them. Doctrine greatly
adorneth a man highly born, but a godly endeavor of Christianity beautifieth him most of all. By none other ways have the
Apostles and martyrs obtained a noble report than by the valiant force of pure doctrine and faith.

A gentle heart (saith Seneca) or a stomach that is noble mov-
eth, provoketh, and stirreth only to things honest. No man
which hath a noble wit delighteth in things of small value, much
less in matters of filthiness or superstition. Chiefly appertaineth
it to men and women of sincere nobility to regard the pure
doctrine and faith. Unto such hath God promised in the scriptures abundance of temporal things, long life, fortunate children, a kingdom durable, with such others (Deut. 28).

"Epistle Dedicatory"

A most worthy conqueror is Gideon, noted in the scriptures for destroying false religion and renewing the kingdom [5v] of faith (Judges 6). So is King Asa for removing the male stews from the prelates abhorring marriage and for putting down idols which his forefathers maintained (1 Kings 15). So is King Jehoshaphat for being courageous in ways of God and for putting down the hill altars and their sacrifices (2 Chron. 17). So is King Jehu, for slaying the idolatrous priests and for breaking and burning their great god Baal, and for making a jakes of their holy Church (2 Kings 10). So is King Hezikiah, for cleansing the house of the Lord from all filthiness, afore his time therein occupied (2 Chron. 29), and for breaking down the brazen serpent and idolatrous images with their altars and sanctuaries (2 Kings 18). So is King Josiah, for suppressing religious persons and altarpriests for consuming their jewels and ornaments and for overthrowing their buggery chambers in the house of the Lord (2 Kings 23). This noble king also destroyed all their carved images, he strewed the dust of them upon their graves that had offered to them, and burnt the priests' bones upon their altars, restoring again [6r] the laws of the Lord (2 Chron. 34). Jesus Sirach reporteth of him finally that he wholly directed his heart to the Lord, and took away all abominations of the ungodly (Ecclus. 49). Besides that is spoken of King David and King Solomon.

Not I only, but many thousands more which will not from henceforth bow any more to Baal, are in full and perfect hope that all these most highly notable and princely acts will revive and lively flourish in your most noble and worthy brother King Edward the Sixth. Most excellent and godly are his beginnings reported of the very foreign nations, calling him for his virtuous, learned, and godly prudent youth's sake the second Josiah. Those his wonderful principles in the eyes of the world,

87

and no less glorious before God, thus being to His honor, that eternal living God continue and prosper to the end, that he may have of them as had these worthy kings before rehearsed, a right noble and famous report. Nobility sought by wicked enterprises and obtained by the same (as in many before our days and in some now of late) is not else but a public and [6v] notable infamy and in the end eternal damnation. Nobility won by the earnest seeking of God's high honor is such a precious crown of glory as will never perish here nor yet in the world to come.

Cain, after a worldly manner or among the ungracious sort, is held noble for slaying his brother; Judas of the prelates (for he received of them a noble reward) for betraying Christ; Herod of the Jews for murdering the innocents. And what is there more worthy of reproach, dishonor, and shame than are these execrable facts? The nature of true nobility (as I said before) is not to rise of vice but of virtue, though many men there seek it. Of the most excellent kind of nobility is he sure (most virtuous and learned lady) which truly believeth and seeketh to do the will of the eternal father, for thereby is he brought forward and promoted into that heavenly kindred (John 1). By that means becometh he the dear brother, sister, and mother of Christ (Matt. 12), a citizen of heaven with the apostles and prophets (Eph. 2), yea, the child of adoption and heir together with Christ in the heavenly inheritance [7r] (Rom. 8). No such children left Socrates behind him, neither yet Demosthenes, Plato, nor Cicero with all their pleasant wisdom and eloquence. No such heritage could great Alexander the Macedonian bequeath to his posterity, neither yet noble Charles, Arthur, nor David.

Of this nobility have I no doubt (Lady most faithfully studious) but that you are, with many other noble women and maidens more in this blessed age. If questions were asked me how I know it? my answer would be this: By your godly fruit, as

the fertile tree is none otherwise than thereby known (Luke 6).
I received your noble book, right fruitfully by you translated
out of the French tongue into English. I received also your
golden sentences out of the sacred scriptures, with no less grace
than learning, in four noble languages, Latin, Greek, French,
and Italian, most ornately, finely, and purely written with your
own hand. Wonderfully joyous were the learned men of our
city, Murseus, Buscoducinus, Bomelius, Lithodius, and Iman-
nus, as I shewed unto them the said sentences, in beholding (as
they then reported) so much virtue, [7v] faith, science, and
experience of languages and letters, especially in noble youth
and femininity. Through which occasion there be of them (I
know) that cannot withhold their learned hands from the publishing thereof to the high praise of God the giver, neither yet
from writing to your worthy grace for studious continuance in
the same. Your said sentences (they say) far passeth the apothegms of Plutarch, the aphorisms of Theognis, the strategems
of Isocrates, the grave golden counsels of Cato, and the manifold morals of John Goldeston, the great allegorizer, with such
other like.

Your first written clauses in four speeches, in Latin, French,
and Italian out of the thirteenth Psalm of noble David, men-
tioneth that the unfaithful reckoneth foolishly in their hearts
there is no God. Whereupon so corrupt they are in their vain
conjectures and so abominable in their daily doings that not
one of their generation is godly. By this does Your Grace unto
us signify that the barren doctrine and good works without
faith of the hypocrites, which in their uncommanded Latin
ceremonies serve their bellies and not Christ [8r] in greed-
ily devouring the patrimony of poor widows and orphans, are
both execrable in themselves and abominable before God. For
though those painted sepulchres have the name of the Lord in

their mouths and greatly boast the good works of the law, yet know they not what belongeth to His true honor, but hate in their wicked hearts both His glorious name and word. The true doctrine of faith and the fear of God will that wicked sort (whom this Psalm wringeth) not hear, but still torment the consciences of miserable wretched idiots for advantage of masses and mumblings. Happy are they of this latter age that in the gospel have received the saving health out of Zion (as Your Grace has done), being clear from the sting of those viperous worms. Blessed be those faithful tutors and teachers which by their most godly instruction have thus fashioned your tender youth into the right image of Christ and not Antichrist. Yea, most blessed be those godly governors and magistrates which have travailed and yet laboriously travail with worthy Moses to bring [8v] God's people clearly out of their most wretched captivity.

Your latter clause in the Greek inciteth us to the right worshipping of God in spirit and verity (John 4), to honoring of our parents in the seemly offices of natural children (Eph. 6), and to the reverent using of our Christian equals in the due ministrations of love (1 Pet. 2). Neither Benedict nor Bruno, Dominick nor Francis (which have of long years been boasted for the principal patrons of religion) ever gave to their superstitious brethren so pure precepts of sincere Christianity. Neither yet Peter Lombarde in his four books of sentences with whose smokey divinity the lousey locusts, monks, canons, priests, and friars have these four hundred years darkened the clear sun, which is the verity of God (Rev. 9). If godly wise men would do no more but confer this learning of yours and of other noble women in these days with the doctrine of Robert Kilwardby, archbishop of Canterbury and cardinal (which the universities of Oxford and Paris were sworn to for maintenance of that

Christianity in the [9r] year of our Lord 1276 by the consent of all masters, regents and non-regents), I doubt it not but they should find just cause to hold up both their hands and praise their Lord God for changing that hell into this heaven. An unsavory gust therefore shall they find, adjoined of the Parisians as necessary divinity to the foresaid sentences of Peter Lombarde.

In your forenamed book, composed first of all by the right virtuous lady Margaret, sister sometime to the French king Francis and Queen of Navarre, and by your noble grace most diligently and exactly translated into English, find I most precious treasure concerning the soul. Wherefore I have added thereunto the title of *A Godly Meditation of the Soul, Concerning a Love toward God and His Christ*. Most lively in these and such other excellent facts express ye the natural emphasis of your noble name. Elizabeth in the Hebrew is as much to say in the Latin as *Dei mei requies*; in English, "The rest of my God." Who can think God not to rest in that heart which sendeth forth such godly fruits? I think none that hath right discretion. [9v] Your pen hath here plenteously uttered the abundance of a godly occupied heart, like as did the virginal lips of Christ's most blessed mother, when she said with heavenly rejoice, My soul magnifieth the Lord and my spirit rejoiceth in God my saviour (Luke 1). Many noble women of French literature have been aforetime in this region, whose nomenclature or rehearsal of names I intend to show in the end of this book, but none of them were ever yet like to those which are in our age. No, neither Cambria, Marcia, Constantia, Agasia, Voadicia, Boudicca, Claudia, Helena, Ursula, Hilda, no such other like. This one copy of yours have I brought into a number to the intent that many hungry souls by the inestimable treasure contained therein may be sweetly refreshed. The spirit of the eternal son of God, Jesus Christ, be always to your excellent grace assistant that ye may send forth more such wholesome fruits of soul and become a nourishing mother to His dear congregation, to their comfort and His high glory. Amen.

Your bound orator, John Bale.

C ertain and sure am I (most gentle reader) that all they which shall peruse this godly book shall not therewith be pleased. For among feeders are always sundry appetites, and in great assemblies of people diverse and variant judgments. As the saying is: so many heads, so many wits. Neither fine painted speech, wisdom of this world, nor yet religious hypocrisy (which for private commodity many men seek) are herein to be looked for. And a reason why, for He that is here familiarly commoned with regardeth no curiosity, but plainness and truth. He refuseth no sinner, but is well contented at all times to hear his homely tale. Hide not thyself from Me (saith He) when thou hast done amiss, but come boldly face to face and common the matter with Me. If thy sins be so red as scarlet, I shall make them whiter than the snow. And though thy deeds be as the purple, yet shall they appear so white as the wool (Isa. 1). For as truly as I live (saith He), no pleasure have I in the death of the sinner but will much rather that he [39v] turn and be saved (Ezek. 33).

If the homely speech here do too much offend, consider it to be the work of a woman, as she in the beginning thereof hath most meekly desired. And yet of none other woman than was most godly minded. Mark David in the Psalter, which was a man both wise and learned, and you shall find his manner in speaking not all unlike to this. Faith (St. Paul saith) standeth not in flourishing eloquence, neither yet in man's politic wisdom, but in the grace and power of God (1 Cor. 2). If the oft repeating of some one sentence engendereth a tedious weariness to the reader, let him well peruse the holy works of St. John the Evangelist, and I doubt it not but he shall find there the same manner of writing. And his occasion is (as all the chief writers affirm) the necessary marking of the precepts of health, or of matter chiefly concerning the soul's salvation. For a thing twice or thrice spoken entereth much more deeply into the remembrance than that [which] is uttered but once.

And as touching the portion that my Lady Elizabeth, the King's most [40r] noble sister, hath therein, which is her translation, chiefly hath she done it for her own exercise in the French tongue, besides the spiritual exercise of her inner soul with God. As a diligent and profitable bee hath she gathered of this flower sweetness both ways and of this book consolation in spirit. And thinking that others might do the same, of a most free Christian heart she maketh it here common unto them, not being a niggard over the treasure of God (Matt. 25). The first fruit is it of her young, tender, and innocent labors. For I think she was not full out fourteen years of age at the finishing thereof. She hath not done herein as did the religious and anointed hypocrites in monasteries, convents, and colleges, in sparing their libraries from men studious and in reserving the treasure contained in their books to most vile dust and worms. But like as God hath graciously given it, so doth she again most freely distribute it.

Such noble beginnings are neither to be reckoned childish nor babyish, though she were a babe in years that hath here given them. Seldom find we them [40v] that in the closing up of their withered age do minister like fruits of virtue. An infinite swarm behold we of old doting bawds and beasts that with consciences laden with sin (as St. Paul reporteth them) taketh every painted stock and stone for their God, besides the small breads that their lecherous chaplains have blown upon. They

94

shall not be unwise that shall mark herein what commodity it is or what profit might grow to a Christian commonwealth if youth were thus brought up in virtue and good letters. If such fruits come forward in childhood, what will follow and appear when discretion and years shall be more ripe and ancient? A most manifest sign of godliness is it in the friends where youth is thus instituted, and a token of wonderfully faithful diligence in the studious teachers, tutors, and daily lookers-on.

Nobility which she hath gotten of blood in the highest degree, having a most victorious king to her father, and a most virtuous and learned king again to her brother, is not in the early spring stained with wanton ignorance, neither [41r] yet blemished with the common vices of dissolute youth, but most plenteously adorned with all kinds of languages, learnings, and virtues, to hold it still in right course. The translation of this work were evidence strong enough, if I had nought else to lay for the matter. But mark yet another much more effectual and clear, at the which not a few learned men in Germany have wondered. In four noble languages, Latin, Greek, French, and Italian, wrote she unto me these clauses following, which I have added to this book not only in commendation of her learned youth but also as an example to be followed of other noble men and women concerning their children. The written clauses are these, which she first wrote with her own hand much more finely than I could with any printing letter set them forth.

Stultus dixit in corde suo, non est Deus. Illi corrupti sunt, & abhominabiles in sua impietate, nullus est qui aliquid boni facit.

Le fol disoit en son coeur, il n'a nul Dieu. Ils sont corumpus & sont abhomi[41v]nables en leur impiete, il n'a nul qui faict bien.

Is stulto disse nel suo core, non v'e alcuno Dio. Corrutti sono & abhominabile nella loro impieta, nissuno e buono.

Ton theon phoboun, tous de goneis tima, tous de Philous aes-
chynou.

The first clause in the three languages, Latin, French, and Italian, comprehendeth this only sentence, as I shewed before in
the Epistle Dedicatory:

> The fool saith in his heart, there is no God. Corrupt they are,
> and abominable in their wickedness (or blasphemies against
> God); not one of them doth good.

The Greek clause is thus to be Englished:

> Fear God, honor thy parents, and reverence thy friends.

Thus hath she given us counsel both to go and to come, to leave
and to take. To [42r] decline from the evil, and to do that which
is good (Ps. 36). To flee from the Antichrist and his great body
of sin or blasphemous cruel clergy and to return to God by a
perfect fear, honor, and love. So lively apothegms, or brief and
quick sentences respecting Christianity, have seldom come
from women. I have searched Plutarch, Boccaccio, Bergomas,
Tertor, and Lander of Bonony, which all wrote of the virtues
and worthy acts of women. But among them all have I found no
counsels so necessary to the commonwealth of our Christianity.
I deny it not but excellent things they uttered and matters of
wisdom wonderful concerning moral virtues. But these most
highly respecteth the kingdom of faith and regiment of the
soul, which Jesus Christ the eternal son of God from heaven by
his doctrine and death so busily sought to clear. Many grave
sentences had they concerning private causes. But universally
these are for all sorts of people, high, low, hale, sick, rich, poor,
learned, and unlearned, that mindeth to have freedom by
Christ's deadly sufferings, or to be delivered from hell, sin,
death, & the devil [42v] by the price of his precious blood.

No realm under the sky hath had more noble women, nor of more excellent graces, than hath this realm of England, both in the days of the Britons and since the English Saxons obtained it by valiant conquest. Gwendolyn the wife of Locrinus the second king of Britain, being unlawfully divorced from him for the pleasure of an whore whom he long before had, tried it with him by dint of the sword, had the victory, and reigned after him as king the space of fifteen years, till her son Maddan came to lawful age. Cordelia the daughter of King Lear and least of all her sisters, as her father was deposed and exiled out of his land, she received, comforted, and restored him again to his princely honor, and reigned alone after his death for the space of five years. Cambra, the daughter of King Belyne and wife to Antenes then king of France, did not only exceed in beauty but also in wisdom, insomuch that she first instructed the noble men how to build cities, castles, and other strongholds, the common people more comely manners, and the women a most see[43r]mly decking of their heads. She made their civil laws which upon her name were called Leges Sycambrorum. She taught them to sow flax and hemp, to water it, dry it, dress it, spin it, weave it, whiten it, and fashion it to all manner of use for the body.

Marcia the wife of King Guythelyne, a lady exceedingly fair, wise, and learned in all the liberal sciences, invented things wonderful by the high practice of her wit. After the death of her husband she reigned seven years as king, till Sicilius her son came to age. She redressed the commonwealth, reformed the gross manners of the people, and made most honest laws called of her name Leges Martiane. So delighted the French king Nicanor in the wisdom, learning, and comely manners of his wife Constantia, the daughter of King Heliodorus, that he not only helped her brother Geruntius in sea battle against the king of Orchades but also sent his most dear son Priamus into Britain to have the selfsame bringing up. The Scottish king Finnanus thought his princely honor most gloriously increased as he had obtained [43v] Agasia, the daughter of King Blegabridus, to be coupled in marriage with Dorstus his son for the manifold graces that he beheld in her. What though the said ungracious Dorstus, in spite of the Britons, did afterward use her most wickedly? Boudicca, a woman both high of stature and stomach, also of most noble lineage among the Britons, perceiving the havoc which the Romans daily made in the land, with great puissance of worthy warriors she invaded them, slew them, hung up their captains, and followed the remnant of them to the very Alps of Italy, where at the latter by reason of daily labors she sickened and so died, even the very glory of woman, saith Ponticus Virunnius.

Voada, the first wife of King Arviragus, a woman of wonderful force and heart, strongly armed herself, her two daughters, and five thousand women more of the Briton blood, in battle against the furious fierce Romans to suppress their tyranny and execrable filthiness in abusing maids, wives, and widows. But as she beheld the victory upon their sides, because she would not come under [44r] their captivity, she poisoned herself and so died. Voadicia, her younger daughter, afterward escaping the hands of the said Romans, with a mighty power of the Britons entered into the Isle of Man and in a night battle there slew them in a wonderful number, destroying their fortresses and holds. Notwithstanding, at the latter being taken, she was beheaded, her elder sister being married to King Marius. Athildis, the daughter of the said King Marius, was also a most noble woman, whom the French king Marcomerus married for only the natural gifts and sciences which she had above other women and had seven sons by her. Claudia Rufina, a noble Briton, witty and learned in both Greek and Latin, having to husband one Aulus Rufus, a learned knight, a poet of Bonony, and a philosopher of the stoical sort, is much commended in Martialis the poet for the epigrams and poems which she then compiled in both those tongues.

Emerita, the sister of King Lucius, which is called the first christened king, a lady most virtuous and faithful, for constantly affirming the verity of Christ [44v] suffered most tyrannous death and was burnt in the fire. Helena Flavia, the daughter of King Coelus, and mother to great Constantine the emperor, was a woman of incomparable beauty and learning. None could be found like her in the arts liberal, neither yet in the fine handling of all instruments of music. She excelled all other in the diverse speeches of nations, especially in the Latin, Greek, and Hebrew. She made a book of the providence of God, another of the immortality of the soul, with certain Greek poems, epistles, and diverse other treatises. Constantia, her daughter, was also a woman of most excellent gifts, had she not in the end declined to the detestable sect of the Aryans by certain hypocritical priests. Ursula Cynosura, the flourishing daughter of Dionothus the Duke of Cornwall, was so nobly brought up in all liberal disciplines that Conanus the king of Little Britain desired her to wife, and as she went thitherward with eleven thousand Britons' wives more, by chance of weather and violence of sea rovers, both she and they perished by the way.

Anna, the sister of Aurelius Ambrosius, [45r] which was afterward married to Loho, the king of Picts, and Anna, the twin sister of King Arthur, are of writers magnified for their diverse and excellent graces. Morgan, a woman of incomparable love toward her parents and country, so secretly and wisely conveyed the body of King Arthur, the most worthy governor of the Britons, that the English Saxons could never come to it to do their violence thereon. Hermelinda, rising of the English Saxon blood, for her excellent beauty and noble behavior became the wife of Cunibertus, the king of Lombardy. Hilda, a noble woman both godly, wise, and learned, not only disputed in the open Synod at Streneshalce in the north country against the prelates concerning their newly found out celebration of Easter and their crown shaving, with other ceremonies, but also wrote a treatise against bishop Agilbert, a Frenchman, the busiest among them. The three daughters of King Alfred, Elfleda, Elfritha, and Ethelgora, were wonderfully expert in the liberal sciences. Eleanor, the wife of King Henry the Second, was learned also and wrote diverse [45v] epistles to Pope Celestine the Third and also to King John, her youngest son.

Joanna, the youngest daughter of the said King Henry, so much delighted in good letters that before she should be married to King William of Sicily she caused her father to send over two learned men of England, Walter and Richard, with a French doctor called Petrus Belsensis to instruct him in them, especially in the art of versifying. And at her coming thither one of those English men was made archbishop of Panorm and the other bishop of Syracuse in recompense of their labors. Margaret, the noble mother of King Henry the Seventh, so plenteously minded the preferment of sciences and going forward of learning that she built in Cambridge for the same purpose the colleges of Christ and of St. John the Evangelist and gave lands for their maintenance, as Queen Elizabeth did before to the Queens College there. Long were it to rehearse the exceeding number of noble women, which in this land of Britain or realm of England have excelled in beauty, wit, wisdom, science, languages, liberality, policies, heroical for[46r]ce, and such other notable virtues, and by reason of them done feats wonderful. Either yet to sort out their names and register them one by one, which have been married out of the same, to emperors, kings, dukes, earls, worthy captains, philosophers, physicians, astronomers, poets, and others of renowned fame and letters, only for their most rare graces and gifts.

Though none in this land have yet done as did among the Greeks Plutarch and among the Latins Boccaccio with other authors aforenamed, that is to say, left behind them catalogues or nomenclatures of famous and honorable women, yet hath it not at any time been barren of them. No, not in the days of most popish darkness as appeareth by Eleanor Cobham, the wife of good Duke Humphrey of Gloucester, brother to King Henry the Fifth, whom Antichrist's grand captains, the bishops then of England, in hate of her name and belief, accused of sorcerous enchantments and experiments of necromancy against their holy horned whorish church and at the last slew her noble husband in a false Par[46v]lement at Bury, by their own hired slaughterman Pole, as they never are without such. If they were worthy praise which had these aforenamed virtues single or after a bodily sort only, we must of congruence grant them worthy double honor which have them most plenteously doubled. As now since Christ's gospel hath risen, we have beheld them and yet see them still to this day in many noble women, not rising of flesh and blood as in the other, but of that mighty living spirit of His which vanquished death, hell, and the devil.

Consider yet how strongly that spirit in Anne Askew set them all at naught with their artillery and ministers of mischief, both upon the rack and also in the fire, whose memory is now in benediction (as Jesus Sirach reported of Moses) and shall never be forgotten of the righteous. She, as Christ's mighty member, hath strongly trodden down the head of the serpent and gone hence with most noble victory over the pestiferous seed of that viperous worm of Rome, the gates of hell not prevailing against her. What other noble women have, [47r] it doth now and will yet hereafter appear more largely by their godly doctrine and deeds of faith. Mark this present book for one, whose translation was the work of her which was but a babe at the doing thereof. Mark also the grave sentences which she giveth forth to the world, and laud that living father of our Lord Jesus Christ, which hath thus taken His heavenly wisdom from the great grave seniors, that only are wise in their own conceits, and given it so largely to children (Matt. 11). That heavenly Lord grant her and other noble women long continuance in the same to His high pleasure. That like as they are become glorious to the world by the study of good letters, so may they also appear glorious in His sight by daily exercise in His divine scriptures, whose nature is in process of time to kindle their minds and inflame their hearts in the love of Christ their eternal spouse as this present book requireth. So be it.

"FOUR CLAUSES OF SACRED SCRIPTURE" (Folio 38v)

These four clauses of sacred scriptures added my Lady Elizabeth unto the beginning and end of her book, and therefore I have here registered them in the end.

Ecclus. 25: There is not a more wicked head than the head of the serpent, and there is no wrath above the wrath of a woman.

Ecclus. 25: But he that hath gotten a virtuous woman hath gotten a goodly possession. She is unto him an help and pillar whereupon he resteth.

Ecclus. 25: It were better to dwell with a lion and dragon than to keep house with a wicked wife.

Ecclus. 7: Yet depart not from a discreet and good woman that is fallen unto thee for thy portion in the fear of the Lord, for the gift of her honesty is above gold.

Elizabeth I (1544)

The 1544 manuscript of the "Glass" was written by an eleven-year-old girl whose authorial intentions are difficult to discern. Her stepmother Catherine Parr and/or the theologian John Bale made emendations that Elizabeth may not have seen before the 1548 printing by Dirik van der Straten in Marburg.[1] The German publishers with whom Bale associated during his exile were generally accurate in their works, however[2] — which cannot be said of either James Cancellar, who published the 1568–70 version, or Roger Ward, who published the 1590.[3] So the best copy-text for Bale's "Epistle Dedicatory" and "Conclusion," as well as Elizabeth's "Four Sentences," is probably the first edition (1548).[4] It would have provided the copy-text for the "Glass," too, were it not for the fortunate existence of the original and reliable manuscript.[5] A photocopy and my modernized transcription of that manuscript, together with Elizabeth's New Year's letter to Catherine Parr, appear below. For problems of orthography and transcription I would refer the interested reader to other sources.[6]

I have not provided a collation of textual variants. For Elizabeth's "Glass," unlike Shakespeare's plays, "the textual comparison of different copies of a document . . . with a view to ascertain the correct text, or the perfect condition of a particular copy"[7] would seem unnecessary and even misleading. Gary Taylor, warning against the often prejudicial use of variorum editions and collations, endorses the view that scholars should work from multiple editions, transcriptions of the manuscript, or photographic facsimiles.[8] Elizabeth's editors may have made "changes" in the various editions for political reasons, however, and she herself may have made "errors" in the translation for personal reasons.

Elizabeth's translation, though not without "inaccuracies," is generally "literal."[9] Some oddities are germane to the question of how the princess may have interpreted this poem about physical and spiritual incest: generally speaking, Elizabeth "cools" Marguerite's sexually "hot" words,[10] engages in less self-abasement,[11] and employs less repetition of words.[12] But more important, a few errors of translation and slips in handwriting seem to bear on Elizabeth's early views of the family or on the later formation of her familial and political theorizing. One example is Elizabeth's apparently confused translation of the passage in the *Miroir* where a cuckolded husband possibly pardons his adulterous wife instead of executing her. Elizabeth, whose mother, Anne Boleyn had been executed by Henry VIII on a charge of adultery, may well have thought of the contrast between the forgiving husband (Christ) and her own unmerciful father (Henry): in the most crossed-out and rewritten part of her manuscript, she translates Marguerite's French ("Assez en est, qui pour venger leur tort, / Par les juges les on faict mettre a mort") as "There be enough of them, which for to avenge their wrong, did cause the judges to condemn ~~him~~ them to die."[13]

Other "errors" involve kinship terms.[14] In translating the following lines, for example, Elizabeth simply skips over the first, which concerns a father's mercy to his child: "Si pere a eu de son enfant mercy / Si mere a eu pour son filz du soulcy / Si frere à soeur a couvert le peché / Je n'ai point veu, ou il est bien caché."[15]

Elizabeth, called "bastard" by her own father, likewise sidesteps the problem of whether a parent can recognize his or her own child. Marguerite's version of the Solomon story suggests that God can distinguish a real child from a false one, but Elizabeth omits the line about the narrator's telling love for her child: "Pour qui voyiéz mon cueur tant travailler."[16]

The question of double lineage and gender is also "misinterpreted" in esoteric fashion. Marguerite writes: "Pere, fille: O bienheureulx lignaige. / Que de doulceur, que de suavité / Vient de ceste doulce paternité." But Elizabeth translates *Pere* as if it were *Mere:* "Mother and daughter: O happy kindred."[17] And when Marguerite refers to a child who will "son bon pere offenser," Elizabeth writes of one who does "offend his mother."[18]

From one perspective the "Glass" is a series of daring spiritualist quotations and interpretive translations of passages not only from ambiguous "Reformation" teachings by the likes of Martin Luther and Guillaume Briçonnet but also, as the marginalia indicate, from the Bible. The biblical marginalia in Marguerite's text, which are often keyed to the French translation of Lefèvre d'Etaples and to the Latin Vulgate, are likely the work of editors; they vary from edition to edition and suggest not so much sources as parallels.[19] Elizabeth's translations of the scripture-based passages are generally closer to Marguerite's French than to the various contemporary English translations, which would have included the Tyndale Bible (1525), the Coverdale Bible (1535), and the Great Bible (1540). These were always the subject of heated debate. For example, in 1543, Tyndale's Bible was prohibited by an Act of Parliament, and this act also required that "no woman (unless she be a noble woman or gentle woman)" should read or use any part of the Bible under pain of fines and imprisonment. Marguerite of Navarre and Anne Boleyn were proponents of Bible translation and distribution, helping translators and readers to break prohibitions.[20]

Elizabeth I

In the transcription that follows, the scripture references that appear in the margins of Elizabeth's manuscript are included, with modernized names for biblical and apocryphal books; chapter and verse numbers are mainly those of the Vulgate.

ELIZABETH'S LETTER TO QUEEN CATHERINE PARR

(Cherry 36, Folios 2r–4v)

To our most noble and virtuous queen, Catherine, Elizabeth her humble daughter wishes perpetual felicity and everlasting joy.

Not only knowing the affectionate will and fervent zeal which your highness hath toward all godly learning as also my duty toward you (most gracious and sovereign princess), but knowing also that pusillanimity and idleness are most repugnant unto a reasonable creature and that (as the philosopher saith) even as an instrument of iron [2v] or of other metal waxeth soon rusty unless it be continually occupied, even so shall the wit of a man or woman wax dull and unapt to do or understand anything perfectly unless it be always occupied upon some manner of study, which things considered hath moved so small a portion as God hath lent me to prove what I could do. And therefore have I as for an essay or beginning (so following the right noble saying of the proverb aforesaid) translated this little book out of French rhyme into English prose, joining the sentences [3r] together as well as the capacity of my simple wit and small learning could extend themselves. The which book is entitled, or named, *The Mirror or Glass of the Sinful Soul*, wherein is contained how she (beholding and contemplating what she is) doth perceive how of herself and of her own strength she can do nothing that good is, or prevaileth for her salvation, unless it be through the grace of God, whose mother, daughter, sister, and wife by the scriptures she proveth herself to be. Trusting also that through His incomprehensible [3v] love, grace, and mercy she (being called from sin to repentance) doth faithfully hope to be saved. And although I know that as for my part which I have wrought in it (as well spiritual as manual) there is nothing done as it should be nor else worthy to come in Your Grace's hands, but rather all unperfect and uncorrect, yet do I trust also that albeit it is like a work which is but new begun and shaped, that the seal of your excellent wit and godly learning in the reading of it (if so it vouchsafe your highness to do) [4r] shall rub out, polish, and mend (or else cause to mend) the words (or rather the order of my writing) the which I know in many places to be rude, and nothing done as it should be. But I hope that after having been in Your Grace's hands there shall be nothing in it worthy of reprehension and that in the meanwhile no other (but your highness only) shall read it or see it, lest my faults be known of many. Then shall they be better excused (as my confidence is in Your Grace's accustomed benevolence) than if I should bestow a whole year [4v] in writing or inventing ways to excuse them.

Praying God almighty the maker and creator of all things to guarantee unto your highness this same New Year's Day a lucky and prosperous year with prosperous issue and continuance of many years in good health and continual joy and all to His honor, praise, and glory.

From Ashridge, the last day of the year of our Lord God, 1544.

"TO THE READER" (Cherry 36, Folios 5r–6r)

If thou dost read this whole work, behold rather the matter and excuse the speech, considering it is the work of a woman which hath in her neither science nor knowledge but a desire that each one might see what the gift of God doth when it pleaseth Him to justify the heart of a man. For what thing is a man (as for his own strength) before he hath received the gift of faith whereby only he hath the knowledge of the goodness, wisdom, and [5v] power of God? And as soon as he knoweth the truth, then is his heart full of love and charity, so that by the ferventness thereof he doth exclude all vain fear and steadfastly doth hope upon God unfeignedly. Even so the gift which our Creator giveth at the beginning doth never rest till He hath made him godly which putteth his trust in God.

O the happy gift which causeth a man to be like unto God and to possess his so desired dwelling! Alas, no man could ever understand it, unless by this gift God hath given [6r] him it, and he hath great cause to doubt of it unless God hath made him feel it in his heart.

Therefore, reader, with a godly mind I beseech thee to take it patiently to peruse this work which is but little and taste nothing but the fruit of it, praying to God, full of all goodness, that in your heart He will plant the lively faith.

Ps 51   Make me a clean heart, O God.

Where is the hell full of travail, pain, mischief, and torment? Where is the pit of cursedness, out of which doth spring all despair? Is there any hell so profound that it is sufficient to punish the tenth part of my sins, which be of so great a number that the infinite doth make the shadow so dark that I cannot account them or else scantly see them, for I am too far entered amongst [7r] them, and that worse is, I have not the power to obtain the true knowledge of one? I feel well that the root of it is in me, and outwardly I see no other effect but all is either branch, leaf, or else fruit that she bringeth forth all about me.

If I think to look for better, a branch cometh and doth close my eyes, and in my mouth doth fall when I would speak the fruit which is so bitter to swallow down. If my spirit be stirred to hearken, then a great multitude of leaves doth enter in mine ears and my nose is all stopped [7v] with flowers. Now behold how in pain, crying, and weeping my poor soul, a slave and prisoner, doth lie without clarity or light, having both her feet bound by her concupiscence, and also both her arms through evil use. Yet the power to remedy it doth not lie with me, and power have I none to cry help.

Now as far as I can see I ought to have no hope of succor but through the grace of God which I cannot deserve, which may raise everyone from death. By His brightness He giveth light to

Ps 51

John 1

my darkness, and His power, [8r] examining my fault, doth
break all the veil of ignorance and giveth me clear understanding not only that this cometh of me but also what thing abideth
in me, where I am, and wherefore I do labor, who He is whom I
have offended, whom also I did obey so seldom. Therefore it is
convenient that my pride be suppressed; and humbly I do con-
fess that, as for me, I am much less than nothing: before my   Job 10 and 30
birth, mire, and after, a dunghill, a body ready and prompt to do
all evil, not willing other study; also subject to [8v] care, sorrow,   Gen 8
and pain, a short life and the end uncertain, which under sin by   Job 14
Adam is sold and by the law judged to be hanged.   Rom 5 and 7
                                                                     1 Cor 15
   For I had never the power to observe even one of the com-   Ps 31
mandments of God. I do feel the strength of sin to be in me.   Rom 7
                                                                     Rom 7
Therefore is my sin no whit the less to be hidden; and the more
it is dissembled outwardly, so much the more it increaseth within the heart. This that God wills I cannot will; and what He
wills not, I oftentimes desire to have. Which things doth con-
strain me [9r] by importable sorrow to wish for the end of this
miserable life through desired death, because of my weary and
ragged life.

   Who shall be he then that shall deliver, and recover such
good for me? Alas, it cannot be a mortal man, for his power and
strength are not such, but it shall be only the good grace of
almighty God, which is never slack to prevent us with His   Rom 5
mercy.

   Alas, what a master! Without having deserved any goodness
of Him but rather served Him slothfully and without cease
offended Him every [9v] day, yet is He not slack in helping me.
He doth see the evil that I have done, what and how much it is,
and how of myself I can do nothing that good is, but with heart   Jer 10
and body so inclined to the contrary that I feel no strength in   Jer 17
me, unless it be to do evil.

He doth not tarry till I humbly do pray Him, or that (seeing my hell and damnation) I do cry upon Him; for with His spirit, He doth make a wailing within my heart greater than I or any man can declare, which asketh the gift whereof the virtue is unknown to my little [10r] power. And this, the same unknown sigh, doth bring me a new desire, showing the good that I have lost by my sin, which is given me again through His grace and bounty which hath overcome all sin.

O my God, what grace and goodness is this, which doth put out so many sins! Now may we see that Thou art full of all good love to make me such an honest turn.

Alas, my God, I did not seek Thee, but I fled and ran away from Thee; and here beneath Thou camest to me which am nothing [10v] but a worm of the earth all naked.

What do I say, "worm"? I do him wrong, I being so naught and forsworn, full of pride, deceit, malice, and treason.

The promise which my friends made when I was baptized, being such always through Thy passion to feel the mortifying of my flesh, to be always with Thee in the cross, where Thou hast nailed (as I do believe) and yielded death dead, and also all sin, which I have oftentimes taken down again and untied; I have broken, [11r] denied, and falsified my promise, and (through pride) I did suchwise lift up my will that (with sloth) my duty toward Thee was forgotten. And the thing which much more is as well the wealth of the promise that I had of Thee on the day of my baptism as also Thy love and promise, I have forgotten all alike.

What shall I say more? Albeit that oftentimes Thou withstoodest mine unhappiness, giving so many warnings by faith and sacraments, admonishing me by preaching and also comforting me by the [11v] receiving of Thy worthy body and holy blood, also promising to put me in the row of them that are in

Rom 8

John 7

Ps 118
Rom 6.8
and Ps 43
Rom 6

Mark 16

Rev 3

perfect innocence; but I have all this goodness put in forgetfulness. Oftentimes have I broken with Thy covenant, for my poor soul was too much fed with ill bread and damnable doctrine, I despising succor and physic such as would have helped me. And if I had been willing to look for it, I know no man whom I had required, for there is neither man, saint, nor angel for whom the [12r] heart of a sinner will change.

Alas, good Jesus! Thou seeing my blindness and that at my need I could have no succor of men, then didst Thou open the way of my salvation. O what goodness and sweetness! Is there any father to the daughter, or else brother to the sister, which would ever do as He hath done? For He came into hell to succor my soul, where against His will she was willing to perish because she did not love Thee. Alas! Thou hast loved her. O charity, fervent and inflamed, Thou [12v] art not slack to love; Thou which lovest everybody, yea, and also Thy enemies, not only forgiving them their offenses but also to give Thyself (for their salvation, liberty, and deliverance) to the death, cross, travail, pain, and suffering.

When I do consider what is the occasion of Thy love toward me, I can see nothing else but love which inciteth Thee to give me this that I cannot deserve.

Then (my God) as far as I can see, I ought to give no thanks for my salvation but only unto Thee, to whom [13r] I owe the praise for it, as to Him which is my savior and creator. Alas, what thing is this? Thou hast done so much for me, and yet art Thou not content to have forgiven me my sins, but also given unto me the right gracious gift of grace.

For it should suffice me (I coming out of such a danger) to be ordered like a stranger; but Thou dost handle my soul (if so I durst say) as a mother, daughter, sister, and wife.

I, Lord, I which am not worthy to ask bread, to come near

Acts 4

1 John 4

Rom 5

Eph 7

1 Tim 1

Eph 2

Luke 15

117

the door of the right [13v] high place where Thy dwelling is! O what grace is this, that so suddenly Thou vouchsafest to draw my soul in such highness that she feeleth herself the ruler of my body. She, poor, ignorant, and lame, doth find herself with Thee rich, wise, and strong, because Thou hast written in her heart the roll of Thy spirit and holy word, giving her true faith to receive it, which thing made her to conceive Thy son, believing Him to be God, man, savior, and also the true remitter of all sins. Therefore dost Thou vouchsafe to assure [14r] her that she is mother of Thy son of whom Thou art the only father.

And, furthermore (O my father) here is a great love, for Thou art not slack of welldoing, since Thy son full of divinity hath taken the body of a man and did join Himself with our ashes, which thing a man cannot understand unless he hath a true faith. It hath pleased Thee to put Him so near us that He did join Himself unto our flesh; then we (seeing Him to be called man) do call Him sister and brother. Now, the [14v] soul (which may say of herself that she is the sister of God) ought to be assured in her heart. After this dost Thou declare with great love how her creation is only the good will which it pleaseth Thee to have always toward her, giving assurance that before her first day (providing for her) Thou hast had Thy love in her, and how (through love) Thou hast begotten her, as (alone) Thou canst do very well. And also how Thou didst put her within this body, not for sleep with sloth but that both of them should have no other [15r] exercise but only to think how to do some service unto Thee. Then the truth maketh her to feel that there is true paternity in Thee.

O what honor, what good and glory hath the soul which doth always remember that she is Thy daughter; and, in calling Thee father, she doth Thy commandments! What is there more? Is that all? No. It pleaseth Thee to give her another name, to call

Phil 4

2 Cor 3
and Rom 16
Eph 2

Rom 5

Phil 2

Eph 1

her Thy wife and she to call Thee husband, declaring how Hos 2 Thou hast freely declared the marriage of her. By the [15v] baptism Thou hast made a promise to give her Thy goods and riches. Thou dost take her sins, for she hath nothing else, which Adam her father did give her.

All her treasures are nothing else but sins which Thou hast taken upon Thee, and paid all her whole debt. With Thy goods 1 Pet 2 and great lands, Thou hast made her so rich, and with so great a jointure, that she (knowing herself to be Thy avowed wife) doth believe to be quit of all that she oweth, esteeming very [16r] little this that she doth see here beneath. She forsaketh her old father, and all the goods that he giveth, for her husband's sake.

Surely (O my God) my soul is well hurt to be fed of such good, as to leave the pleasure of this world for the same which is everlasting, where peace is without war. I marvel how she (for joy) doth not lose her wit, countenance, and speech.

Father, father, alas, what ought I to think? Shall my spirit be so bold to take upon him to call Thee father? Yea, and also our father, for so hast Thou said [16v] in the *pater noster.* Matt 6

But to call me a daughter, hast Thou so said? I beseech Thee tell it me. Alas, yea, for (with great sweetness) Thou saidst: Daughter, lend me thy heart. O my God, instead of lending, he Prov 23 is ready to give himself wholly unto Thee. Receive him, then, and do not permit that anybody put him far from Thee: so that forever (with faithful steadfastness) he may love Thee with a daughterly love.

Now, my Lord, if Thou be my father, may I think that I am Thy mother? For I cannot [17r] perceive how I should conceive Thee, which hast created me. But Thou didst satisfy my doubt when in preaching (stretching forth Thy hands) Thou didst say: Those that shall do the will of My father, they are My Matt 12 brethren and mother.

I believe then (hearing or reading the words that Thou didst say and hast said by Thy holy prophets) the same also, which (through Thy good preachers) Thou dost daily declare unto men, believing (and desiring steadfastly to fulfill it) that through love I have begotten Thee. [17v] Therefore without any fear will I take upon me the name of a mother: Mother of God. O sweet virgin Mary, I beseech thee be not sorry that I take up such a title. I do neither steal nor pretend anything upon thy privilege. For thou (only) hast above all women received so great honor that no man can in himself comprehend how He hath been willing to take in thee our flesh.

Luke 1

For thou art mother and perfect virgin, before, after, and in His birth. Thou didst bear and [18r] nourished Him in thy holy womb. Thou didst follow Him at His preaching and also when He was troubled. Now to speak short, thou hast with God found the grace that our enemy (through malice and deceit) had caused Adam and his posterity to lose.

Luke 1

Through Eve and him we had lost it, and by thy son it hath been yielded unto us again. Therefore hast thou been rightly named full of grace, for thou lackest neither grace nor virtue since He (which is the best among them that be good, also [18v] the spring of all goodness, grace, and power, which hath created in thee so pure innocence that thou art the example of all virtues) hath built in thee His dwelling and temple. He (through love) did conform Himself with thee, and thou art transformed with Him. Therefore, if any man should think to give thee greater praise than God Himself hath done, it were a blasphemy. For there is no such praise as the same is which cometh from God.

Rom 5
John 1
Luke 1

Also hast thou had so steadfast and constant a faith that by grace [19r] she had the power to make thee godly. Therefore I will not take upon me to give thee greater praise than the honor which the sovereign Lord hath given unto thee. For thou art His corporeal mother and also (through faith) His spiritual mother. Then I (following thy faith with humility) am His spiritual mother.

Alas, my God, of the fraternity that Thou hast toward me through Thy humbleness in calling me sister, didst Thou ever say anything of it? Alas, yea, for Thou hast broken the kindred of my old [19v] father, calling me daughter of adoption.

Well, then, since we have but one father, I will not fear to call Thee my brother, for so hast Thou said by Solomon in his ballad, saying, My sister, thou hast wounded my heart with the sweet look of one of thy eyes and with one of thy hairs. Alas, good brother, I wish for nothing else but that in wounding Thee I might find myself wounded with Thy love. Song of Sol 4

And likewise Thou dost call me wife, showing that Thou lovest me, and call me (by true jealous love), [20r] My dove, rise up my spouse. Therefore shall I say with loving faith, Thou art mine and I am Thine. Thou dost call me love and fair spouse. If so it be, such hast Thou made me. Alas! Doth it please Thee to give me such names? They are able to break a man's heart and to kindle him by such love when he thinketh upon the honor which is greater than he hath deserved. Song of Sol 2

Mother, mother: but what child is it? It is of such a son that my heart doth break for love. My God, my son, O Jesus, what [20v] speaking is this! Mother and daughter: O happy kindred. O what sweetness doth proceed of the same paternity! But what daughterly love and reverent fear ought I to have toward Him? My father, yea, and my creator, my protector and my conservator. To be Thy sister, alas, here is a great love. Now dost Thou break my heart in the middle. Make room for the same so sweet a brother, so that no other name be written in Thee but only my brother Jesus, the son of God. For unto no other [21r] man will Ps 26 and 30

121

I give place, for all the grudging and baiting that they can do unto me.

Keep my heart then, my brother, and let not Thy enemy enter in it. O my father, brother, child, and spouse, with hands joined, humbly upon my knees, I yield Thee thanks and praise that it pleaseth Thee to turn Thy face toward me, converting my heart and covering me with such grace that Thou dost see no more my evils and sins. So well hast Thou hidden them that it seemeth Thou hast put them in [21v] forgetfulness. Yea, and also they seem to be forgotten of me, which have committed them, for faith and love causeth me to forget them, putting wholly my trust in Thee only.

James 3

Then, my father, in whom lieth unfeigned love, whereof can I have fear in my heart? I confess that I have done all the evil that one man can do and that, of myself, I am naught. Also that I have offended Thee as the prodigal child did, following the foolish trade of the flesh, where I have spent all my substance and also all the [22r] abundance of goods which I had received of Thee. For poverty had withered me even as hay, and yielded my spirit dead for hunger, seeking to eat the reliefs of swine; but I found very little savor in such meats. Then I (seeing my living to be so miserable) did return unto Thee, O father. Alas I have sinned in heaven, and before Thee; I am not worthy (I tell it before every man) to be called Thy child, but (O bountiful father) do no worse unto me, but as to one of Thy household servants. [22v]

John 6
Luke 15

Alas, what love and zeal is this? For Thou wouldst not tarry my coming and prayer, but (stretching forth Thy hand) receivedst me, when I did think that Thou wouldst not see me. And instead of having punishment, Thou dost assure me of my salvation.

Where is he then that shall punish me when my father shall

deny him my sin? There is no judge that can condemn any man, unless God himself would damn him. I fear not to have lack of goods since I have God for my father. [23r] My enemy shall do me no harm, for my father shall undo his power. If I owe anything, He shall pay it for me. If I have deserved death, He (as a king) shall give me grace and pardon and deliver me from prison and hanging.

But here is the worse: what mother have I been? For after I had received the name of a true mother, then have I been too rude unto Thee. For after I had conceived and brought Thee forth, I left reason; and being subject unto my own will, not taking heed unto Thee, [23v] I fell asleep and gave place to my great enemy: the which in the night of ignorance (I being asleep) did steal Thee from me, craftily, and in the place she did put her child which was dead. So did I lose Thee by my own fault, which thing is a hard remorse for me. Now have I lost Thee by mine own fault, because I took no heed to keep Thee.

1 Kings 3 [Note: Present 1 and 2 Sam. and 1 and 2 Kings were formerly cited as 1, 2, 3, and 4 Kings].

My enemy, my sensuality (I being in my beastly sleep) did steal Thee from me and gave me another child having no life in him, which is called sin, whom I will not have, for I do ut[24r]terly forsake him. She affirmed that he was my own, but I knew him to be hers, for as soon as I came to the light of the grace which Thou hadst given me, then I knew my glory to be changed when I saw the dead child not to be mine. For the same which was alive (whom she had taken away) was my own. Between Jesus and sin is the change so apparent. But here is a strange thing: this old woman causeth me to keep him which is dead, whom she saith to be mine, and so she will maintain.

O [24v] Solomon, true judge! Thou hast heard this lamentable process, and ordained (contenting the parties) that my child should be divided in two parts. The false woman agreeth it should be so, but I (remembering Him to be my own son) was rather content to lose Him, than to see His body parted in two pieces (for true and perfect love is never content with one half of this that she loveth). But I would rather weep for my whole loss than to recover but one half. My mind should [25r] not be satisfied if I had recovered one half without life. Alas! give her rather the child which is alive; better it is for me to die, than to see Jesus Christ divided. But (O my Lord) Thou didst look better to it than I, for Thou (seeing the pain that I did suffer, and how I did rather forsake my right than to see such cruelness) saidst, This is the true mother, and caused them to give me my child again.

1 Kings 3

O sweet Jesus, have I found Thee, after having proved if I did love Thee, I who had [25v] lost Thee, yet didst Thou return unto me? Alas, dost Thou vouchsafe to come again to her which, being let with sin, could not keep Thee? O my sweet child, my son, my nourisher, of whom I am right humble creature, do not permit that ever I do leave Thee, for I repent myself of the time passed.

Now come, my sensuality, with sins of all qualities, for thou hast not the power to make me receive the child which is dead. The same that I have is strong enough to defend me, and He shall not permit that [26r] thou do take Him away from me. He is already as strong as any man is; therefore may I sleep and take rest near of Him. For He shall keep me better than I could keep Him. Then (as I think) I may take rest.

Ps 23

O what a sweet rest it is, of the mother and the son together. My sweet child, O my God, honor and praise be unto Thee only, so that everybody may perceive how it hath pleased Thee me less than nothing to call a mother. The more that the thing is strange and hard to be done, [26v] the more ought Thy goodness have praise for it.

And also, I find myself more bound unto Thee than ever I

did, for it pleaseth Thee to have retained me for Thy sister. I am sister unto Thee, but so naughty a sister that better it is for me to hide such a name; for I (forgetting the honor and adoption of so noble kindred, also Thy so sweet a brotherly behavior toward me) did rise against Thee and (not remembering my faults, but going far from Thee) did agree with my brother Aaron, willing to give judg[27r]ment against Thy works, and also grudging against Thee privily, which thing causeth me to have a great remorse in my conscience.

Num 12

O bountiful God, brother, and true Moses, which doth all things with goodness and justice, I have esteemed Thy deeds to be wicked, being so bold and saying rashly, Why hast Thou married a strange woman? Thou givest us a law, and punishment if we do not fulfill it; and Thyself would not be bound to it, forbidding us the thing which Thyself didst. For Thou dost forbid us to kill [27v] any man; and Thou dost kill and spared none of three thousand that Thou caused to be slain. Also God gave us commandment by Thee, that we should not marry the daughter of a stranger, but Thou tookest Thy wife among them. Alas, my brother, I told Thee a great many such words, which I know well to be foolish, whereof I do repent; for the lively voice of God took me up before I went out of the place. What didst Thou of my sin? Alas, my brother, Thou wouldst not have me to be punished but rather [28r] wouldst for my health and salvation, in asking for this great benefit, that it should please God to mitigate His judgment. Which thing Thou couldst not obtain, for I became a lazar, so that when anybody should look upon me, he might say that I had not been wise.

Exod 32

Num 12

And so was I put (like a lazar) from the tents and habitation of the people, for a soul cannot have greater punishment than to be banished from the company of them that are good and holy [28v] because that a sick body may mar them which be in health. But what didst Thou, seeing my repentance? For Thou didst help that my penance was soon ended. By true love Thou didst pray for me, and then did I return.

O what brother who, instead of punishing His foolish sister, would cleave unto her! For injury, grudge, and great offense, Thou gavest her grace and love in recompense. Alas, my brother, this is too much. Thou shouldst not do such a good turn unto such a poor woman as I am. I have [29r] done ill, and Thou givest me good for it. I am Thine, and Thou didst say that Thou art mine. Thine I am, and so will I be forever. I fear no more the great foolishness of Aaron, for no man shall loose me from Thee.

Ps 26

Now then that we are brother and sister together, I care but little for all other men. Thy lands are my own inheritance. Let us then keep (if it pleaseth Thee) but one household. Since it pleaseth Thee to humble Thyself so much as to join Thy heart with mine, in making Thyself a lively man, I do right humbly thank Thee. [29v] And as for doing it as I ought, it lieth not in my power. Take my meaning then, and excuse mine ignorance, since I am of so great a kindred as to be Thy sister. O my God, I have good cause to praise, to love, and to serve Thee unfeignedly and not to desire or fear anything but Thee only. Keep me well, then, for I ask no other brother or friend.

If any mother hath taken any care for her son, if any brother hath hid the fault of his sister, I never saw it (or else it was kept wondrous secret) that any husband would forgive [30r] his wife after she had offended and did return unto him. There be enough of them which for to avenge their wrong did cause the judges to condemn them to die. Others, seeing their wives sin, did not suddenly spare their own hands to kill them. Others also (seeing their faults appear) did send them home again to their own friends. Others (seeing their ill deeds) did shut them

in a prison. Now, to speak short, look upon all their complexions, for the end of their pretense is no[30v]thing else but punishment. And the less harm that ever I could perceive in punishing them is this, that they would never see them again. Thou
shouldst rather make the sky to turn than to make the agreement between the husband and his wife when he knoweth truly
the fault that she hath done or else hath seen and found her in
doing amiss.

Wherefore (O my God) I can find no man to be compared
unto Thee. For Thou art the perfect example of love; and now
[31r] (more than ever I did) I do confess that I have broken
mine oath and promise.

Alas, Thou hadst chosen me for Thy wife and didst set me up   Hos 2
in great dignity and honor (for what greater honor may one
have than to be in the place of Thy wife, which sweetly taketh
rest near to Thee), of all Thy goods queen, mistress, and lady,
and also in surety both of body and soul. I so vile a creature,
being ennobled by Thee. Now (to tell the truth) I had more and
better than any man can desire. [31v] Therefore my heart hath
cause to sigh always, and with abundance of tears my eyes to   Ps 94; Ezek 36
come out of my head. My mouth cannot make too many ex-
clamations, for there is neither old nor new writings that can
show so pitiful a thing as the same which I will tell now. Shall or
dare I tell it? May I pronounce it without shame? Alas, yea, for
my confusion is to show the great love of my husband; therefore I care not if for his worship I do declare my shame.

O my savior, which [32r] died and was crucified on the cross
for my sins, this deed is not such as [a father] to leave his son
and as a child to offend his mother or else (as a sister) to grudge
and chide against her brother. Alas, this is worse; for the offense
is the greater where more love and knowledge is. And the more
we receive of God familiarity and benefits, the offense is the
greater to deceive Him.

I which was called spouse and loved of Thee as Thine own soul, shall I tell the truth? Yea, I have left, forgotten, and run away from Thee. [32v] I did leave Thee to go at my pleasure. I have forsaken Thee to choose a worse. I did leave Thee (O spring of all goodness and faithful promise), I did leave Thee. But whither went I? Into a place where nothing is but cursedness. I have left my trusty friend and lover worthy to be loved above all other. I have left Thee through my own ill will. I have left Thee, full of beauty, goodness, wisdom, and power. And (for the better to outdraw myself from Thy love) I have taken Thine enemy, which is the devil, the world, [33r] and the flesh, whom to overcome Thou hast fought so sore on the cross to put me in liberty whom they had a long time kept prisoner, slave, and so bound that no man could cause me to humble myself. And as for the love and charity that I should have toward Thee, they did quench it so that the name of Jesus my husband (which before I had found so sweet) was to me tedious, and I did hate it so that oftentimes I did jest at it. And if any man (we hearing a sermon) should say unto me, The preacher saith well, [33v] I will answer, It is true. But my words did flee away as a feather doth. And I went never to the church but for manner's sake. All my deeds were but hypocrisy, for my mind was in other places. I was annoyed when I heard speak of Thee, for I was more willing to go at my pleasure.

Now to speak short, all this that Thou didst forbid me, I did it; and all that Thou commandedst me to do, I did eschew it; and all this (O my God) because I did not love Thee. [34r]

Yet for all that I did hate, forsake, run away, and betray Thee, because I should give Thy place to another, hast Thou suffered that I should be mocked, or else beaten, or killed? Hast Thou put me in dark prison, or banished, setting nought by me? Hast Thou taken away again Thy gifts and jewels, to pun-

Deut 32

Gal 4

Prov 1

Joel 2

ish me for my unfaithful sins? Have I lost my jointure, which
Thou hast promised me, because I did offend against Thee?
Am I accused by Thee before [34v] the judge as a naughty
woman should be? Yet, hast Thou forbidden me that I should
never present myself before Thee (even as reason was) and also
that I should never come to Thy house? O true, perfect husband and friend, the most loving among all good lovers! Alas, Luke 15 and 18
Thou hast done otherwise. For Thou soughtest for me diligently when I was going in the most deep place of hell, where
all the evils are done. I that was so far from Thee, both heart
and mind out of the true way, [35r] then didst Thou call upon Ps 44
me, saying, My daughter, hark and see and bow thy hearing toward Me. Forget, also, the same manner of people, with whom
thou didst run away from Me and also the house of thine old
father, where thou hast dwelled so long. Then the king full of
godliness shall desire thy company.

But when Thou sawest that this sweet and gracious speaking
did me no good, then Thou beganst to cry: Come unto Me all Matt 11
ye which are weary with labor. I am I that shall receive and feed
[35v] you with My bread.

Alas, I would not hark unto all these words; for I doubted
whether it were Thou, or else a simple writing, that so said. For
I was so foolish that without love I did read Thy word. I saw and
understood well that the comparisons of the vineyard which Deut 32
brought forth thorns and poisons instead of good fruit, Thou Isa 5
saidst all of this of me which had so done. Considering also that
when Thou didst call thee me wife, saying, Come again, Sul- Song of Sol 3
amite, all this Thou didst speak because I should my sin leave. [Note: Shula-
[36r] And of all these words, I did as though I had understood mite is a name
never a word. by which the
Beloved is
But when I did read Jeremiah the prophet, I confess that I called].
had in the reading of it fear in my heart and shame in my face. I

will tell it, yea, and with the tears in my eyes, and all for Thy honor and to suppress my pride. Thou hast said this by Thy holy prophet: If a woman hath offended her husband and left him to go with another man, they never saw that the husband would take her again. Is [36v] she not esteemed to be polluted and of no value? The law doth consent to put her in the hands of the justice, or else drive her away and never see her or take her again. But thou, which hast made separation of My bed, and did put thy false lovers in My place and committed fornication with them, yet, for all this, thou mayst come unto Me again, for I will not be angry against thee. Lift up thine eyes, and look up, then shalt thou see in what place thy sin had led thee, and how thou liest down in the earth. O poor soul, look where [37r] thy sin hath put thee: even upon the highways, where thou didst wait and tarried to beguile them that came by, even as a thief doth which is hidden in wilderness. Therefore (having fulfilled thy pleasure) thou hast infected (with fornication) all the earth which was about thee. Thine eye, thy forehead, and thy face had lost all their good manner; for they were such as those of an harlot, and yet thou hadst no shame of thy sin.

And the surplus that Jeremiah saith, which things constraineth me to know my wretched life and [37v] to wish (with sorrowful sighs) the day, the hour, the month, the year, and the time that I did leave Thee, yielding myself condemned and worthy to be forever in the everlasting fire. The same fear (which doth not proceed of me, but cometh of Thee and exceedeth all pleasure) had almost put me in despair as often as I did remember my sin, if it hath not been that Thou never leftest me. For as soon as Thou knewest my will bowed to obey Thee, then (putting in me a lively faith) Thou didst use Thy [38r] clemency and goodness; so that after I knew Thee to be Lord, master, and king (of whom I ought to have fear), then found I

Jer 3

Prov 15

my fear to be quenched, believing that Thou were so gracious, good, sweet, and pitiful [a] husband that I (which should rather hide me than show myself) was not afraid to go and seek for Thee; and in seeking I found Thee.

But what didst Thou then? Hast Thou refused me? Alas (my God) no, but rather excused me. Hast Thou turned Thy face from me? No, for Thy sweet look hath penetrated my heart, wounding him to the [38v] death, giving me remorse for my sins. Thou hast not put me back with Thy hand, but with both Thine arms and with a sweet and manly heart Thou didst meet with me by the way, and not reproaching my faults, embracedst me. I could not see, beholding Thy countenance, that ever Thou didst perceive mine offense; for Thou hast done as much for me as though I had been good and honest, and didst hide my fault from everybody in giving me again part of Thy bed, and also showing that [39r] the multitude of my sins are so hidden and overcome by Thy great victory that Thou wilt never re-member them. So Thou seest nothing in me but the grace, gifts, and virtues which it pleaseth Thy goodness to give me.

O charity, I see well that Thy goodness doth consume my lewdness, and maketh me a godly and beautiful creature. This that was mine Thou hast destroyed it and made me so perfect a creature that Thou hast done me as much good as any husband can do unto his wife, giving me a faithful [39v] hope in Thy promises.

Now I have (through Thy good grace) recovered the place of Thy wife. O happy and desired place, gracious bed, throne right honorable, seat of peace, rest of all war, high step of honor separate from the earth! Dost Thou receive this unworthy crea-ture, giving her the scepter and crown of Thine empire and glorious realm? Who did ever hear speak of such a thing as to raise up one so high which of herself was nothing, and maketh of a great value this that [40r] of itself was naught.

131

Alas, what thing is this? For, I casting mine eyes on high, I see in Thee goodness so unknown, grace and love so uncomprehensible, that my sight is left invisible. Then am I constrained to look down; and, looking down, I do see what I am and what I was willing to be. Alas, I do see in it the lewdness, darkness, and extreme deepness of my evils; also my death, which by humbleness closeth mine eye; the admirable goodness of Thee, and the unspeakable evil which is in me; Thy highness and right pure majesty, [40v] my right fragile and mortal nature; Thy gifts, goods, and beatitude, my malice and great unkindness; how good Thou art unto me, and how unkind I am unto Thee; this that Thou wilt, and this that I pursue. Which things considered causeth me to marvel how it pleaseth Thee to join Thyself unto me, seeing that there is no comparison between us both; for Thou art my God, and I am of Thy work. Thou art my creator, and I am Thy creature. Now, to speak short, I cannot define what it is of Thee, [41r] for I know myself to be the least thing that can be compared unto Thee.

O love, Thou madest this agreement when Thou didst join life and death together; but the union hath vivified death. Life dying and life without end hath made our death a life; death hath given unto life quick death. Through such death I (being dead) received life, and by death, I am ravished with Him, which is alive. I live in Thee, and, as for me, I am dead, for death is nothing else to me but the coming out of a prison. [41v]

Death is life unto me, for through death I am alive. This mortal life yieldeth me full of care and sorrow; and death yieldeth me content. O what a goodly thing it is to die, which causeth my soul to live, delivering her, through this mortal death, exempt from miserable death and equal unto God, with so mighty a love that, unless she doth die, she languisheth always.

Is not, then, the soul blameless which would fain die to have

Heb 3

such life? Yea, surely, for she ought to call the death her well   Phil 1
beloved [42r] friend.

O sweet death, pleasant sorrow, mighty key, delivering from sorrow all those which, trusting in Thee and in Thy passion, were mortified because they did trust in Thee and in Thy death; for with a sweet sleep Thou didst put them from the death which caused them to lament.

O how happy is the same deadly sleep unto him who when he waketh doth find (through Thy death) the everlasting life! For the death is no other thing to a Christian man but a liberty from his mortal bond. And [42v] the death which is fearful to the wicked is pleasant and agreeable to them that be good.

Then is death (through Thy death) destroyed. Therefore,   Heb 2
my God, if I were rightly taught, I should call death life, end of labor, and beginning of everlasting joy. For I know that long life doth let me from Thy sight.

O death, come and break the same obstacle of life, or else love, do now a miracle. Since I cannot yet see my spouse, transform me with Him, both body and soul, and then shall I the better tarry for the [43r] coming of death. Let me die, that I may live with Him, for there is none that can help me unless it be thou only.

O my savior, through faith I am planted and joined with   Rom 11
Thee. O what union is this, since (through faith) I am sure of Thee. And now I may call Thee son, father, spouse, and   John 1
brother. Father, brother, son, husband: O what gifts Thou dost give by the goodness of those names. O my father, what paternity; O my brother, what fraternity; O my child, what delectation; O my [43v] husband, O what conjunction! Father full of humility, brother having taken our similitude, son engendered through faith and charity, husband loving in all extremity.

But whom dost Thou love? Alas! It is she which Thou hast

withdrawn from the snare wherein through malice she was bound, and gave her the place, name, and office of a daughter, sister, mother, and wife. O my savior, the same sweetness is of great savor, right pleasant and of a sweet taste, if any man speak [44r] unto Thee or else hear Thee. And calling Thee (without any fear) father, child, and spouse, hearing Thee I do hear myself to be called mother, sister, daughter, and spouse. Alas! now may the soul (which doth find such sweetness) be consumed by love.

Is there any love that may be compared unto this, but it hath some evil condition? Is there any pleasure to be esteemed? Is there any honor, but it is accounted for shame? Is there any profit to be compared unto this? Now, to speak short, [44v] is there any thing that more I could love? Alas no, for he that loveth God doth repute all these things worse than a dunghill. Pleasure, profit, and honor of this world are but trifles unto him which hath found the love of God. For such love is so profitable, honorable, and abundant that she only contenteth the heart and yieldeth him so content (as I dare say) that he never desireth or would have other thing. For whosoever hath God (as we ought to have Him), he that asketh [45r] any other thing is a superfluous man.

Now, thanked be God, through faith have I recovered and gotten the same love; therefore I ought to be satisfied and content. Now I have Thee, my father, for the defense of the foolishness of my long youth. Now have I Thee, my brother, to succor my sorrows wherein I find no end. Now I have Thee, my son, for the only stay of my feeble age. Now have I Thee, true and faithful husband, for the satisfying of my whole heart and mind. Now since I have Thee, I do forsake [45v] all them that be in the world. Since I hold Thee, Thou shalt escape me no more. Since I see Thee, I will look upon nothing that should

Jer 3
Song of Sol 4.5

Phil 3

Ps 106

Song of Sol 3

keep me from the beholding of Thy divinity. Since I do hear Ps 84
Thee, I will hear nothing that letteth me from the enjoying of Song of Sol 3.8
Thy voice. Since it pleaseth Thee to put me so near Thee, I will
rather die than to touch another man. Since I serve Thee, I will
serve no other master. Since Thou hast joined Thy heart with
mine, if he doth depart from it, let him be punished forever. For
[46r] the departing from Thy love is worse than any damnation
is. I do not fear the pain of ten thousand hells as much as I do to
lose Thee one day of the week.

Alas, my God, my father, and creator, do not suffer that the
devil (inventor of all sin) hath such power that he make me to
lose Thy presence. For whosoever hath once felt the loss of Ps 7 [37]
Thy love, he shall say that I would rather be bound forever in
hell than to feel what he shall feel by the loss of Thy love one
moment of time.

O my savior, do not permit that [46v] ever I do depart from
Thee. But (if it pleaseth Thee) put me in such a place that my
soul, through wantonness or sin, be never loosed from Thy
love. For, in this world, I cannot have perfectly this my desire,
which things considered maketh me fervently and with all my
heart to desire the departing from this miserable body, not
fearing the death nor any of her instruments. For what fear
ought I to have of my God which (through love) hath endeav-
ored Himself and suffered death wherein He was not bound,
but be[47r]cause He should undo the power that this mortal 2 Tim 1
death had.

Now is Jesus dead, in Whom we are all dead; and through His
death He causeth every man to live again. I mean those which,
through faith, are partakers of His passion. For even as death,
before the great mystery of the cross, was hard unto everybody, Ecclus 4
there was no man but was feared withal, considering the copula-
tion of the body and soul, their order, love, and agreement,

where the extreme sorrow was in the departing one from another. [47v] But since it hath pleased the sweet lamb to offer
Himself upon the cross, His great love hath kindled a fire within
our heart so vehement that every Christianman ought to esteem
the passage of death but a play or pastime and so to provoke one
another to die. For even as fear of death did retard us, even so
love ought to give us a desire to die. For if true love be unfeignedly within the heart of a man, he can feel no other thing, because that love is so great of itself that she keepeth all the room
and putteth [48r] out all other desires, not suffering anything in
him but God only. For wheresoever true and perfect love is, we
do neither remember fear nor sorrow.

If our pride (to get honor) maketh us to seek for death with
so many means; if (to have a foolish pleasure) a man putteth
himself in jeopardy of his life; if a man (to get riches) doth put
his life in danger for the value of a shilling; if the will to rob, or
to kill, to beat, or to beguile causeth oftentimes the mind of a
man to turn so that he [48v] doth not see the danger of death
when he will do any ill or else avenge himself of any man; if the
strength of sickness or the disease of a melancholy causeth a
man to wish for death and oftentimes (as doth) drown, hang, or
kill himself, for such evil and desire is so great that he causeth a
man to choose death for liberty; if so it be, then, that these great
pains, full of evil and imperfection, causeth them not to fear the
hazard of death, and it seemeth unto them that it cometh too
late, alas, what ought true and laudable love [49r] do? What
ought the love of the creator do? Should she not stir so the
heart of a man that he (being transported with such affection)
should feel no other thing in him? Alas, yea, for death is a
pleasant thing to the soul which is in love with God and es-
teemeth the passage easy, through which she cometh out of a
prison. For the hard way (through which she cometh to em-
brace her husband) cannot weary her.

Isa 53

1 John 4

Ps 115
Phil 1

O my savior, how good the same death is, through which we shall have the end of all sorrow, by whom also we shall [49v] enjoy Thy sight and be transformed unto the likeness of Thy majesty.

O death, (through Thy deed) I trust to have so much honor that upon my knees (in crying and weeping) I do desire thee. Come quickly, and make an end of my pain and sorrow.

O happy daughters, right holy souls, joined in the city of Jerusalem, open your eyes and (with pity) look upon my desolation. I beseech ye that in my name ye will tell unto my God, my friend and king, how at every hour of the day I do lan[50r]guish for His love. Ps 119
Song of Sol 5

O sweet death, through such love come to me, and with love bring me unto my God. O death, where is thy sting and dart? Alas, they are vanished from my eyes, for rigor is changed into sweetness. Since my friend did suffer upon the cross for my sake, His death doth so encourage my heart that Thou art under [wondrous?] gentle to me, if I might follow Him. O death, I beseech thee come to put the friend with His love. 1 Cor [15]

Now since death is so pleasant a life that she pleaseth me more than feareth [50v] me, then I ought to fear nothing but the true judgment of God. All my sins with His just balance shall be weighed and shown openly. This that I have done, also my thought and word, shall be better known than if it were written in a roll. And we may not think that charity would offend justice and truth, for whosoever doth live unfaithfully shall be punished in the everlasting pain. God is just, and His judgment is righteous. All that He doth is just in all things. Alas, what am I, considering my righte[51r]ousness, I wretched and poor creature? For I know that all the works of just men are so full of vices that before God they are more filthy than dirt or any other filthiness. What shall it be, then, of the sins which I Luke 12
and Matt 10

Ps 7

Job 15

Mic 7

Isa 64

Ps 129 and 37

do commit, whereof I do feel the burden importable? I can say nothing else but that I have won damnation.

Is this the end? Shall despair be the comfort of my great ignorance? Alas, my God, no, for the invisible faith causeth me to believe that all things which are impossible to men are possible unto Thee. [51v] So that Thou do convert my work (which is nothing) into some good work. Then, O Lord, who shall condemn me, since He (which is given me for a judge) is my husband, my father, and my refuge?

Matt 19

Rom 5 and 8

Ps 89
and 1 Tim 2

Alas, what father doth never condemn his child but doth always excuse and defend him? Then I see I have no other accuser but Jesus Christ which is my redeemer, whose death hath restored us our inheritance, for He made Himself our man of law, showing His so worthy merits before God, wherewith my [52r] great debt is so surmounted that in judgment she is accounted for nothing.

1 John 2
and 1 Tim 2

O redeemer, here is a great love, for we find but few such men of laws. O sweet Jesus, it is unto Thee that I am a debtor, for Thou dost pray and speak for me. And moreover, when Thou dost see that I am poor, Thou dost pay my debt with the abundance of Thy goods. O incomprehensible sea of all goodness! O my father, dost Thou vouchsafe to be my judge, not willing the death of the sinner? O Jesus Christ, true fisher [52v] and savior of the soul, friend above all friends, for Thou, being my man of law, excused and did speak for me where Thou couldst justly accuse me.

Isa 53

Heb 7
Rom 8
Ezek 18

Matt 4

I fear no more to be undone by any man, for the law is satisfied for all. My sweet spouse hath made the payment so abundant that the law can ask nothing to me, but she may have it of Him. For (as I believe) He hath taken all my sins to Him and gave His goods and riches.

[1] Pet 2

O my savior (presenting Thy virtues), Thou dost content the

[53r] law. When she will reproach me my sins, Thou dost show her how willingly in Thine own flesh Thou hast taken the charge of them through the conjunction of our marriage; also how upon the cross, through Thy passion, Thou hast satisfied it. Moreover, Thy charity hath given me this that Thou hast deserved. Therefore (since Thy merit is my own) the law asketh nothing of me.

Then will I fear no more the judgment, but with desire, rather than by force, I do tarry for the time that [53v] I shall see my judge and hear of Him a just judgment. Yet I know that Thy judgment is so just that there is no fault in it and that my unfaithfulness is worthy to suffer the cruelness of hell. For if I do only consider my deserving, I can see nothing in it that can keep me from the fire of hell. True it is that the torment of hell was never prepared but for the devil, and not for a reasonable man; nevertheless, if any man hath put his mind to be like unto the devil, then he ought (as the devil shall) to be [54r] paid with such a reward.

But if a man, through contemplation, doth hold of the angel virtue, goodness, and perfection, so that he doth obtain heaven, which is a place of like deserving, then shall the vicious be punished with him to whom he did join himself. And since he followed Satan, he must keep such place as is prepared for him. Now, I considering the diversity of both sorts, it comforteth my spirit but little, for I cannot deny but I am more like unto the devil than to the [54v] angel. Wherefore I fear and tremble, for the living of the angel is so godly that I am nothing like him (this I do confess); but as for the other, I am so like unto him, of malice in custom, that of his pain and torment I ought to be partaker. For the cruel sin which hath bound me in hell is great, and sin is strong with letteth nothing come from him and feareth not that any man cometh to assail him. He which is strong

Ps 84

Wisd. of Sol 18

Matt 25

139

Luke 11   knoweth not how his strength goeth away [55r] when a stronger man than he cometh. Sin is strong which bringeth us into hell, and I could never see that any man, by merit and pain, could vanquish hell, save only He which hath made such assault through charity (He being humbled to the cross) that He hath bound and overcome His enemy, broken hell and his power, so that he hath no further strength to keep any soul prisoner which hath put her trust in God.

Then, believing and trusting in the power that God hath, I do set by hell and sin [55v] not a straw. For whereof can sin annoy me, unless it be to show how my God is merciful, strong, mighty, and vanquisher of all the evil which is within my heart? If my sin forgiven is the glory of my savior, I ought likewise to believe that also my glory is increased therewith, acknowledging that I am planted and joined with Him. His honor only doth honor all His, and His riches doth replenish everyone of goods.

Then is hell, and sin, overcome by Him. O glutton hell, where is Thy defense? Thou [56r] villain, sin, where is thy power? O death, where is thy sting and victory, which are so much spoken of? Instead of death, thou givest us life, and so dost thou contrary unto thy will. And also, thou sin, which would draw everybody unto damnation, thou dost serve us as a ladder to reach unto the goodly city of Jerusalem. For thou wouldst by thy cursed nature that our maker should lose His creature. But through love and grace Thou dost cause her to come again and submit herself unto God more than ever she did. [56v] His great goodness doth make thee to lose the pain which thou dost take all the whole week. Therefore hell hath not had all the number which he did pretend to have, because the shadow and strength of His passion is such a protection to the soul that she ought to fear neither death, sin, nor hell.

Is there anything, then, that can hurt me if God be willing,

Phil 2
Eph 4

1 Cor 15

Rom 5

through faith, to draw me unto Him? I mean faith such as we must have to obtain the right high gift from above, and also Eph 2 such faith which, through charity, [57r] doth join the humble servant unto his master. I, being joined unto Him, ought to have no fear of travail, pain, or else sorrow. For whosoever willingly doth suffer any manner of death or sorrow (as Christ did), he doth feel in such torment great consolation for his soul. Knowing that as for myself I am weak and with God I am right strong, by His comfort I may do all things; for His love is so Phil 4 steadfast and everlasting that she varieth for nothing of this world.

Who can then outdraw me from His grace? Surely the [57v] Rom 8 great height of heaven nor the deepness of hell nor the breadth of all the earth, neither death nor sin (which doth war every day against me) can separate me one day from the great love and charity that my father, through Jesus Christ, hath unto me. For His love is such that He loveth me which doth not love Him, and if I love Him, then shall I feel His love to increase because my love is not worthy to love Him. But I desire His love to be mine, which I feel such as though it were my own. His desire is to love me, and [58r] through His love He causeth my heart to be inflamed with love, and through such love He findeth Himself so well beloved that His own deed yieldeth Him content and not my own love or strength. Contenting Himself, His love doth increase more in me than I can desire of Him.

O true lover, spring of all charity, and the only purse of the heavenly treasure, ought I to think, dare I to say, what Thou art? May I write it? Can any mortal man comprehend Thy goodness and love? And if Thou dost print it within any man's [58v] heart, can he express it? No, surely, for the capacity of no man can comprehend the unmeasurable goodness which is in Thee. For natural reason doth show us how there is no com-

Ps 144

parison between an eternal and a mortal thing; but when, through love, the mortal is joined with the eternal, the mortal thing is so full of the eternal that she cannot find the end of it, for she hath more good within her than she can hold. Therefore doth a man (which hath this love) think that all the world is within him.

Even as we see that the [59r] sun with only one sparkle of his light doth blind the eye of a man, and yet doth she hide her great light (but ask the eye what he hath seen: the eye will say that he hath seen the whole clarity of the sun; but that is a lie for he, being blinded with a little sparkle, could not see the whole clarity of the sun; and nevertheless he is so content it seemeth unto him, if he had so much light in him as the same sparkle was, that he should not be able to suffer it), even so the soul which (through faith) doth feel one sparkle of the love of God [59v] then doth find this fire so great and marvelous, so sweet and good, that it is impossible unto her to declare what thing the same love is. For a little that she hath felt doth yield her mind

Ecclus 24

satisfied and desiring more of this whereof she hath enough. So doth she live desiring, languishing, and sighing. The heart doth feel well that he hath received too much of it, but he hath conceived such desire in this too much that he always desireth to receive the thing which he cannot have, neither is he worthy to receive. He knoweth the [60r] good that he hath already to be unspeakable, and yet would he have more of this whereof he cannot understand? He can neither feel nor think the good which is in him.

Then it lieth not in my power to tell what thing the love of God is, since I have no knowledge of the ferventness thereof. He that thinketh to have all this love within his heart cannot truly declare what thing it is. Happy is he which hath such abundance that he may say, My God, I have enough of it. He which hath this love within him dare not speak of it for fear that in speaking he should [60v] let it go (unless it be for the salvation of his neighbor, to edify him).

The impossibility of the declaration of this love, then, shall make me hold my peace. For there is no saint so perfect, if he will speak of the love of the high God, of His goodness, sweetness, grace, and of all the things which pertaineth unto Him, he shall, looking below, stop his mouth.

I, then, worm of the earth, less than nothing, I ought to cease and not to speak of the highness of this love. But too much unkindness should be in me if I had written nothing, having this done to satisfy to a [61r] better wit than mine is. For he that would hide the goodness of so good a master should commit a sin worthy to be punished with the everlasting pain. Therefore come, O happy Paul, which hast tasted so much of the same sweet honey, being blinded for the space of three days and ravished unto the third heaven. Now I beseech thee, satisfy my ignorance and fault and tell me what thou hast seen with such a vision. Acts 9 and 2 Cor 12

Hark what he saith: O unspeakable highness of the great treasure and riches of the spring of all wisdom, science, and pa[61v]tience, Thy judgments are incomprehensible and Thy ways are unsearchable to all our wits. O good saint Paul, thy words causeth us to marvel that thou, having knowledge of such secrets, would speak no further of it. But yet, tell us what thing we trust to have one day through such love. Rom 11

Hark, and ponder the words which he saith: There was never any man that did see, or ears could never hear, neither any man could comprehend this that God hath prepared for his good friends. 1 Cor 2

Would he speak any further? [62r] No, yet all this that he saith is for nothing else but to provoke us to love and to esteem this that he can neither declare nor name, and to draw our hearts, love, and hope to desire this which no man also can either see, feel, or think what it is and yet causeth many men to die for His love.

O the right great gift of faith, whence so much good cometh that he causeth one to possess the thing which he cannot comprehend. Faith joined with truth bringeth forth hope, whereby perfect charity is engendered; and charity is God, as thou knowest. Therefore, if [62v] we have charity, we have God also. Then is God in us, and all we are in Him, and He in all men. If we have Him through faith, then have we a greater treasure than any man can tell.

Now to conclude. Since so great an apostle as Saint Paul is willing to speak no further of God and of His love, according to the example of his right wise teachings I will hold my peace. But following his word, albeit that I acknowledge myself to be but mire and dust, yet may I not fail to give graces and thanks unto God of all the goods [63r] and benefits undeserved which pleaseth Him to give me. Unto the king of heaven, immortal, invisible, our mighty God only and incomprehensible, be all honor, praise, glory, and love forever.

1 John 4

1 Tim 1

The Manuscript

TO OVR MOST ~~IN~~ NOBLE AND
vertuous quene KATHERIN, Eliza
beth her humble daughter wisheth
perpetuall felicitie and euerlasting ioye

NOT ONELY knowing the affe-
ctuous wille, and feruent zeale, the
with your highnes hath towardes
all godly lerning, as also my dutie
towardes you (most gracious and
souerayne ^{princes}) but knowing also that
pusilanimite and ydlenes are most
repugnante vnto a reafonable creature, and that (as the philofopher
fayeth) euen as an inftrument of yron

folio 2r

or of other metayle, waxeth soone
rusty, onles it be continualy occupied.
Euen so shall the witte of a man, or
woman, waxe dull, and vnapte to
do, or vnderstand any thing psittely.
onles it be alwayes occupied vpon
some maner of study Wiche thinges
consydered, hath moued so small a
portion, as god hath lente me, to
proue what i could do And therfore
haue i (as for a seye, or beginninge (fo
lowing the right notable sayeng of the
prouerbe afore sayd) translated this
lytell boke out of frenche ryme, in to
englishe prose ioyning ŷ sentences

folio 2v

together as well as the capacitie of
my symple witte: and small lerning
coulde extende themselues. The wich
booke is intytled, or named y̆ͤ mirour
or glasse, of the synnefull soule. where
in (this is conteyned, how she(beholdi̧g
and contempling what she is) doth
perceyue how, of herselfe, and of her
owne strenght, she can do nothing
that good is, or preuayleth for her
saluacion: onles it be through the
grace of god. whose mother, daugh
ter, syster, and wife, by y̆ scriptures
she proueth herselfe to be. Trusting
also, that through his incōprehen

sible loue grace, and mercy, she (be
ynge called from synne to repen
taunce) doth faythfully hope to be
saued. And althoughe i knowe y
as for my parte, wich i haue wrought
in it, the (as well spirituall, as manuall)
there is nothinge done as it shulde
be. nor els worthy to come in youre
graces handes, but rather all vnper
fytte and vncorecte: yet do i truste
also that oubeit it is like a worke wich
is but newly begonne, and shapen, y
the style of youre excellent witte, and
godly lerninge, in the redinge of it (if
so it vouchefe youre good highnes to do)

folio 3v

shall rubbe out, polishe and mende
(or els cause to mende) the wordes (or
rather the order of my writting) the
wich i knowe in many places to be
rude, and nothinge done as it shuld
be. But i hope, that after to haue ben
in youre graces handes: there shall
be nothinge in it worthy of reprehen
sion: and that in the meane whyle
no other (but your highnes onely) shal
rede it, or se it, lesse my sauttes bere
knowen of many. Than shall they be
better excused (as my confidence is in
youre graces accoustumed benenolence)
than if i shuld bestowe a whole yere

folio 4r

in writtinge, or inuentinge wayes for
to occupie them. Prayeng god almigh
ty the maker and creatoure of alle
thinges to garaunte vnto youre high
nes thesam newe yeres daye, a lucky
and a prosperous yere, with prospe
rous yssue, and continuance of many
yeres in good helthe and contynuall
ioye, and all to honnoure, praise, and
glory. Frome asherige, the laste daye
of the yeare of our lord
god, 1544

folio 4v

To the reader

If thou doest rede thys whole w
worke, beholde rather the matter,
and excuse the speche, consydering
it is the worke of a woman, wiche
hath in her neyther science, or know
ledge, but a desyre that eche one
might se, what the giste of god doth
when it pleaseth hym to iustifie the
harte of a man. ffor what thinge is
a man (as for hys owne strenght)
before that he hath receyued the giste
of fayth, wherby onely hath ye know
ledge of the goodnes, wysedom, and

folio 5r

power of god. and as foone as he
knoweth the truthe, than is his hart
full of loue, and charitie. fo that by
the feruentenes therof. he doth exclu
de all vayne feare, and ftedfastely
doth hope vpon god vnfaynedly.
Euen fo the gifte the wich oure crea
tour giueth at the beginninge. doth
neuer reste. tyll he hath made hym
godly. wich putteth hys trust in god
O the hapy gifte wich caufeth a mā
to be like vnto god. and to poffeffe
hys fo defyred dwellinge. Alas no
man coulde neuer vnderstande it, on
les by this gifte god hathe gyuen

folio 5v

hym it, and he hath greate cause to
doute of it, onles god hath made hym
sele it in to hys harte. Therfore reader,
with a godly mynde i heche beseche
the to take it pacientely to peruse this
worke, wich is but lytell, and taste
nothinge but the frutte of it, praienge
to god full of all goodnes, that in
your harte he will plante
the liuely fayth.

THE glasse of the synnefull soule.

Make me a cleane harte; O god.

WHERE is the hell full of trauayle
payne, mischiefe, and turmente where
is the pytte of cursydnes, out of the
wich doth springe all despaire. Is her
there any hell so profunde, that is suf
ficiente to punishe the tenth parte of
my synnes, wich be of so great a nū
ber, that the infinite doth make the
shadow so darke that i can not ac
compte them, or els scantly se them.
ffor i am to farre entred emongest

folio 6v

them and that worse is, i haue not y
power to obtayne the true knowled
ge of one. I fele well that the roote of
it is in me. and outwardly i se no
other effecte but all is eyther brauns
che leaffe, or els frutte that she brin
geth furth all aboute me. Ifi thinke
to loke for better, a braunche cometh
and doth close myne eyes. and in
my mouth doth fall when i wolde
speake the frutte wich is so bytter to
swalowe down. If my spirite be sty
red for to kirken: than a great mul
titude of leaffes doth entre in myne
eares and my nose is all stoped

folio 7r

[with flowres] Now behold, how in
[primier] prime and wepinge my se
poore soule captue, and prisonnere
doth lye, withoute clartie, or light
hauinge both her fete bound by her
concupiscence. and also both her
armes through yuell vse. yet ý power
to remedye it, doth not lye in me, and
power haue i none, to cry helpe. Now
aserfourth as i can setiought to haue
no hope of succoure, but through ý
grace of god, wiche i can not deserue.
the wiche maye rayse eueryone frō
death. By thys brightenes he geueth
light to my darkenes. and his power.

examininge my fautte, doth breake
all the vayle of ignorauncy, and geueth
me cleare vnderstanding, not onely
that thys cometh of me, but also what
thinge abydeth in me, where i am
and wherfore i do laboure, who he
is whom i haue offended, to whom
also i did obey so seldom. Therfore
it is conuenient that my pryde be
supressed, and humbly i do confesse
that, as for me, i am muche lesse thā
nothinge: before my byrthe, meere
and after, a dongehyll. A body redy
and prompt to do all yuell, not wil
linge other study, also subiette to

Iob. 10.
and. 20.

gene. 8.

folio 8r

iob odro fold iob. and payne: a shorte
lyfe: and the ende vncertayne: the
rom wich vnder ... by adam is folde
and.. and by the lawe iudged to be hange
i corinthis ffor i had neuer the obserue. onely.
psal. 31. _power to_
one of the comaundementes of god
rom I do fele the strenght of synne to be
in me: therfore is my sinne nowhitt
the lesse to be hydden. and y more
disembled outwardly harte. so
much the more he encreasyth w...
rom thine the harte. Thys that god will
i can not wille: and what he will
not: i oftentimes desyre to haue se...
Wich thinges doth constrayne me

folio 8v

by importable sorowe, to wishe for
the ende of thys myserable life, throug
desyred death, bycause of my wery
and ragyd life. Who shall be he
than that shall delyuer, and recou
uer suche good for me Alas, it can
not be a mortall man. ffor his power
and strenght is not such, but it
shall be the onely good grace of al
mighty god, wich is neuer slake to
preuente vs with hys mercy. Alas,
what a mayster withoute to haue
serued any goodnes of hym but ra
ther serued hym sloughtfully, and
withoute ceasse offended hym euery

rom.s.

folio 9r

daye, yet is he not flake in helping me
He doth fethe yuell that i haue done,
what, and how muche it is, and how,

hiere 10 of myfelfe, i can do nothinge y^t good

hiere 17 is, but with harte, and body fo enclined
to the contrary, that i fele no ſtrenght
in me, onles it be for to do yuell. He
doth not tary tyll i humbly do
praye hym, or that (feynge my hell
and damnacion) i do cry vpon
hym, ffor, with hys fpirite, he doth

rom.8 make a wallinge withyne my hart,
greater than i, or any man, can de
clare, wich afketh the gifte, wherof
fvertue is vnknowen to my lytell.

folio 9v

power. And this, the same vnknowen
highe, doth bringe me a newe desyre,
shewinge the good that i haue loste
by my synne, wiche is giuen me a=
gaine, through his grace, and bontie,
wich hath ouercomed all synnes
O my god. what grace, and good
nes is this, wich doth put out so=
many synnes. Nowe maye we=
se that thou arte full of all good=
loue, to make me such an honeste
turne. Alas my god, i did not
sele the, but i fled, and raune awaye
frome the, and here beneth thou = thon=
camest to me, with vnknowinge=

folio 10r

but an worme of the earth all na
zed what do i saye, worme i do
hym wronge, beynge so naughte
and forsworne full of pride, deʒ
eyte, malice, and treason. The
promes wiche my frendes made
when i was baptised, beyng such
allwayes through thy passion to
rom. 6 8
and fele the mortifieng of my fleshe
to be allwayes with the in the
crosse, where thou hast nayled
(as i do belieue) and yelded death,
deeu, and also all synne, wiche
wich i haue often tymes raken down
againe, and vntied. I haue brozen

folio 10v

denied and justified my promesse,
and (through pryde) i dyd suchewise,
lyfte vp my wille. that (with sloughte)
my duetie, twardes the was forgotten
And the thinge wiche muche more
is: as well the welhte of the promes
that i had of the, on the daye of my
baptifme, as also thy loue and pro
messe i haue forgotten all a lilze.
What shall i say more: albeit that
often tymes thou witstoudest mijn
vnhapynes, geuinge so many war
ninoes, by faythe, and sacramentes
admonishinge me by preaching
and also conforting me by the

pota,

folio 11r

receyuing of thy worthy body and
holy bloude also promyinge to put
me in the rowe of them that are
in parfaitte innocency: but i haue
all these goodnes put in forgetful
nes. Often tymes haue i broken
with the conuenante. ffor my poore
foule was to moche fede of with
yll bread and damnable doctrine
i despysinge fuccoure and phificke
as wolde haue helped me
and if i had ben willinge to lolze
for i knowe no man whom i had
requyred for there is neyther man
fainte or els aungell for whom the

folio 11v

harte of a sinner will chaunge. Alas
good iesus: thou seynge my blyndnes
and that at my nede i could haue
no succoure of men, than didest ↣   actes 4.
thou opene the waye of my salua
cion. O what goodnes and swittenes
Is there any father to the daugther,
or els brother to the syster, wiche
wolde euer do as he hath done. //
ffor he came in to hell for to suc ↣   1. ihon 4
coure my soule, where against his
wille she was willinge to perishe //
by cause she did not loue the. alas //
thou has loued her. O charitie ↣   1 corint 1
feruente, and inflammed thou ↣

art not flake to loue: thou, wiche
louest euery body, yea, and alfo
rom.s. thye enmyes: not only forgauinge
them their offences, but alfo to gue
thyfelfe (for their faluacion, libertie
and deliuraunce) to the deathe, ſe
crofse, trauayle, payne, and fouf
fring. Whan i do confydere what
is the occafion of thy loue twardes
ephe. me; i can fe nothinge els but loue
wich inciteth the to geue me this
that i can not deferue. Than (my
god) as ferfourth as i can fe, i ought
i timo. to geue no thankzes for my falua
cion but onely vnto the, to whom

folio 12v

I owe the prayse for it, as to hym
wich is my sauioure and creatour.
Alas what thinge is this thou hast
done so muche for me, and yet art
thou not contente to haue forgiuen
me my synnes, but also gyuen
vnto me the right gracious gyfte
of grace. ffor it shuld suffise me (i
cominge out of suche a daunger)
to be ordred like a straunger: but
thou doest handle my soule (if so
i durst say) as a mother, daugther
syster and wife. I lord, i wich am
not worthy, for to aske bread, to
come neare the dore of the ryche

ephe. z

luke. s

folio 13r

highe place, where thy dwellinge is.
O what grace is this, that so sodely
thou vouchesafest to drawe my soule
in suche hignes, that she feleth herselfe
the rular of my body. She poore, //

ignoraunte, and layme, doth synde
herselfe with the riche, wise, and strög

bycause thou hast written in her harte
the rolle, of thy spirite, and holy word

geuenge her true sayth to receyue it.
wiche thinge made her to cöceyue
thy sonne: beleuinge hym to be god.
man, sauyoure, and also the true //

remitter of all sinnes. Therfore ☞
doest thou vouchesafe to assure //

her that is mother of thy sonne
whom thou art the onely father
And furthermore (o my father) here
is a greate loue. ffor thou art not
flatze of well doynge, sythe that
thy sonne full of diuinite, hath talze
the body of a man, and did ioyne
himselfe with oure ashes, wiche thing
a man can not vnderstand, onles
he hath a true fayth. It hath plea
sed the to put hym so neere vs,
that he did ioyne hymselfe vnto
oure fleshe. than we (seynge hym
to be called man) doo call hym
syster, and brother. Nowe, these

philip.

folio 14r

soule (wich may say of herselfe, that
she is the Systre of god) ought to be
assured in her harte. After this doest
thou declare with great loue, howe
her creacion is onely the good wille.
wich it pleasyth the to haue alwayes
twardes her: geuyng assuraunce y̅

ephe.i before her first daye (prouiding for
her) thou hast had thy loue in her,
and how (through loue) thou hast
begotten her, as (alone) thou canest
do very well. And also how thou
 out her withine this body
not for slepe withsloughte, but that
both of them shuld haue no other

exercice, but onely to thinke howe
to do you some seruice vnto the:
than the truth maketh her to tell
that there is true paternite in the.
O what honnoure, what good and
glory hath the soule, wich doth
alwayes remember, that she is thy
daughter: and, in callinge the father,
she doth thy comaundementes.
What is there more, is that all, no:
it pleaseth the to gyue her an other
name, to call her thy wife, and
she to call the, husbande. decla
ringe how thou hast frely decla
red the mariage of her. By the

folio 15r

baptisme th'ou haddest ~~made~~ hast
made a promesse to giue her thy
goodes, and riches. Thou doest take
her synnes. ffor she hath nothinge
els, the wiche adam her father did
giue her. All her treasures are no
thinge els but synnes, wiche thou
hast taken vpon the, and payed
all her whole debte. With thy
goodes, and great laundes, thou
hast made her so riche, and with
so greate a ioynter, that she (know
inge herselfe to be thy auowed
wife) doth beleue to be quitte of
all that she oweth, estiming very

1.peter.2.

folio 15v

lytell this that she doth se here be
neth. She forsakzeth her olde father,
and all the goodes that he geueth
for herhusbandes salze Surely (o my
god) my soule is well hurte, to be sede
of suche good, for to leaue the plea
sure of this worlde, for thesame wich
is euerlasting, where peace is without
warre. I meruaile howe she (for ioye
doth not lese her witte, côtenaunce,
and speche. Father father, alas
what ought i to thinlze: shall my
spirite be so bolde to talze vpon
hym to call the, father yc, and also,
oure father, for so hast thou said

folio 16r

math.6. in the pater noster. But to call me,
a daughter. hast thou so sayd, I be
seche the tell it me. alas, ye, ffor (with
great swittenes) thou saydest, daug
prouer. 23. ther. lende me thy harte: O my
god, in stedde of lending, he is redy
to giue hymselfe wholy vnto the.
Receyue hym, than, and do not
permitte, that any body put hym
farre frome the: so that foreuer
with faythfull stedfastenes) he may
loue the, with a daugtherly loue
Nowe my lorde, if thou be my fa
ther, may i thinke me to be youre
that i am thy mother. ffor i can not

folio 16v

perceyue howe i shuld conceyue
the wich hast created me. But thou
          satisfie
didest my doutte when in preaching
(stretching furth thy handes) thou
didest say: Those that shall do
the wille of my father; they are
my brethern, and mother. I beleue
than that (heeringe, or reding the
wordes, that thou didest saye, and
hast sayd by thy holy prophettes
thesame also wich (through thy
good preachers) thou do dayly de
clare vnto men; beleuing, and de
ringe stedfastely to fulfille it) that
through loue i haue begotten the

math 12.

folio 17r

Therfore withoute any feare will
i talze vpon me the name of a
mother. Mother of god: o fwitte
virgin mary. I befeche the be not fory
that i talze vp fuche a titell: I do
neyther fteale, or pretende any
thinge vpon thy priuilege. ffor
thou (onely hast aboue all wome
luke reccaued fo great honnoure; that
no man can not in hymfelfe
comprehende, howe he hath ben
willinge to talze in the our flefhe.
ffor thou art mother, and perfytt
virgin, before, after, and in hys.
byrth. Thou didest beare and

norished hym in thy holy wombe.
Thou didest folowe hym at hys
preaching, and also when he was
troubled. Nowe to spelze shorte,
thou hast with god founde the gra   luke.i
ce, that oure enmy (through malice
and deceyte) had caused adam, and
hys posterite to lese. Through eue,
and hym, we had loste it and, by   rom.s
thy fonne, hath ben yelded vnto   ihon.i
vs againe. Therfore hast thou ben
ryghtely named, full of grace; for   luke.i
thou lakest, neyther, grace or ver
tue fyth that he (wich is the beste
emonge them that be good also

folio 18r

the spring of all goodnes, grace and
power, wich hath created in theso
pure innocency that thou art the
example of all vertues) hath buylded
in the, his dwellinge, and temple He
(through loue) did conforme himselfe
with the, and thou art transformed
with hym. Therfore, if any man
shuld thinke to geue the greater
prayse than god hymselfe hath
done, it were a blasphemy. ffor
there is no suche prayse, as thesame
is wich cometh frome god. Also
hast thou had so stedfaste, and
constante a fayth, that by grace

folio 18v

she had the power to make the god
ly. Therfore i wil not take vpon
me to gyue the greater prayse, than
the honnoure wich the soueraync
lorde hath gyuen vnto the. ffor
thou art his corporall mother, and
also (through fayth) his spirituall
mother. Than, (folowinge thy faith
with humilitie) am thys spirituall
mother. Alas my god: of the frater
nite that thou hast twardes me
through thy humblenes, in callinge
me, syster, didest thou euer fayd
any thinge of it: alas, ye, ffor thou
hast broken the kinrede of myne

folio 19r

olde father, callinge me, daugther of
adoption. Well, than, syth that we
haue but one father, i wil not feare
to call the, my brother. ffor so hast
thou sayd by salomon in his ballet,
cantic. 4. sayenge. my syster, thou hast won
ded my harte with the switte loke
of one of thy eyes, and with one
of thy heeres. Alas good brother.
I wishe for nothinge els, but that
in wondinge, thou might synde my
self wonded with thy loue. And
likewise thou doest call me, wife,
shewinge that thou louest me,
and callme (by true louenateur

folio 19v

my doue, ryfe vp my fpowfe. Ther cantic,z
fore fhall i fay, with louing faith,
thou art myn, and i am thyne.
Thou doeft call me, loue, and faire
fpowfe: if fo it be, fuche haft thou
made me Alas; doth it pleafe the
to geue me fuche names: they are
hable to breake a mans harte, and
to kindle hym by fuche loue, when
he thinketh vpon the honnoure
wich is greater than he hath defer
ued. Mother, mother: but what
childe is it; it is of fuche a fonne y
my harte doth breake for loue.
My god my fonne: O iefus what

folio 2or

~~speche~~ spekzing is this : mother and
daugther : O hapy kzinrede . O what
swittenes doth procede of thesame
paternite . But what daugtherly
loue , and reuerent feare ought i to
haue t&wardes hym . My father : ye
psal , 26.
and , 30. and my creatoure . my protectoure
and my conseruatoure : to be thy
syster :. alas here is a greate loue :
Nowe doest thou brealze my hart
in the middes : malze rowme so
thesame so swette a brother : so
no other name be written in the
but onely my brother iesus the
sonne of god . for vnto no other

folio 20v

man wil i geue place for all the
grudginge, and heyttinge ẏ they
can do vnto me. Kepe my harte
than, my brother, and lett not thy
enmy entre in it. O my father, bro
ther, childe, and spowse: with my
handes ioyned, humbly vpon my
knees, i yelde the thankes, and
praise, that it pleaseth the to turne
thy face twardes me, conuerting
my hart, and coueringe me with
such grace, that thou doest se
no more my yuels, and synnes
so well hast thou hydden them,
that it semeth thou hast put them

in forgetfulnes. yea, and also they
seme to be forgotten of me, wich
haue comitted them, ffor, faith, and
loue, cauſeth me to forgett them,
putting wholy my truste in the
onely. Than, my father, in whom
lyeth vnſayned loue: wherof can
i haue feare in my harte. I confeſſe
that i haue done all the yuell that
one man can do, and that, of my
ſelfe, i am naught, alſo that i haue
offended the, as the prodigal childe
did, folowing the foliſhe tradde
of the fleſhe, where i haue ſpent
all my ſubſtancy, and alſo all the

iames, 3.

abundance of goodes: wich i had ré
ceiued of the ffor, pouertie had we
thered me, euen as hey, and yelded
my spirite deed for hunger, selzyng
to eate the reliefz of swinne: but i
founde very lytell sauoure in such
meates Than (seyng my liuynge
to be so miserable) did returne   iohn. 6.
vnto the, O father. Alas i haue sinned
in heauen, and before the: I am   luke. 15.
not worthy (i tell it afore euery
man) to eall myselfe be called thy
childe, but (o bountiesull father)
do no worse vnto me, but as to
one of thy householde seruauntes

Alas what loue, and zeale is thys :
ffor thou woldest not tary my com
ming, and prayer, but (ſtretching
furth thy hande) receuedyſt me :
when i did thinkze that thou wol
dest not ſe me: and in ſtedde to
haue puniſhemente, thou doest aſ
ſure me of my ſaluacion. Where
is he, than, that ſhall puniſhe me
when my father ſhall denye hym
my ſynne. There is no iudge that
can condemne any man, onleſſe
god himſelſe wolde damne hym.
I feare not to haue lakze of goodes,
ſyth i haue god for my father.

folio 22v

My enmy shall do me no harme,
ffor my father shall vndowe hys
power. If i owe any thing, he shal paye
it for me. If i haue deferued death
he (as a lzinge) shall geue me gra
ce, and pardon, and delyuer me
frome prifon, and hanging. But
here is the worfe: what mother se
haue i ben: ffor after that i had
receued the name of a true mother
than haue i ben to rude vnto the.
ffor after that i had conceyued,
and brought the furth; i lefte rea
fon, and fubiette borfe vnto my owne
will, not talzing hide vnto the,

folio 23r

i fell aflepe, and gaue place to my
great enmy: the wich in the nyght.
of ignoraunce (i beyng aflepe) did
fteale the frome me, craftely, and in
the place fhe did put her childe wich
was dead. So did ilefe the by my
owne faute, wich thinge is a harde
remorfe for me. Nowe haue i loste
the by mine owne fautte. by caufe i tolze
no hyde to lzepe the. My enmy. my
fenfualite (i beyng in my beastely
flepe) did fteale the frome me. and
gaue me an other childe hauinge
no life in hym. wich is called fynne.
whom i will not haue ffor i do yt

folio 23v

terly forsalze hym She affyrmyd
that he was mijn owne, but i
lznewe hym to be hers. ffor as foone
as i came to the light of the grace
wich thou haddest geuen me, than
i lznewe my glory to be chaunged
when i fawe the deed child not to
be mijn: ffor thefame wich was a
liue (whom fhe had talzen awaye)
was mynowne. Betwene iefus, and
fynne, is the chaunge fo apparent,
But here is a ftraunge thing: This
olde woman caufeth me hym wich
is dead, whom fhe fayeth to be
mijn: and fo fhe will maytene. O

folio 24r

ſalomon true iudge, thou hast herd
this lamentable proces, and or
deyned (contenting the parties)
that my child ſhuld be diuided
in two partes The ſalſe woman
agreeth it ſhuld be ſo: but i (re
membring hym to be my owne
ſonne) was rather contente to
leſe hym, than to ſe his body par
ted in two peces (ſſor, true, and
parſaitte loue is neuer contente
with one halſe of this that ſhe
lou⁽ᵗʰ⁾) but i wolde rather wyppe
ſor my whole losſe than to reco
uer but one halſe. My mind ſhuld

folio 24v

not be satisfied, if i had recouered
one halfe withoute life. Alas geue
her rather the childe wiche is a
liue: better it is for me to dye, thā
to se iesuschrist dyuided. But (o my
lorde) thou didest lolze better to
it, than i, ffor, thou (seynge the
payne that i did suffer, and howe
i did rather forsalze my ryghtie
than to se suche cruelnes) saydest,
this is the true mother and cau   z.king.z
sed them to gyue me my childe
againe. O swítte iesus, haue i
founde the after to haue proued
me, if i did loue the, i. who had

folio 25r

loste the, yet didest thou retourne
vnto me. Alas doest thou vouchafe to
come againe to her wiche, beynge
let with fynne, coulde not kepe the,
O my fwitte childe, my fonne, my
nourriture, of whom i am ryght
humble creature, do not permytte
that euer i do leaue the; ffor i repent
myfelfe of the tyme paffed. Nowe
come, my fenfualitie, with fynnes of
all qualities, ffor thou hast not the
power to make me receyue ý childe
wich is dead. Thefame that i haue
is ftronge inough for to defende
me, and he fhall not permitte that

thou do take hym awaye frome
me. He is alredy as ftrong as any
man is: therfore maye i flepe, and
take reste neere of hym, ffor he fhal
kepe me better, than i could kepe
hym. Than (as i thinke) i maye //
take reste. O what a fwitte reste
it is, of the mother, and the fonne
togyther. My fwitte childe: O my
god; honnoure, and praife be vnto
the, onely, fo that euery body maye
perceyue, howe it hath pleafed
the, me leffe than nothing to call
a mother: the more that ẏ thing
is ftraunge, and harde to be done.

folio 26r

the more ought thy goodnes haue
praise for it. And also, i finde myself
more bounde vnto the, than euer i
did for this that it pleaseth the to
haue reteyned me for thy syster. I
am syster vnto the, but so naughty
a syster, that better it is for me to
hyd suche a name: ffor i(forgettinge
the honnoure, and adoption of so
noble Izmrede; also thy so switte a
brotherly behauoure towardes me)
did ryse against the, and (not reme
bring my sauttes, but goynge farre
nomez frome the) did agree with my bro
ther aaron, willinge to giue iudge

folio 26v

mente againste thy worlzes, and also
grudging againste the, priuely, wiche
thinge causeth me to haue a great re //
morse in my conscience. O bountiefull
god, brother, and true moses, wich
doth all thinges with godnes, and
iustice. i haue estimed thy dedes
to be wiclzed, beynge so bolde, and
sayenge rashely, why hast thou
married a straunge woman. Thou
gyuest vs a lawe, and punishemēt
if we do not sulfille it, and thyselfe,
wolde not be bounde to it. forbiding
vs the thinge wich thyselfe dedyst //
ffor thou doest forbide vs to lzde //

folio 27r

no man; and thou doest kille and
exo. zz. speared none of thre thousande that
thou caused to be slayne. Also god
gaue vs commaundemente by the
that we shuld not marry y̆ daugꝏ
ther of a straunger: but thou tokest
thy wife emonge them. Alas my bro
ther, i tolde the a great, many of such
wordes, wiche i knowe well to be ⸗
folishe, wherof i do repente: ffor y̆ ⸗
truely voyce of god toke me vp ꝛ
afore i went oute of the place. What
didest thou of my synne: alas my
brother thou woldest not haue ⸗
nume. iz. me to be punished; but rather ꝰ

folio 27v

woldest for my helthe, and salua
cion, in askinge for thys great be
nesite, that it shuld please god to
mitigate hys iudgemente. The
wiche thinge thou couldest not
obtayne; ffor i became a lazare,
so that whan any body shulde
loke vpon vpon me, might saye
that i had not ben wise. And
so was i put (like a lazare) frome
the tentes, and habitacion of the
people: ffor a soule can not haue
greater punishemente, than to be
banished frome the company of
them that are good, and holy

folio 28r

bycause that a sylze body maye
marre them wiche be in helthe. But
what didest thou, ffor seynge my
repentaunce; ffor thou didest helpe
that my penaunce was soone ended
By true loue, thou didest pray for
me, and than did i returne. O
what brother, who, in stedde to pu
nishe hys folishe syster, wolde
cleaue vnto her. ffor iniury grudge
and greate offence, thou gauest her
grace, and loue in recompense. Alas
my brother this is to moche, thou shul
dest not do fuche a good turne vnto
fuche a poore woman as i am. I haue

folio 28v

done yll, and thou geuest me good //
for it. I am thine, and thou didest say
that thou art myn. Thyne i am, and
so will i be for euer. I feare no more //
the great folishenes of aaron. ffor no
man shall lose me frome the. Nowe
than that we are brother, and syster
togyther, i care but lytell for all other
men. Thy laundes are my owne ☞   psal. z o.
inheritaunce, lett vs than kzepe (if it
pleafeth the) but one husholde. Syth
it pleafeth the to humble thyfelfe fo
moche, as to ioyne thy harte with ☞
myn, in makzinge thyfelfe a lyuely //
membre do ryght humbly thankze the

and as for to do it as i ought, it lieth
not in my power. Take my meaning
than, and excuse myne ignoraunce,
syth that i am of so great a kinrede
as to be thy syster: O my god, i haue
good cause to praise, to loue, and to
serue the vnsaynedly and not to de.
syre, or seare any thing, but the onely
Kepe me wel, than, ffor i aske no
other brother, or frende. If any mo
ther hath taken any care for her
sonne; If any brother hath hyd the
fautte of hys syster: I neuer sawe it
(or elles it was kepte wonders secrette)
that any husbande wolde forgiue

folio 29v

his wife, after that she had offended
hym an did returne vnto hym.

There be inoughe of them, wiche for
to auenge their wronge, did cause
the iudges to condemne ~~hym~~ them to dye.
Other seynge their wiues synne,
did not soudaynely speare theyr
owne handes to kzille them. Other
also(seynge their fauttes to appeare)
did sent them home agayne to
their owne frendes. Other (seynge
their yll dedes, did shutte them in
a prison. Nowe to spelze shorte,
lolze vpon all theyr complexions,
ffor the ende of their pretence, is no

folio 30r

thinge els, but punißhemente. And ȳ
leße harme that euer i coulde per
ceyue, in punißhinge them: thys it
is, that they wolde neuer ſe them
agayne. ~~ſhuldest rather.~~ Thou
ſhuldest rather malze the ſtye to
to turne, than to malze the agre
ment betwne the huſbande, and
hys wiſe, whan he lznoweth truly
the ſautte that ſhe hath done. or
els hath ſene, and founde her in
doynge amiße. Wherfore (O my
god) i can ſinde no man to be cō
pared vnto the: ſſor thou arte the
parſaitte example of loue, and now

folio 30v

(more than euer i did) i do confeſſe,
that i haue brolzen myne othe, and
promeſſe. Alas thou haddest cho
ſen me for thy wſe. and didest ſett
me vp in great dignitie, and hon
noure.(ſſor what greatter hōnour
may one haue than to be in the
place of thy wiſe, wich ſwittely ta
lzeth reste nere to the) of all thy
goodes, quene, maistres, and lady
and alſo in ſuretie, both of body
and ſoule. i ſo vile a creature, be
ynge ennobliſhed by the. Nowe,
(to tell the truth) i had more, and
better than any man, can deſyre,

osea, 2.

folio 31r

Therfore, my harte hath cause to
syghe alwayes, and with habun &
psal.94. daunce of teares myne eyes to come
out of my head. My mouthe can
not make to many exclamacions,
ffor, there is neyther olde, or newe
writtinges, that can shewe so pitie
full a thinge, as thesame is, wiche i
will tell, nowe. Shall, or deare i tell
it, maye i pronounce it withoute
ezech.36. shame: alas, ye, ffor, my confusion
is for-to shewe the great loue of &
my husbande, therfore i care not,
if for his worship, i do declare my
shame. O my sauioure wiche &

folio 31v

dyed, and was crucified on the //
croſse, for my ſynnes: thys dede is ſo
not ſuch as to leaue hys ſonne, and,
as a childe, to offende hys mother: //
or elles (as a ſyster) to grudge, and
chyde agaynst hys brother. Alas //
thys is worſe: ffor, the offenſe is the //
greater, where more loue, and know
ledge is. And the more we receyue //
of god familiarite, and beneſites, the
offenſe is the greater to deceyue hym.
I, wich was called ſpowſe, and loued
of the, as thyne owne ſoule. Shall i //
tell the truth; ye, I haue lefte forgotten and raunne awaye frome the. //

folio 32r

I did leaue the, for to go at my plea=
sure. I haue forsaken the for to
choyce an worse. I did leaue the (o
spring of all goodnes, and faythfull
promesse. I did leaue the; but whether
went i; in a place where nothinge
is but cursydnes. I haue leste, my
trusty frende, and louer worthy to
be loued aboue all other. I haue
leste the, through myne owne yll
will. I haue leste the, full beautie, good
nes, wisedom, and power: And (for
the better to wi outdrawe myselfe
frome thy loue) i haue taken thyne
enmy with is the dyuell, y world

deuto.zz.

folio 32v

and the fleshe: for whose to ouercome
thou hast soghte so sore on the crosse
for to put me in libertie. whom they
had a longe tyme kzepte prisonnere,
slaue, and so bounde, that no man,
coulde cause me to humble myselfe.
And, as for the loue, and charitie, y
i shuld haue towardes the; they did
quenshe it; so that the name of iesus
my husbande (wich before i had so
founde so swite) was to me, tedious,
and i did hate it, so that oftentimes,
i did geaste at it. And if any man
(he hearinge a sermon) shuld saye
vnto me; the preacher sayeth well

gala, 4.

prouer, 1

folio 33r

i wil anſwere it is true: but my w
wordes ~~doth flee~~ did flee awaye as
a ſether doth: and i went neuer to
the church but ſor maner ſalze
all my dedes were but ypocriſy ſſor
my mynde was in other places
I was enoyed when i herde ſpealze
of the: ſſor. ~~my mynde was in~~
~~other places~~ i was more willinge
to go at my pleaſure. Nowe to
ſpelze ſhorte all this that thou di
dest ſorbide me, i did it and all ſ
thou cõmaundedest me to do: i
did eſchue it, and all thys (O my
god) by cauſe i did not loue the

folio 33v

yet for all thys that i did hate, for
salze, raune a waye, and betrayed
the, bycause i shuld geue thy place
to an other: hast thou suffered y
i shuld be mod molzed, or elles bea ~~ioel z~~
ten, or lzilled: Hath thou ~~fett me~~
put me in darlze prison, or bani
shed syttyng nought by me. ꝰ
Hast thou talzen awaye agayne
thy gyftes, and iouyelles, for to pu
nishe me of my vnsaythful ~~turne~~
sinnes. Haue i loste my iointer
wich thou hadyst promysed me
bycause i did offende against the
Am i accused by the afore the

folio 34r

iudge, as a naughty woman shuld
be, yet, hast thou forbiden me, that
i shuld neuer presente myselfe be
fore the (euen as reason was) and
also that i shuld neuer come to thy
house. O true parsaitte husbande
and frende, the moste louinge //
emonge all good louers. Alas //
thou hast done otherwise: ffor //
thou soughtest for me diligently,
when i was goynge in the most
depe place of hell, where all the
good yueles are done. I that //
was so farre frome the, both hart
and mynde oute of the true way

like as and, ie

folio 34v

than didest thou call vpon me, say
enge. My daughter : hartze, and se
and bowe thy hearinge towardes
me. Forget, also, the same maner of
people, with whom thou didest
raune awaye frome me, and also
the house of thyne olde father, where
thou hast dwelled so longe : than
the lzinge full of godlines shal desyre
thy company. But, when thou sawest
that thys fwitte, and graciouse spe
lzing, did me no good: than thou
begannest to cry. Come vnto me
all ye wich are werey with laboure,
I am i that shall receyue, and seat

psal. 44

math. 11

folio 35r

you with my bread . Alas i wolde
harke
not vnto all thefe wordes : ffor i dou
ted whether it were thou, or els a
fymple writtinge, that fo fayd . ffor i
was fo folifhe that without loue i
thy
did rede your worde" I fawe , and
vnderftoude well that the compa
deuto.33 rayfons of the vineyarde , wich brou
efay.5 brought furth thornes , and poy
fons in ftedde of good frutte ; thou
faydeft all this of me , wich had fo
done . Confideringe alfo that when
call
thou dideft the wife , fayenge , come
cante,7 againe , falamite ; all this thou dideft
fpeke bycaufe i fhuld my fynne leaue

folio 35v

and of all these wordes, i did as
though i had vnderstand neuer //
a worde. But when i did rede ie //
remy the prophet, i confesse that //
i had in the reading of it, feare
in my harte, and shame in my //
face. I will tell it, ye, and with ȳ //
teares in myne eyes, and for thy //
honnoure, and to supresse my
pride. Thou hast fayd this by
thy holy prophet. If a woman
hath offended her husbande, and
lefte hym for to go with a other
man: they neuer fawe that the huf
bande wolde talze her againe. I

hiere 3

folio 36r

she not estimed to be poluted, and of no
value. The lawe doth consente to put
her in the handes of the iustice, or els
dryue her a waye, and neuer se her, or
tolze her againe. But thou wich hast
made separacion of my beade, and
did put thy false louers in my place
and commyted fornicacion with
them: yet, for all thys thou mayest
come ynto me againe ffor I will
not be angry against the: lyfte vp
thyne eyes, and lolze vp, than shalt
thou se in what place thy synne had
leade the, and how thou lyest downe
in the earth. O poore soule, lolze here

thy synne hath put the: euen vpon the
hyghe wayes, where thou didest wayte,
and taryed for to begyle them that //
came by. Euen as a thief doth wich
is hydden in wildernes. Therfore (ha
uinge fullfilled thy pleasure) thou hast
infected (with fornicacion) all the so
earth wiche was aboute the. Thyne eye
thy forehed, and thy face, had loste
all their good maner. ffor they were
suche as those of an harlotte, and //
yet thou haddest no shame of thy //
synne. And the surplus that ieremy
sayeth. Wich thinges constrayneth //
me know my wretched life. and

folio 37r

to wishe (with sorowfull syghes) the
daye, the houre, the moneth, the yere
and the tyme, that i did leaue the
yeldinge myselfe condemned, and
worthy to be for euer in the euerla
stinge fyre. Thesame feare (wiche
prouer. 15. doth not procede of me, but cometh
of the, and excedeth all pleasure)
had almoste put me in despayre
as often as i did remember my
synne: if it hath not ben that thou
neuer leftest me. ffor as soone as
thou knewest my wille bowen for
to obey the: than (puttinge in me
a luely fayth) thou didest vse of thy

folio 37v

clemency, and goodnes. so that after ∥
i knewe the, to be lord, maister, and
kinge (of whom i ought to haue feare)
than founde i my feare to be quenshed
beleuinge that thou were fo gracious
good, fwitte, and pitiefull hufbande,
that i (wich rather hyd me, than to
shewe myfelfe) was not a feare to go
and feke for the: and in fekinge i
founde the. But, what didest thou,
than, hast thou refufed me: Alas (my
god) no. but rather excufed me.
Hast thou turned thy face from me,
no. ffor, thy fwitte loke hath pene ∥
tred my harte, wonding hym

death. geuinge me remorse of my //
synnes. Thou hast not put me backe

luke. 15. with thy hande : but with both thyn
armes, and with a swifte and man
ly harte, thou didest mete with me.
by the waye: and not reprochinge
my sauttes, embrassedst me. I could
not se, beholding thy contenance. //
that euer thou didest perceyue my
myne offence. ffor. thou hast done
as moche for me, as though i had
ben good, and honeste. and didest
hyd my sautte from euery body my
my geueng me againe the parte of //
thy hedde. and also shewinge that

folio 38v

the multitude of my synnes are so //
hydden, and ouercome by thy &
great victory, that thou wilt neuer
remember them; so thou seist nothing
in me but, the grace, gystes, and ver
tues, wich it pleaseth thy goodnes //
to gyue me. O charitie: i se well y //
thy goodnes doth consume my le
udnes, and maketh me a godly //
and beautiefull creature. Thys that
was myn thou hast destroyed it //
and made me so parsaitte a creature
that thou hast done me as muche //
good, as any husband can do ynto
hys wife, geuenge me a faythfall &

folio 39r

hope in thy promesses. Nowe i
haue (through thy good grace) reco
uered the place of thy husbande
wife. O hapy, and desyred place,
gracious bedde, trone ryghthono
rable, seate of peace, rest of all
warre, hygh steppe of honnoure,
separate from the earth: doest thou rece
thys vnworthy creature, gyuinge
her the sceptre, and crowne of
thyne empire, and glorious realme
Who did euer heare speke of such
a thinge; as to rayse vp one so high.
wich of herselfe was nothing, and
maketh of a great value, thys ẏ

of it selfe was naught Alas what thing
is thys. ffor, i casting myne eyes an
high, i se in the goodnes so vnknowen,
grace, and loue so incomprehensible
that my syght is leste inuisible Thā
am i constrayned to loke down://
and lolzing down, i do se what i //
am, and what i was willinge to be
Alas i do se in it the leudnes, darke
nes and extreme depenes of my so
yuelles. Also my death, wiche by so
humblenes closeth myne eye. The //
admyrable goodnes of the; and ẙ
vnspekeable yuell wich is in me. //
Thy hignesse, and right pure maieste.

folio 4or

my ryht fragile, and mortall nature.
Thy gyftes, gooddes, and beatitude,
my malice, and great vnkidnes //
Howe good thou art vnto me, and
howe vnkind i am vnto the, Thys
that thou wilt: and this that i pur
fhue. Wich thinges confidered, cau
feth me to meruayle, how it plea
feth the to ioyne thyfelfe vnto me.//
feynge that there is no comparay fō
betwene vs both: ffor thou arte
my god, and i am of thy worke
Thou arte my creatore, and i am
thy creature. Nowe to fpeke fhorte,
i cannot define what it is of the //

folio 40v

ffor i knowe myselfe to be the lest
thinge that can be compared vnto
the . O loue ,thou madest thys a—
grement , when thou didest ioyne
life , and death togyther: but there
vnion hath viuified death . Life dy
enge , and life without ende , hath//
made oure death a life . death hath
geuen vnto life . quycke death . .
Through such death (i beyng decd)
receyued life , and by death , i am//
rauished with hym , wich is aliue .
I liue in the , and , as for me , i am
decd . ffor , death is nothinge els to//
me , but the . cominge oute of a prison .

folio 41r

Death is life vnto. ffor through d
death, i am aliue. This mortall life
yeldeth me full of care, and sorowe:
and death yeldeth me contente.
O what a goodly thinge it is, to
dye, wich causeth my soule to liue.
in delyuringe her, trough thys mor
tall death, exempt from miserable
death, and equall vnto god, with
so mighty a loue. that (onlES she
doth dye) she languisheth alwayes
Is not, than, the soule blameles wich
wolde ffne dye, for to haue such
philip i life. ye surely. ffor she ought to
call the death her welbeloued

folio 41v

frende. O swittc death, pleasaunte
sorowe, mighty keye, delyuringe //
from sorowe, all those, wich tru //
stinge in the, and in thy pafsion //
were mortified, bycause did truste
in the, and in thy death. ffor, with
an swittc slepe, thou didest putt //
them frome the death, wich caused
them to lamente. O how hapy is //
thesame deedly slepe vnto hym, the
wiche when he waketh, doth sinde
(through thy death) the euerlasting
life. ffor, the death is no other thing
to a christen man, but a libertie //
frome hys mortall baunde. And //

folio 42r

the death wich is fearefull to $\mathring{y}$ wiked
is pleasante. and agreable to them $\mathring{y}$
be good. Than is death (through //
thy death destroyed. Therfore, my
god, if i were rightely thaught, i //
shuld call the death, life, ende of //
laboure, and begyning of euerlastig
ioye. ffor i knowe that the longe //
life doth lett me frome thy syght //
O death, come, and breake thesam
obstacle of life. or els loue do nowe
a myracle. Syth that i can not yet
se my spowse: transforme me with
hym, both body, and soule: and //
than shall i the better tary for $\mathring{y}$ //

cominge of death. lett me dye, that
i maye liue with hym: for there is
none, that can helpe me, onles it be
thou onely. O my sauioure, through
fayth, i am plaunted, and ioyned
with the. O what vnion is thys.//
fyth (through fayth) i am sure of //
the, and nowe i maye call the: ☞
fonne, father, fpowfe, and brother.
Father, brother, fonne, hufband
O what giftes thou doest gyue.//
by the goodnes of thofe names.//
O my father: what paternite. O
my brother: what fraternite. O //
my childe: what dilection. O my

rom. 11.

ihon. 1.

folio 43r

husband: O what conionction.//
Father full of humilitie. Brother//
hauinge taken our similitude. Sōne
engendred through faith, and cha
ritie. husbande louing in all extre
mite. But whom doest thou loue.
Alas it is she, the wich thou hast //
withdrawen frome the snare,//
wherein, through milice, she was
bounden, and gaue her y̆ place
name, and office, of a daughter,ꝭ
syster, mother, and wife. O my sa
uioure: thesam swittenes is of great //
fauoure, rightpleasaunte, and of //
a swittetost, y̆ any may speke ꝭ

vnto the, or els heare the . And cal
linge the (withoute any feare) father
childe, and spowse : hearing the.
i do heare myselfe to be called,
mother, syster, daughter, and spe
spowse. Alas, nowe may e͛ soule
(wich doth finde suche swittenes) to
be consumed by loue. Is there any
loue that may be compared vnto
this, but it hath some yuell condi
cion Is there any pleasure to be //
estimed Is there any honnoure, //
but it is accounted for shame. Is //
there any profitte, to be compared
vnto this . Nowe to speke shorte, //

here, 3

cantic, 4. 5

folio 44r

is there any thinge. that more i co
could loue, alas no: ffor. he ẏ loueth
god. doth repute all thefe thinges

philip, 3. worfe than a donge hyll. Plefure
profitte, and honnoure of thys
worlde, are but trifles vnto hym
wich hath founde the loue of
god. ffor fuche loue is fo profita
ble, honorable, and abundante:

pfal. 106. that, fhe onely, contenteth ẏ harte
and yeldeth hym fo contente (as i
deare faye) that he neuer defyreth
or wolde haue other thinge. ffor
whofoeuer hath god (as we ou
ought to haue hym) he that afketh

folio 44v

any other thinge, is a superfluous //
man. Nowe, thanked be god, throug
faith, haue i recouered, and gotten //
thesam loue: w therfore i ought to
be satisfied, and contente. Nowe i //
haue the, my father, for the defence
of the folishenes of my longe youth
Nowe haue i the, my brother, for to
succoure my sorowes. wherin i find
no ende. Nowe i haue the, my sone,
for the onely stey of my feble age. //
Nowe haue i the true, and fayth //
full husband, for the satisfieng of //
my whole harte, and mynd. Nowe
syth that i haue the. i do forsake //

folio 45r

all them that be in the world. Syth

cantic.3. that i holde the: thou shalt escape
me no more. Syth that i se the: i will
loke vpon nothing that shuld kepe
me frome the beholding of thy diui

psal.84. nite. Syth that i do heare the: i will
cantic.3.8 heare nothinge that letteth me from
the enioyenge of thy voyce. Syth y͏͏ͤ
it pleaseth the to put me so neere the:
i will rather dye, than to touche an
other man. Syth that i serue the: i
will serue no other maister. Syth
that thou ioyned thy harte with
myne: if he doth departe frome it:
lett hym be punished for euer. ffor

folio 45v

the departinge frome thy loue, is
worse, than any damnacion is. ⁓
I do not feare the payne of ten ⁓
thousande helles, as moche as i do
to lese the, one daye of the weke. ⁓
Alas, my god, my father, and cre
atour: do not suffer that the dyuell
(inuentour of al synne) hath suche //
power that he maketh me to lese thy
presence. fforwho-soeuer hath ones //
fell the loste of thy loue: he shall say,
rather
that i wolde be bounde for euer in //
hell, than to fele that he shall do: by y
loste of thy loue one moment of tyme
O my sauioure, do not permitte that

psal. 7

folio 46r

euer i do departe frome the. But (if it
pleaseth the) put me in suche a place
that my soule, through wantonnes, or
synne be neuer lowsed frome thy
loue. ffor, in this worlde. i can not
haue persettely. this my desire. wich
thinges considered, maketh me fer
uently, and with all my harte, to de
sire the departinge frome this mise
rable body, not fearing the death,
nor any of her instrumentes. ffor
what feare ought i to haue of my
god. wich (through loue) hath ende
uoured hymselfe. and suffred death.
wherin he was not bounde: but by

folio 46v

cause he shuld vndowe the power
that this mortall death had. Nowe
is iesus deed, in whom we are all
deed: and through hys death, he
causeth euery man to liue agayne.
I meane those, wich, through sayth,
are partakers of hys passion. ffor.
euen as the death, before the greate
mystery of the crosse, was hard vnto
euery body, and there was no man
but was feared withall: considering
the copulacion, of the body, and soule
their order, loue, and agremente.
where the extreme sorowe, was in
the departinge one frome an other

right margin:
2 timoth, 1

ecclesiastic

folio 47r

But ſyth it hath pleaſed to the ſwitt
lambe, to offer himſelfe vpon the croſſe,
hys greate loue hath kindled a ſyre
withine our harte. ſo vehemente: y͏ͭ
euery chriſtenman ought to eſtime
the paſſage of death, but a pleye, or
paſſetyme: and ſo to prouoke one
an other to dye. ſſor. euen as ſeare //
of death did retarde vs: euen ſo ;//
loue ought to gyue vs a deſyre to //
dye. ſſor. if true loue be vnſaynedly
withine the harte of a man; he can
not ſele no other thinge; bycauſe y͏ͭ
loue is ſo greate of it ſelfe, that ſhe ꝭ
kepeth all the rowme, and putteth

oute all other desyres: not suffring
any thinge in hym, but god onely.
ffor (whersoeuer true and perfytte //
loue is, we do neyther remember
feare, or els forowe. If oure pryde,
(for to get honnoure) maketh vs to
feke for death, withfo many mea
nes. If (for to haue a folifhe plefure)
a man putteth hymfelfe in ieopardy
of his life. If a man (for to get riches)
doth put hys life in dāuger, for the
value of a fhelinge. If the wille to //
robe, or to kille, to beate, or to beoyle
caufeth often times the mynde of a
man to turne, fo that he knoweth

folio 48r

doth not se the daunger of death whē
he will do any yll, or els auenge hym
selfe of any man. If the strenght of //
sykenes, or the desease of an melēcoly,
causeth a man to wishe for deathe :
and often tymes (as doth) drowen
hange, or kille hymselfe ffor, suche
yuell, and desire, is so great, that he
causeth a man to choyce death. for
libertie. If so it be, than these greate //
paynes, full of yuell, and imperfectiō
. causeth them not to seare the hasard //
of death, and it semeth vnto them
that it cometh to late. Alas what
ought true, and laudable loue //

folio 48v

do. What ought the loue of the //
creatore do: shulde she not styrre //
so the harte of a man. that he(beyng
transported with such affection)shuld
sele no other thinge in hym; Alas, ye
ffor death is a pleasaunte thinge to ꝭ   psal, us.
soule wich is in loue with god and //
estimeth the passage easy, through ꝭ //   philip.i.
wich she cometh out of a prison. ffor
the harde way (through the wiche //
she cometh for to embrasse her hus //
band) can not wery her. O my sauiour
how good thesame death is, through
the wich we shall haue the ende of //
all sorowe, by whom also we shall ∾

folio 49r

enioye of thy fyght, and be transfor
med vnto the likenes of thy maieste
O death (through thy dede) i truste
to haue fo moche honnoure, that
wpon my knees (in crienge, and //
wepinge) i do defire the come quic
kely, and make an ende of my peine
and forowe. O hapy daughters, //
right holy foules, ioyned in to the //
citie of iherufalem: opene your eyes,
and (with pitie) loke vpon my de
folacion. I befeche ye, that in my //
name) ye will fay tell vnto my god
my frende, and kinge, howe, at //
euery houre of the day, i do lan //

pfal. ii 9.

cantic, s.

folio 49v

guishe for hys loue. O swittе death,
through suche loue come to me, and
with loue, bringe me vnto my god
O death: where is thy stinge. and dart. 1.corinth.
alas they are vanished frome myne
eyes, for rigoure is chaunged in to //
swittenes. Syth that my frende did suf
fer death vpon the crosse for my //
sake hys death doth so encourage my
harte. that thou art vnders gentyll
to me. if i might folowe hym. O de
death i beche the beseche the come to
put the frende with hys loue. Nowe, //
syth that death is so pleasaunte a life //
that she pleasyth me more tha feareth

folio 5or

fea me: than i ought to feare nothing
but the true iudgemente of god All
my synnes with hys iuste balaunce
shall be weyd, and shewen openly.
Thys that i haue done, also my the//
thought, and worde shall be better
knowen, than if it were written in a
rolle And we may not thinke that
charitie, wolde offende iustice, and
truth ffor, whosoeuer doth liue vn
faythfully, shall be punished in the
euerlasting peine. God is iuste, and
hys iudgemente is righteous All y
he doth is iuste in all thinges Alas
what am i, considering my right

luke, 12.
and math, 10

psal, 7

folio 50v

ousnes : I wretched and poore crea iob, 15.
ture. ffor i knowe, that all $\tilde{y}$ workes
of iuste men are so full of vices, that miche 7.
before god, they are more sylthy, thã
durth, or any other sylthines What esay. 64.
shall it be, than, of the synnes wich psal. 129
i do comitte, wherof i do fele the and 7 1.
burden importable : I can saye no //
thinge els, but that i haue wone //
damnacion. Is thys the ende : shall
despayre be the conforte of my great
ignoraunce : Alas, my god, no : ffor..
the muifible faith, causeth me to be
leue that all thinges wich are vnpof
fible to men, are possible vnto the // math 19

folio 51r

So that thou do conuerte my worke

rom.5. and,8. (wich is nothinge) in some good worke

Than. O lorde, who shall condemne

me syth that he (wich is geuen me

for a iudge) is my husband. my fa

ther, and my refuge. Alas what

psal,89. and timoth,2. father, who doth neuer condemne

hys childe: but doth alwayes excu

se and defende hym. Than ise to

haue no other accuser, but iesuschrist

wich is my redemer, whose death

hath restored vs.oure inheritaunce

1.ihon 2. and 1.timo.2. for he made hymselfe oure man a

lawe, shewynge hys so worthy me

rites afore god, wherwith my g=

folio 51v

great dette is so surmonted, that in
iudgemente she is accompted for
nothinge. O redemer, here is a
great loue: ffor we synde but sewe
such men of lawes. O switte iesus
it is vnto the, that i am a detter: ffor   esay 5
thou doest pray, and speke for me   hebr. 7
And moreouer, when thou doest   rom. 8
se that i am poore, thou doest paye
my dette, with the abundance of
thy goodes. O incomprehensible
see of all goodnes. O my father,
doest thou vouchase to be my
iudge, not willinge the death of   ezech. 18
the synner. O iesuschriste true fysher   math. 4

folio 52r

and sauioure of the soule : frend, aboue
aboue all frendes. ffor. thou beyng
my man a lawe, excused, and did
speke for me, where thou couldest //
iustely accuse me. I feare nomore
to be vndone by any man, ffor the
lawe is satisfied for all. My swette //
spowse hath made the payment //
so abundante, that the lawe can //
aske nothing to me, but she maye
haue it of hym. ffor (as i beleue) he
peter. 2. hath taken all my synnes to hym.
and gaue me hys goodes and ri
ches. O my sauioure (presenting thy
vertues) thou doest contente thow

folio 52v

ehes lawe; when she will reproche
me my synnes, thou doest shewe her
howe willingly in thyne own fleshe
thou hast taken the charge of them
through the coniunction of oure
mariage Also howe vpon ẙ crosse,
through thy passion, thou hast satis
fied for it Moreouer thy charitie
hast hath gyuen me this ẙ thou
hast deserued. Therfore (syth that
thy merite is myne owne) the lawe   psal. 84
asketh nothing of me. Thā will
i feare no more the iudgemente,
but with desyre, rather, than par
force, i do tary for the tyme, that

folio 53r

i shall se my iudge, and heare of h-
hym, a iuste iudgemente. yet, i knowe
that thy iudgemente is so iuste, that
there is no saute in it: and that myne
vnfaithsulnes is worthy to suffer //
the cruelnes of hell. ffor, if i do only
consydere my deseruing, i can se no
thinge in it, that can kepe me from
the syre of hell. True it is, that the //
turmente of hell was neuer prepared but for the dyuell, and not for
a reasonable man. Neuertheles, if
any man hath put hys mynde //
to be like vnto the dyuell: than he
ought (as the dyuell shall) to be //

folio 53v

payed with such a rewarde. But
if a man, through contemplacion.
doth holde of the aungell vertue
goodnes, and perfection, so that
he doth optayne heauen, wiche is
a place of like deseruinge than shall
the viciouse be punished with hym   sapien.
to whom he did ioyne hymselfe.
And syth he solowed satan, he
muste kepe suche place as is prepa-   math. 25.
red for hym. Nowe i considering
the diuersitie of both the sortes, it
consorteth my spirite but lytell
for i can not denye but i am more
like vnto the dyuell than to the

folio 54r

aungell. Wherfore i feare, and tremble: ffor the liuinge of the aungell is so godly, that i am nothing like vnto hym (this i do confesse) but, as for the other. i am so like vnto hym, of malice in custome, that of hys payne, and turmente, i ought to be partaker of it. ffor. the cruell synne wich hath bound me in hell is so great; and synne is stronge wich letteth nothinge come from hym, and feareth not that any man cometh to asayle hym He wich is stronge, knoweth not how his strenght goeth a waye when

luke 11

folio 54v

a stronger man than he cometh
Synne is stronge, wich bringeth //
vs in to hell, and i coulde neuer se
that any man, by merite, and //
payne, coulde vainquishe helle, //
saue onely he, wich hath made such
assaute through charitie (he being
humbled to the crosse) that he hath philip .2.
bounde, and ouercome his enmy, bro ephesi.4.
ken hell, and his power, so that he
hath no further strenght to kepe any
soule prisonnere, the wich hath put //
her truste in god. Than, beleuinge, //
and trustinge in the power that god
hath, i do not sett by hell, and sinne

folio 55r

not a strawe. ffor. wherof can synne
rmoye me. onles it be for to shewe.
how my god is mercyfull, stronge
mighty. and vanquisher of all the
yuell wiche is withme my hart. If
my synne forgiuen is the glory of
my sauioure. i ought likewise beleue
that also my glory is increased there
with. knowledginge that i am pla
ned. and ioyned with hym. Hys
honnoure onely. doth honore all
hys. And his riches doth replenishe
euery of goodes. Than is hell. and
synne ouercomed by hym. O glouto
hell where is thy defence: Thou

folio 55v

villayne synne: where is thy power
O death. where is thy stinge. and i.corinth.15.
victory. wich are so muche spoken
of. In stedde of death. thou geuest
vs life. and so doest thou contrary
vnto thy wille. And also. thou sine.
wich wolde drawe euery body vnto
damnacion; thou doest serue vs of
a ladder, for to reshe vnto the goodly
citie of iherusalem. ffor. thou woldest
by thy curfed nature, that our maker
shulde lese hys creature. But through
loue. and grace. thou doest cause her rom.5.
to come againe, and submitte herselfe
vnto god, more than euer she did.

folio 56r

His greate goodnes. doth make the to
lefe the payne, wich thou doest take,
all the whole weke. Therfore hell hath
not had all the number, wich he did
pretende to haue: bycaufe that the //
fhadowe. and ftrenght. of his pafsio.
is fuch a protection to the foule, that
fhe ought to doute, neyther deathe,
fynne, or hell. Is there any thinge, tha
that can hurte me, if god be willinge,
through fayth, to drawe me vnto
hym: I meane, fayth fuche as we
mufte haue for to obtayne, right
highe gifte frome aboue, and alfo
fuche fayth, wich, through charitie

ephe .z.

folio 56v

doth ioyne the humble seruante, vnto
hys maker. I beynge ioyned vnto hym,
ought to haue no feare of trauayle,
payne, or els sorowe. ffor whosoeuer
willingly doth suffer any maner of
death, or sorowe (as christ did) he
doth fele in suche turmente greate
consolacion for hys soule. Knowinge
that, as for myselfe i am weake: and
with god, i am right stronge. By his
conforte i may do all thinges. ffor   philip. 4
hys loue is so stedfaste, and euerlastig
doth suffer that she varieth for nothig
of thys world. Who can, than, oute   rom, 8
drawe me frome hys grace. Surely the

folio 57r

greate heyght of heauen, nor the depe
nes of hell, nor the breade of all the
earth, neyther death, or synne (wiche
doth warre euery daye againste me)
can not separate me one daye frome
the great loue, and charitie, that my
father, through iesuschriste, hath vnto
me. ffor hys loue is such, ŷ he loueth
me wiche doth not loue hym: and
yf i loue hym, than shall i fele hys
loue to increase, bycause that my loue
is not worthy to loue hym: but i do
fyre hys loue to be myne, the wiche
i fele such as thoughe it were myne
owne, hys desyre is to loue me, and

folio 57v

through hys loue, he causeth my hart
to be inflamed with loue: and throug
suche loue, he fyndeth hymselfe so wel
beloued: that hys owne dede yeldeth
hym contente, and not myne owne
loue, or strenght. Contentinge hymselfe,
hys loue doth increase more in me //
than i can desyre of hym. O true /
louer. springe of all charitie, and the
onely purse of the heauenly treasure
Ought i to thinke, deare i to saye //
what thinge thou art. maye i wrytteth
Can any mortall man conprehende /
thy goodnes, and loue: and yf thou /
does printe it withine any mannes /

folio 58r

harte, can he expresse it. No surely: ffor
the capacitie of no man can not comprehende the vnmesurable goodnes
wich are in the ffor naturall reason
doth shewe vs, how there is no com-
parayson betwene an eternall, and
a mortall thinge: but whē, throughe
loue the mortall is ioyned with the
eternall, the mortall thinge is so full
of the eternall, that she can not synde
the ende of it. ffor she hath more ge-
good withine her, than she cā holde:
therfore doth a man (wich hath this
loue) thinke that all the worlde is
within hym. Euen as we se, that the

psal.144

folio 58v

sunne with one onely sperkell of hys
light doth blynde the eye of a man
and yet doth she hydde her greater
light; but, aske to the eye what he hath
sene: the eye will say that he hath sene
the whole clartie of the sunne; but that
is a lye. ffor he (beyng blinded with
a lytell sperkell) coulde not se the
whole clartie of the sunne, and neuer
theles he is so contente, that it semeth
vnto hym, if he had so much light,
in hym, as the same sperkell was, that
he shuld not be able to suffer it. Euen
so the soule wich (through fayth) doth
fele one sperkell of the loue of god. thā

doth she fynde thys fyre so great, and
meruaylous so swittc, and good, that
it is vmpossible vnto her to declare
what thinge thesame loue is. ffor aly
tell that she hath felthe, doth yelde
her mynde satisfied and desyringe
more of thys wherof she hath ynough
So doth she liue desyringe, and lan
guishinge, and seghynge The harte
doth fele well that he hath receyued
to muche of it: but he hath conceyued
suche desire, in thys to muche, that
he allwaes desyreth to receyue the thig
whiche, he can not haue, neyther is
he worthy to receue Hc knoweth the

lesiastic, z4

folio 59v

good that he hath alredy to be vnspe
keable, and yet wolde he haue more
of thys wherof he can not skille. He
can neyther fele, or thinke the good
wich is in hym Than, it lyeth not in
my power to tell what thinge ẙ loue
of god is. syth that i haue no know
ledge of the feruentenes therof. He that
thinketh to haue all this loue withine
his harte, can not truely declare what
thinge it is Hapy is he wich hath
suche abundance, that he maye saye:
My god i haue inoughe of it. He wiche
hath this loue withine hym, dar not
of it for feare that in speckinge he shuld

folio 6or

let it go sonles it be for the saluacion of
hys neigboure, to edifie hym. The im=
posibilite of the declaracion of this loue.
than, shall make me to holde my p[er]=
peace: ffor there is no sainte so parfaite
if he will speke of the loue of the highe
god, of hys goodnes, suittenes, grace,
and of all the thinges wich perteyneth
ynto hym he shall lokinge a lowe,
stoppe hys mouthe. I than, worme of
the earth, lesse than nothinge, ought
to ceasse, and not to speake of ye highnes
of thys loue. But to muche vnkindnes
shuld be in me, if i had written nothig
hauinge thys done for to satisfie to a

folio 6ov

better witte than myne is. ffor he that
wolde hydde the goodnes of so good
a maister, shulde comitte a synne,
worthy to be punished with ÿ euer
lastinge payne. Therfore come o ha
py paule wich hast tasted so muche
of the same swette honny, beynge blin
ded for the space of thre dayes, and
rauished vnto the thyrde heauen. Now
I beseche the satisfie myne ignoraunce,
and faulte, and tell me what thou //
hast sene with such an vision. Harke //
what he sayeth. O vnspekeable hignes
of the greate treasure, and riches of ÿ
springe of all wisedome, science, and pa

actes. 9 and
2. corin. 12.

rom. 11.

folio 61r

cience: thy iudgementes are incompre
hensibles. and thy wayes are vnserchea
bles vnto all our wittes. O good sainte
paule: thy wordes causeth vs to mer
uayle, that, thou hauinge knowledge
of suche secrettes, wolde speake no &
further of it. But yet, tell vs what th
thinge we truste to haue one daye &
through suche loue. Harke, and pou
der the wordes wich he sayeth. There
1.cor,2. was neuer no man that did se, nor //
eares coulde neuer heare, neyther no
man coulde comprehende, thys that
god hath prepared for hys good //
frendes. Wolde he speake any further

folio 61v

No: yet all thys that he sayeth, is for no
thinge els, but to prouoke vs, to loue ,//
and to estime thys that he can neither
declare, or name, and to drawe our
hartes, loue, and hope to desyre thys
wich no man also can neyther se/
sele, or thinke what it is, and yet cau
seth many men to dye for hys loue O
the right greate gifte of fayth, whens
so muche good cometh, that he causeth
one to possede the thinge wich he can
not comprehende. Fayth ioyned with truth
bringeth furth hope, wherby parfaitte
charitie is engendred: and charitie is
god, as thou knowest. Therfore if   1 ihon. 4

we haue charitie, we haue god also.
Than is god in vs, and all we are in
hym, and he in all men. If we haue
hym throughe fayth, than haue we
a greater treasure, than any man can
tell. Now to conclude: Syth that
so greate an apostell as faynte paule
willeth to speke no further of god
and of hys loue: Accordinge to the
exemple of hys rightwise teachinges
i will holde my peace. But folowing
hys worde, howbeit that i knowledge
myselfe to be but meere, and duste: yet
may i not fayle to giue graces, and
thankes vnto god, of all the goodes

folio 62v

and benefyttes vndeserued, wich plea
seth hym to geue me. Vnto y kinge 1.timoth,1,
of heauen, immortall, inuisible, oure
mighty god onely, and incompre
hensible be all honnoure, praÿse, glo
ry, and loue, for
euer.

folio 63r

GLOSSARY

CHRONOLOGY

NOTES

BIBLIOGRAPHY

& INDEX

Glossary of Proper Names in Bale

Abraham [né Abram]: Biblical patriarch, to whom God promised numerous descendants.

Aeneas: Trojan hero. Common ancestor of Romans and Britons.

Agasia: Wife to King Finnanus's son Dorstus. Daughter of king Blegabridus.

Albion: Cited by Holinshed as one of the kings of Britain. Also ancient name for the British Isles (one tradition has it that Rome was a colony of Alba Longa) before Brutus gave them their new name.

Alexander the Macedonian [the Great]: Lived 356–23 B.C. Pupil of Aristotle. Regent of Macedonia at age sixteen.

Alfred [the Great]: Saxon king. Ruled 871–99; died 901 A.D. Translated the Molmutine Laws into English and the Lex Martiana (Mercian Law) into Saxon. Like Elizabeth, he made a translation of Boethius's *Consolation of Philosophy*. By his wife Ealhswith, Alfred had two sons (Edward [Eadward], who succeeded him, and Aethelward) and three daughters (Elfleda, the Lady of the Mercians; Elfritha, married to Baldwin, count of Flanders; and Ethelgora, abbess of Shaftesbury).

Anna: Sister of King Arthur. Wife of Lotho of Lodonesia.

Anna: Sister of Aurelius Ambrosius. Wife of Lotho of Lodonesia. Conflated with the Anna above.

Antenes [Anthémius]: Protohistorical fifth-century French king.

Aristotle: Greek philosopher, fourth century B.C.

Arthur: King of the Britons, sixth century. Illegitimate son of Utherpendragon, who was brother of Aurelius Ambrosius. National hero; champion of Christendom. United the British tribes against the invading Saxons; defeated Romans.

Glossary of Proper Names in Bale

Arviragus [Prasutagus]: King of Britain. Second son of Cymbeline. Defeated British army. Boudicca was his first wife; his second was Genvissa [Gwenissa], daughter of Roman Emperor Claudius, mother of Marius, and grandmother of Athildus. An Arviragus appears in Shakespeare's *Cymbeline* and Chaucer's "Franklin's Tale."

Aryans: Fourth-century Christian sect. Denied that Jesus was consubstantial, or of the same essence as God.

Asa: Third king of Judah, c. 915–875 B.C. In removing idols, he did not spare his grandmother Maachah, who occupied the special dignity of "King's Mother," in the Jewish court: Asa burned the symbol of Maachah's religion.

Askew, Anne: Lived 1521–47. Protestant martyr, burned at stake for arguing against transubstantiation. Made friends with the heterodox thinker Joan Boucher in London; may have been supported by Catherine Parr; called an "undoubted citizen of heaven" by Bale (in Askew, *The Lattre Examinacyon*).

Athildis: Daughter of King Marius. Wife of the French king Marcomerus. Sometimes associated with Saint Alkeld [Athilda].

Augustine: Saint. Sent by Pope Gregory I to convert the English, 596 A.D. First Archbishop of Canterbury.

Augustine Friars: One of the four mendicant orders. Luther went forth from an Augustinian Hermit congregation in Germany.

Aulus Rufus Pudens: A Roman knight. Husband of Claudia Rufina.

Aurelius Ambrosius [Ambrosius Aurelianus]: Second son of Constantine II. Fifth-century champion of common British and Roman ancestry. Led Romans and those of Roman descent against the Saxons.

Beline [Belyne, Belinus]: King of Britain. Ruled in concert with Brenne for five years.

Benedict [of Nursa]: Saint. Founder of Western monasticism. Composed *Regula Monachorum* (c.515 A.D.).

Glossary of Proper Names in Bale

Bergomas [Bergomensis], Jacobus: Author of *Supplementum Chronicarum*, completed 1483.

Berosus [Berossus]: Priest of Bel at Babylon. Published in Greek the history of his country during the reign of Antiochus II (250 B.C.); some extracts survive.

Blackfriars: The Dominican Friars or Preachers. They wore black habits.

Blegabridus: King of Britain after Sisillus [Sitsiltus, Cecil] and before Arcimalus Archiuall.

Boccaccio, Giovanni: Lived 1313–75. Author of *De casibus virorum illustrium* (bk. 9 is a source of John Lydgate's *Fall of Princes*), and of *De claris mulieribus*, as well as the better-known *Decameron*.

Bomelius, Henricus [Frederik Samuel Knipscheer]: Author of *The Summe of the Holye Scripture & Ordynary of the Christen Teaching* . . . , which appeared in English in 1535.

Boudicca [Boadicea, Bundīca, Bundwyca, Bunnduca, Voada, Voadicea, Woda]: First-century queen of the Iceni. First wife of Arviragus, an ally of Rome who shrewdly made Nero his co-heir. When he died (60 A.D.), the Romans annexed and pillaged the Iceni territory. According to Tacitus Boudicca was flogged, and her daughters were raped. As British warrior queen, she led a great uprising against the Romans, followed by her suicide.

Brenne [Brennius]: King of Britain. Ruled in concert with Beline for five years.

Bruno [of Cologne]: Saint. Founder of the Carthusian order, 1086 A.D.

Brutus [Brute, Brut]: First king of the Britons. Great-grandson of Aeneas.

Buscoducinus [Busciducinus, Buscoducensis], Nicolaus: In 1512, edited the works of Hugh of St. Victor, the twelfth-century scholastic theologian and mystic philosopher; in late 1520s and early 1530s, edited the dialogues of the third-century Syrian Christian martyr Lucian of Samosata.

Byntre [Binham, Bynham], William: Benedictine. Author of *Contra positiones Wiclevi*, which is not known to be extant, though Wycliffe's reply is.

Cadwalder [Cadwallader, Cadwalader]: Last of the British kings discussed by Geoffrey of Monmouth. Went to Rome, where he was confirmed in the faith of Christ by Pope Sergius; died there in 689 A.D.

Cain: Eldest son of Adam and Eve; killed his brother Abel (Gen. 4).

Cambra: Daughter of King Belyne. Wife to Antenes, the king of France. See Leges Sycambrorum.

Cato: Probably Dionysus Cato, author of *Dionysii Catonis disticha de moribus ad filium.*

Celestine III: Pope 1191–98.

Cham [Ham]: Either the second or the youngest son of Noah (Gen. 10).

Chamesene: Applied by Bale to King Albion. The Chamavi are a German tribe mentioned by the Roman historians; cf. also Noah's son Cham and the Moabites' idol Chamos (against which Josiah instituted his policies).

Charles: Charlemagne, king of the Franks (768–814) and emperor of the West (800–814). Founder of the Holy Roman Empire.

Chrisostomos [Chrysostom], John: Born in Antioch. Saint. Lived 345?–407. Called "golden-mouthed" because of his eloquence.

Cicero, Marcus Tullius: Roman statesman and orator, famous for his eloquence. Lived 106–43 B.C.

Claudia Rufina [Gladys Ruffyth]: Some say that Timothy, Saint Paul's associate, was a son of Claudia by Aulus Rufus Pudens, but see 2 Tim. 1. Martial addressed an epigram to Aulus on the occasion of his marriage to Claudia; there is another to Claudia herself.

Coelus [Coellus, Coel]: King of Britain, c. 125 A.D. Ruled after Marius and before Lucius. Submitted to Senator Constantius.

Constantia: Daughter to Helena (Flavia?). Presumably daughter of Constantius Chlorus. Half-sister of Constantine the Great.

Glossary of Proper Names in Bale

Constantia: Wife to King Nicanor. Daughter of King Heliodorus. Sister of Geruntius.

Constantine I: Called "the Great." Lived. c. 274–337. Son of Constantius Chlorus and Helena, whom Saint Ambrose describes as an innkeeper; the suggestion is that Constantine was perhaps illegitimate.

Constantine I: King of Britain. Son of Constantius and Helena (daughter of Coelus, King of Britain). Conquered Rome and became "overlord of the world." Conflated with Constantine the Great.

Cordelia [Cordilla]: Youngest daughter of King Lear.

Cunibertus [Cunincpert]: Seventh-century king of Lombardy. Husband of Hermelinda.

Dardanus: Priam the Trojan is regularly called *dardanides*.

David: King of Israel. Reputed author of the Psalms.

David: Patron saint of Wales, born c. 500 A.D. Presided over two Welsh synods. Bishop of Moni Judoerum, afterward Saint David's. He moved the ecclesiastical government associated with the name "Saint David's" to the headland of Mynyw, or Menevia.

Demosthenes: Greatest of the ancient Athenian orators.

Dionothus [Dionethus]: Duke of Cornwall. Father of Ursula Cynosura.

Dominick: Saint. Lived 1170–1221. Founder of Dominican order.

Dorstus: Son of Finnenus. Married Agasia; said by Bale to have used her wickedly.

Duns Scotus, John: Lived c. 1265–1308. Franciscan. Wrote commentaries on Aristotle and Peter Lombardus.

Dunwallo [Dunvallo] Molmutius: King of Cornwall. Father of Beline and Brenne. Gave Britain the Molmutine Laws (see Leges Martiane).

Ebranck: Early British king.

Egbert [Ecgbert]: King of the West Saxons. Crowned 802; died 839.

Glossary of Proper Names in Bale

Edward IV: King of England, 1461–83.

Edward VI: King of England, lived 1537–53. Only child of Henry VIII by his third wife, Jane Seymour. Like Elizabeth, received a fine education. Succeeded his father at the age of ten. Recalled Bale from German exile. During his iconoclastic rule many church images, pictures, and stained-glass windows were removed or destroyed.

Eleanor [Alenor] of Aquitane: Divorced wife of French King Louis VII (marriage annulled on the basis of consanguinity). Wife of King Henry II of England. Mother of King John. Dressed as an Amazon warrior leading her own troops in the Second Crusade (1147–49).

Eleanor [Alenor] Cobham: Mistress, then wife (1430) of Humphrey, Duke of Gloucester. In 1441 she was charged with practicing sorcery against Henry VI, condemned, and her accomplices executed.

Elizabeth: Lived 1437–92. Queen of Edward IV of England; daughter of Richard Woodville. Her daughter Elizabeth (1465–1503), was queen to Henry VII and mother of Henry VIII.

Emerita: Sister of King Lucius. Patron of Chur (Switzerland). She was beaten, imprisoned, and burned alive. Her relics are in the monastery church at Chur.

Finnanus [Finnaeus]: Protohistorical Scottish king.

Francis I: King of France, 1515–47. Brother of Marguerite of Navarre.

Francis of Assisi: Saint. Lived 1182–1226. Bale refers to the 1224 Monte Alverno "Miracle of the Stigmata," marks (possibly made upon the skin with a hot iron), resembling the wounds on the crucified body of Christ.

Geruntius [Gerontius]: Brother-in-law of Nicanor. Son or son-in-law of Heliodorus.

Gideon: Fifth judge of Israel. Involved in destruction of Baal's altar.

Grayfriars: Franciscan Friars or Minors. They wore gray habits.

Glossary of Proper Names in Bale

Guythelyne [Guithelin, Guithelinus]: King of Britain. Married Marcia.

Gwendolyn [Guendolena]: Wife of Locrinus. Mother of Maddan. After Locrinus deserted her for his mistress Estrildis, Gwendolyn killed him in battle, ruled for fifteen years, then passed the kingship to Maddan and herself became ruler of Cornwall.

Helena Flavia: Saint. Died 330 A.D. Ambrose says she was an innkeeper. Mother of (the illegitimate) Constantine the Great by Constantius Chlorus (the Pale, or Flavius Valerius Constantius). "Divorced" by Constantine when he became Caesar.

Helena: Daughter to King Coelus. Wife of Constantius. Mother of Constantine I. Coel had educated her expressly to succeed him, and for years Helena seemingly ruled *iure hereditario* with her husband and later in behalf of her young son, who eventually conquered Rome. It is not clear how independent was her rule from that of her husband and son, just as it is unclear "how far the Empress Matilda in history was to reign independently of her second husband" (Tatlock, *Legendary History*, p.286). Conflated with Helena Flavia.

Heliodorus [Helidurus, Elidurus]: King. Father of Constantia. Identified in Ponticus Virrunius, as father of Geruntius; also in Holinshed.

Hengist [Engist]: With his brother Horsa, chieftain of one of the Teutonic/Saxon bands that settled England.

Henry II: King of England, 1154–89. Son of Geoffrey Plantagenet (Count of Anjou) and Matilda (daughter of Henry I). Married Eleanor of Aquitane in 1152. Father to Joanna, wife of William of Sicily.

Henry V: King of England, 1413–22.

Henry VII: King of England, 1485–1509. Son of Margaret Beaufort. Father of Henry VIII.

Hermelinda [Eoremenlind]: Wife of Cunibertus, king of Lombardy. Of English Saxon descent.

Herod [Antipas]: Son of Herod the Great, whom the Romans named "King of the Jews." It was to him that Pilate sent Jesus.

Hezekiah [Ezechias]: A king of Judah.

Hilda [Hild]: Saint. 614–680 A.D. Converted to Christianity by the preaching of Saint Paulinus, Roman missionary who joined Augustine in Kent. Founded at Whitby the double monastery of Brothers and Sisters (among whom was Caedmon, the English Christian poet). Argued at the Synod of Whitby or Streneshalce in 664 (or 663), a meeting to decide whether the date of Easter should be determined by Roman or Celtic church custom.

Humphrey, Duke of Gloucester: Lived 1391–1447. Fourth son of Henry IV. Made Duke of Gloucester by Henry V. Suspected of designs on Henry VI's life; died in custody. Famous as patron of letters.

Hunt, Walter [Venantius]: Carmelite friar. Died 1478. Wrote in Latin some thirty treatises, several of which were against women who preach.

Iles [Yles] of the Gentiles: According to a gloss in the Genera Bible, the Jews applied this term to all lands separated from them by the sea.

Isocrates: Athenian orator. Lived 436–338 B.C.

Japhet [Japheth]: Youngest or (in another, probably earlier, tradition) second son of Noah (Gen. 10). "Father" of one of the three groups into which the nations of the world were divided. Luther saw the Germans as first of all nations by right of their descent from Ashkenaz, whose biblical genealogy is traceable back through Gomer, Japhet, and Noah to Adam.

Jehoshaphat [Josaphat]: King of Judah; son of Asa. Ally of Israel.

Jehu: King of Israel. Killed priests of Baal.

Jesus [Son of] Sirach: Flourished 200 B.C. Author of the apocryphal wisdom book commonly called *Ecclesiasticus*, canonical in Roman Catholic Bible.

Glossary of Proper Names in Bale

Joanna [Johanna]: Lived 1165–99. Queen of Sicily. Daughter of Henry II and Eleanor of Aquitane. Brought up in the double-monastery abbey of Fontevrault.

John [Lackland]: King of England, 1199–1216. Youngest son of Eleanor of Aquitane and Henry II. Quarreled with Pope Innocent III (1207–13), who laid England under an interdict in 1208, excommunicated the king in 1209, and suggested that French king should invade and depose John. John had to acknowledge Stephen Langton as Archbishop of Canterbury, and Langton encouraged barons to bring demands against John; the Magna Carta thus confirms the liberties of the church, but Innocent III suspended John for not being against the baronial demands. Langton's manuscripts are listed in Bale's own *Index Britanniae Scriptorum*. On Bale's *Kyng Johan* (c.1538), see my Introduction.

Josiah [Josias]: King of Judah. Succeeded his father Amon at the age of eight. Reestablished the worship of Jehovah.

Judas [Iscariot]: One of the twelve apostles. Betrayed Christ for money.

Kilwardby [Kylwardby], Robert: Archbishop of Canterbury, 1272–78. A Dominican, he was the first member of a mendicant order to reach high office in England. Writings include *De ortu scientarium*, *De tempore*, *De universali*, and some commentaries on Aristotle. Promoted legislation (1275–90) eliminating feudalism and establishing the parliamentary system.

Lander of Bonony [Leander of Bologna]: Friar. Author of *Libro Primo della deca prima delle historie di Bologna, di F. Leandro degli Alberti Bolognese, dell'ordine de F. Predica, Tori.*

Lear: King. Died 42 B.C. Father of Cordelia.

Leges Martiane [Lex Marciana, Mercian Law]: Given to Britain by Dunwallo Molmutius, translated into English by Alfred — but really, says Bale, the work of Marcia.

Leges Sycambrorum: Attributed by Bale to Cambra. She would appear to have married into the Sicambres, who were antagonists to the Salians (see Dareste's discussion of the Mérovingien dynasty).

Locrinus: Second king of Britain. Oldest son of Brutus. Killed by his wife Gwendolyn.

Lombarde [Lombardus, Lombard], Peter: Twelfth century Italian theologian, bishop of Paris.

Lotho [Loth]: King of Lodonesia; afterward king of Norway. King of the Picts, says Holinshed. Said to be husband to Anna, Arthur's sister, and (perhaps by way of conflation) Anna, Aurelius Ambrosius's sister.

Lucius: Son of the king Coelus. First Christian king of England. Geoffrey of Monmouth says that he died in 156 A.D. and was the first king publicly to profess Christianity. Bede reports that King Lucius of Britain sent letters to Eleutherius, who had obtained the bishopric of Rome, praying to be made a Christian: "The Britons afterwards continued in the right faith till the reign of Diocletian."

Maddan: British king. Son of Gwendolyn.

Marcia [Martia]: Succeeded her husband Guythelyne on the throne. Devised the Leges Martiane, which King Alfred put into English. What we still have of these laws concerns the *wergild*: literally, man-money.

Marcomerus: French king. Husband of Athildis.

Margaret Beaufort: Lived 1443–1509. Countess of Richmond. Mother of Henry VII. Aided scholars and encouraged writers. Translated the (spurious) fourth book of Thomas à Kempis's *Imitatio Christi*.

Marius: Son of Arviragus. Succeeded his father as king. Established friendly relations with Rome.

Martialis [Martial], Marcus Valerius: Roman epigrammatist of the first century A.D. His reference to Claudia appears in bk. 4, epigram 13, of his *Epigrammaton*.

Maydestone [Maidstone], Richard: Died 1396. Author of *Contra Wiclefistas*.

Glossary of Proper Names in Bale

Milverton, John: Died. 1487. Prior of the Carmelite house at Oxford. Defended the Carmelites Henry Parker and Thomas Holden in their preaching of the doctrine of evangelical poverty. Opposed by William Ive [Ivy], excommunicated and imprisoned in the castle of Saint Angelo by Pope Paul II in 1464. It is alleged that Milverton had been chosen bishop of Saint David's, but owing to the accusations against him, he was never consecrated. Apparently none of his writings survive.

Nicanor: French king. Husband of Constantia.

Ninus: Founder of Nineveh. Son of Belos or Bel. Married Semiramis; after his death, which she was accused of causing, she erected a monument to Ninus.

Orchades [Oracedes]: Orkney archipelago (off Scotland). Arviragus, king of Britain, made his submission to Claudius, who with his assistance conquered the Orkney Islands.

Petrus Blesensis [Peter of Blois]: Archbishop of Bath and author. Flourished 1190.

Plato: Ancient Greek philosopher.

Plutarch [Plutarchus]: Lived c. 46–120 A.D. Greek author of *Parallel Lives* and *Opera moralia*.

Pole, William de la: Lived 1396–1450. Fourth Earl and first Duke of Suffolk. Hired killer of Eleanor Cobham.

Ponticus [Ludovicus] Virunnius: Author of *Britannicae Historiae*, published in 1534.

Porphyry: Lived c. 232–304. Greek scholar and neo-Platonic philosopher, born in Syria. Defended paganism and opposed Christianity. His *Chronicles* cover the period from the capture of Troy to 270 A.D.

Priamus: Son of Nicanor.

Raimundus [Raymond of Peñafort]: Saint. Lived c. 1176–1275. Dominican. Author of *Decretalium Gregorii*.

Richard [Palmer]: Bishop of Syracuse (1155 A.D.). One of two tutors sent by Henry II to accompany his daughter Joanna at her marriage to King William of Sicily.

Romulus: With his brother Remus, a descendant of the Trojan Aeneas and founder of Rome.

Seneca, Lucius Annaeus: First-century moralist, moneylender, and tutor to Nero. Bale suggests that he was friendly to British nationalism; however, Seneca's actions were partly responsible for the uprising in Britain in the first century A.D., whose heroine, Boudicca, Bale praises.

Socrates: Ancient Greek philosopher.

Solomon: King of Israel, second son of David and Bathsheba. On the frequent comparison between Elizabeth and Solomon later in the sixteenth century, see King, *Tudor Royal Iconography*, pp. 255–56. Legend had it that Solomon was remarkable not only for his wisdom (to which Marguerite of Navarre's *Miroir* alludes) but also for his connection with the Queen of Sheba, whom the book ascribed to him (Canticles, or Song of Solomon) calls "My sister, my wife."

Stanbery [Stanbury, Stanbridge], John: Died 1474. Carmelite. Confessor to Henry VI. Took Lancastrian side during Wars of the Roses.

Streneshalce [Whitby], Synod of: Crucial moment in the development of British Christianity. Held in 663 or 664 to reconcile differences between Roman and Celtic Christianity; the latter flourished in Britain from the time of the withdrawal of the Roman army in the mid-fifth century until the meeting of this synod.

Theognis: Greek elegiac poet of Megara, sixth century B.C.

Trojan War: Troy fell in the twelfth century B.C.

Ursula Cynosura: Saint and Christian martyr. Daughter of the British prince Dionothus. One of the ten thousand virgins whom the Romans put to death.

Varro, Marcus Terentius: Roman scholar, 116–27 B.C. Among chief works was *Antiquitates rerum humanarum et divinarum antiquitates.*

Glossary of Proper Names in Bale

Voada: Likely a variant of Boudicca, first queen of Arviragus.

Voadicia: Younger daughter of Boudicca.

Walden: Thomas Netter of: Lived c. 1375–1430. Carmelite. *Fasciculi zizaniorum Johannis Wyclif*, apparently his, provides our only contemporary account of the Lollards. Author of *Doctrinale catholicae ecclesiae contra Wiclevistas et Hussites* (1523). Was present at the examination of Sir John Oldcastle. Said to have preached a sermon against the Lollards in which he reproved Henry V for his slackness. Henry V chose him for his confessor.

Walter: Bishop of Palermo. Second tutor sent by King Henry II to accompany his daughter Joanna at her marriage to King William of Sicily.

Whitefriars: The Carmelites (Bale's order). They wore white mantles over brown habits.

William (the Bad) of Sicily: Twelfth-century king of Sicily. Husband of Joanna.

William [the] Conqueror: Norman king, conquered Britain, ruled 1066–87. Sometimes called William the Bastard.

Wycliffe [Wiclif], John: English religious reformer, c. 1320–84. Organized a body of itinerant preachers, the "poor priests." Author of *Two Short Treatises against the Order of the Begging Friars*. Subject of works by Byntre and Thomas Netter of Walden. Bale's relevant works include *A Brief Chronicle concerning . . . Sir John Oldcastle* (Oldcastle had had Wycliffe's works transcribed and distributed; some people say he was the model for Shakespeare's Falstaff.) Wycliffe's supporters came to be known as Lollards.

Chronology

c.1300	Margaret Porete writes *Mirror of Simple Souls*.
1491	Henry VIII is born to Henry VII and Elizabeth of York.
1492	Marguerite of Navarre is born.
1495	John Bale is born.
1507	John Bale enters Carmelite monastery at Norwich. Anne Boleyn is born.
1509	Marguerite of Navarre marries the Duke d'Alençon. Henry VIII marries Catherine of Aragon, widow of his brother Arthur.
1515	Francis I of France, brother to Marguerite of Navarre, is crowned.
1516	Mary Tudor (Mary I) is born to Henry VIII and Catherine of Aragon.
1520	Francis I and Henry VIII hold interview at Field of Cloth of Gold.
1521	Henry VIII is named Defender of the Faith by Pope Leo X.
1525	Brother Martin Luther marries Sister Catherine von Bora.
1527	Anne Boleyn becomes the mistress of Henry VIII. Marguerite of Navarre marries Henri d'Albret.
1528	Thomas More calls Luther's marriage "incestuous."
1531	Marguerite of Navarre's *Miroir de l'âme pécheresse* is published.
1532	Rabelais's *Pantagruel* is published.
1533	Montaigne is born. Henry VIII declares his marriage to Catherine of Aragon null and void on grounds of "incest."

Henry VIII marries Anne Boleyn in secret (she was four months pregnant).

Elizabeth is born (in September).

1534   Teresa of Avila joins the Carmelite Order.

Act of Supremacy is passed.

1535   Thomas More is beheaded.

Henry VIII suppresses monasteries and confiscates their property.

1536   Anne Boleyn is beheaded; the charges included "incest" with her brother.

Thomas Cramer declares marriage of Catherine of Aragon and Henry VIII null and void.

Elizabeth is declared illegitimate.

Henry VIII marries Jane Seymour.

1537   Lady Jane Grey is born, great-granddaughter of Henry VII.

Edward VI is born to Henry VIII and Jane Seymour.

Jane Seymour dies.

1540   Henry VIII marries and divorces Anne of Cleves.

Henry VIII marries Catherine Howard.

Bale flees to Germany.

1542   Catherine Howard is beheaded.

Mary Stuart (Mary, Queen of Scots) is born.

1543   Henry VIII marries Catherine Parr.

1544   Elizabeth completes her "Glass of the Sinful Soul."

1545   Calvin writes "Against the Libertines."

1547   Catherine Parr's *Lamentacion of a Synner* is published.

Henry VIII dies.

Francis I dies.

Edward VI is crowned.

John Bale, on the accession of Edward VI, returns to England.

1548   Bale's edition of the "Glass," *A Godly Medytacyon of the Christen Sowle*, is published in Germany.

1549   Marguerite of Navarre dies.
       Edward VI authorizes the first Prayer Book by Thomas
       Cranmer.

1552   Edward VI excludes Mary and Elizabeth from
       succession and devises it to Jane Grey.

1553   Edward VI dies.
       Mary Tudor is crowned.
       Elizabeth sides with Mary against placing Jane Grey
       on throne.

1554   Jane Grey is beheaded.
       Mary imprisons Elizabeth.

1555   Mary Tudor reestablishes Roman Catholicism in
       England and accepts Cardinal Pole as chief adviser.

1556   Thomas Cranmer, Elizabeth's godfather, is burned at
       the stake.

1558   Elizabeth succeeds Mary I on the throne.
       John Bale receives stall in Canterbury.

1559   Elizabeth is crowned by the Bishop of Carlisle, most
       other bishops refusing to recognize her as head of the
       Church.
       Elevation of the host is discontinued in England.
       Marguerite of Navarre's *Heptameron* is published.

1563   John Bale dies.
       Elizabeth promulgates Cranmer's Thirty-Nine Articles
       and abstains from parliamentary extension of the Act of
       Supremacy, rendering Protestantism and patriotism
       synonymous.
       Mary Stuart claims succession to Elizabeth.

1565   Mary Stuart marries her cousin Henry Stewart, Lord
       Darnley.

1566   Mary Stuart gives birth to a son (James VI of Scotland;
       James I of England).

1568   Mary Stuart is imprisoned.

1568–82 Three editions of Elizabeth's *Godly Medytacyon* are
       published in England.

Chronology

Notes

1. The poem appeared also in 1538 and 1539; and in 1547 and 1548 it was published as part of Marguerite's *Marguerites*.

2. For the view that Anne Boleyn entered the service of Marguerite of Navarre (then Duchess of Alençon), see Perry W. Ames, Introduction to Elizabeth, *Mirror of the Sinful Soul*, p.31. The two queens knew each other as early as Queen Claude's coronation at St. Denis in 1516; and both attended a banquet in France in 1518 and the Field of Cloth of Gold in 1520 (Eric Ives, *Anne Boleyn*, pp.38–42). Anne Boleyn served Queen Claude, wife of Francis of Angoulême (crowned Francis I of France in 1515) and sister-in-law to Marguerite of Navarre, for about seven years.

3. Anne Boleyn and Marguerite of Navarre had a well-documented correspondence in 1534–35. In October 1535, moreover, the English were anxious to interest the French envoys in the young Princess Elizabeth (Ives, *Boleyn*, pp.41, 341). Maria Dowling, "Anne Boleyn and Reform," argues that Anne was a dedicated Church reformer.

4. Ames, Introduction to Elizabeth, *Mirror*, p.31, writes: "We may conclude that the copy . . . had belonged to her mother, who may have obtained it from her former friend and mistress [Marguerite of Navarre]." See m.52, below.

5. Renja Salminen (Commentary in Marguerite, *Miroir*, p.253) says Elizabeth used the edition of December 1533 printed by Antoine Augereau in Paris; but Anne Lake Prescott, ("The Pearl of the Valois and Elizabeth I," p.66) says Elizabeth used the edition of 1539.

6. For the letter, see MS Cherry 36, Bodleian Library, fols.2r–4v (reproduced below, pp.111–12), and Elizabeth, *Letters*, pp.5–7. On Elizabeth's needlework, see J. E. Neale, *Queen Elizabeth*, p.12. At about this time Elizabeth gave as gifts to members of her family other holograph translations as well — an English translation of John Calvin's *Institution Chrétienne* to Catherine Parr (1545); Latin, French, and Italian translations from Catherine Parr's *Prayers, or Meditations* to Henry VIII (1545); and a Latin translation of Bernardino Ochino's *De Christo sermo* to her brother, the ten-year-old Ed-

ward (1547). On a probable role of Catherine Parr as editor, see Salminen, *Miroir*, p.257.

7. Elizabeth asks her stepmother to "rub out, polish, and mend (or else cause to mend) the words (or rather the order of my writing) the which I know in many places to be rude, and nothing done as it should be" (MS Cherry 36, fol.4r; Elizabeth, *Letters*, p.6).

8. John Bale, 1495–1563, went at the age of twelve to the Carmelite convent at Norwich but converted to Protestantism in 1533 — thanks partly to the teachings of Lord Wentworth. He caused a great scandal when he gave up his monastic habit and married Dorothy — a marriage which, like Luther's, Thomas More would have called incest. Bale's principal antiquarian work was the *Illustrium majoris Britanniae scriptorum* (1548), which discusses, among other writings, the manuscripts in the libraries of the religious orders before their houses were destroyed in the Dissolution. Bale's chief literary work was *Kynge Johan* (c. 1538). Written in the English "mother tongue" (*in idiomate materno*), it "marks the transition between the old morality play and the English historical drama" (EB, s.v. "Bale," p.248). Appearing some fourteen years before Thomas Norton and Thomas Sackville's *Gorboduc* and thus probably the first English "history play," *Kynge Johan* represents John as a champion of the English people against Roman rites and rights ("This noble Kynge Johan, as a faythfull Moses / Withstode proude Pharao for his poore Israel"); the people do not enter the promised land until the time of Henry VIII ("Till that duke Josue, whych was our late Kynge Henrye, / Clerely brought us out in to the lands of mylke and honye"). See also "Bale and British Nationhood," below.

9. This portrait is ascribed by some to Hans Holbein the Younger, but it was probably designed in 1547 by an unknown artist (Ames, Introduction to Elizabeth, *Mirror*, p.7). Holbein died of the plague in 1543. John N. King (*Tudor Royal Iconography*, pp.209–10) says that Elizabeth's kneeling before Christ with the Bible in hand suggests Protestant learning, and he draws our attention to a comparable woodcut in Bale, *Illustrium majoris Britanniae scriptorum*, showing Edward VI as a studious king standing at a lectern (King, *English Reformation Literature*, pl.6).

10. A transcription of Elizabeth's manuscript did appear in Renja Salminen's 1979 edition (published by a Finnish academic journal) of Marguerite of Navarre, *Le miroir de l'âme pécheresse*. For further bibliographical information, see R. Steele, "English Books Printed Abroad, 1525–48"; Ruth Hughey, "A

Note on Queen Elizabeth's 'Godly Meditation'"; and H. H. E. Craster, "An Unknown Translation by Queen Elizabeth."

11. Horace Walpole published the first important list in 1758: see his *Catalogue of the Royal and Noble Authors of England*. In the years 1545–47 Elizabeth gave other beautifully prepared translations to members of her family (see note 6 above), not all mentioned by Walpole and his successors (see Bibliography for locations of manuscripts; cf. Salminen, *Miroir*, p.255, and King, *Tudor Royal Iconography*, p.251).

12. Elizabeth's translations include Boethius's *Consolation of Philosophy*, Plutarch's *On Curiosity*, and Horace's *On the Art of Poetry*—the last written as late as 1598. On supposed inaccuracies in these translations, see Caroline Pemberton's preface to Elizabeth, *Englishings*, p.xi. The claim that Elizabeth did not take the trouble to be accurate is not beyond dispute: as Leicester Bradner pointed out long ago (in Elizabeth, *Poems*, p.xii), "a thorough study of Elizabeth's work [the "Glass"] as a translation is much to be desired."

13. For relevant literary analysis of Marguerite's *Miroir*, see Reta Mohney Bernardo, "The Problem of Perspective," chap.2. Several biographers have felt that Marguerite's *Miroir* is excessively dreary; Salminen (*Miroir*, p.82) repeats the related charge that the poem is "without logical plan."

14. Roger Ascham, who helped to oversee Elizabeth's education, acquired fame for his own beautiful handwriting, and in a letter to Jakob Sturm he praised the beauty of Elizabeth's. Her 1544 manuscript of the "Glass" is written in one of the finest italic hands of the English Renaissance. Bale writes in his "Conclusion" (reproduced below, pp.93–102): "The written clauses are these, which she wrote first with her own hand much more finely than I could with any printing letter set them forth" (fol.41r); and one critic has claimed that the princess's manuscript, though of little worth in itself, is "of visual [interest], as an example of italic handwriting."

15. The first half of the sixteenth century saw the beginnings of a major shift in the education of royal and aristocratic women. By the nineteenth century John Stuart Mill could write in *The Subjection of Women* (p.493) that "princesses, being more raised above the generality of men by their rank than placed below them by their sex, have never been taught that it was improper for them to concern themselves with politics; but have been allowed to feel the liberal interest natural to any cultivated human being, in the great transactions . . . in which they might be called on to take a part. The ladies of reigning families are the only women who are allowed the same range of interests and freedom of development as men" (cited in Betty Travitsky, *The Paradise of*

Women, p.191). There was some traditional resistance, of course, to the education of upper-class women (see Merry E. Wiesner, "Beyond Women and the Family"; and Mary Ellen Lamb, "Cooke Sisters"). And sometimes that resistance came from advisers hired by the royal family itself: Juan Luis Vives's regressive *Instruction of a Christian Woman* (1529), for example, was commissioned by Catherine of Aragon for her daughter, Mary (Carlos G. Norena, *Juan Luis Vives*, p.304). But generally speaking, in the 1520–30s daughters were beginning to be educated equally with the sons of forward thinking fathers, including preeminently Thomas More (Frances Murray, "Feminine Spirituality in the More Household"). And by 1581, it was argued that Elizabeth's education itself was proof that the education of women should be advocated; see, e.g., Richard Mulcaster, *Positions . . . for the Training Up of Children*, p.173.

16. In "Spaces for Further Research," Alice Jardine (*Gynesis*, p.95) remarks that women were relatively active as writers during the Renaissance and raises Joan Kelly-Gadol's question "Did Women Have a Renaissance?"

17. Thomas Bentley's *Monument of Matrones* included Catherine Parr's *Lamentacion of a Sinner* and *Prayers, or Meditations*, Elizabeth Tyrwhitt's *Morning and Euening Prayers*, Elizabeth I's *Mirror*, and other devotional literature. Catherine Parr was, according to some critics, "the first woman to publish her work in English with the intention of influencing the public" (Travitsky, *Paradise*, 38). Roland Bainton (*Women of the Reformation*, p.165) calls her *Lamentacion* "one of the gems of Tudor devotional literature," and her *Prayers* is central to the tradition of devotional writing: "I am in prison, and bounden with fetters of sorrowe, till thou O Lord, with thy gratious presence vouchsafe to visit me, and to bring me againe to libertie and joie of spirit, and shew thy favourable countenance unto me" (in Bentley, *Monument*, sig. L5r; cited in John King, "Patronage and Piety," p.47). In the same tradition might be mentioned Anne, Jane, and Margaret Seymour's *Mortum Margaritas Valesiae*, which describes Marguerite of Navarre as burning with the delicious kisses of Christ or in the ecstasy of the divine bridal couch, and which refers to the notion (here of Jane Seymour) that Marguerite will soon see her beloved brother again (pp.100, 84, 74; cf. Prescott, "Pearl," p.74). See too St. Teresa's *Meditations on the Song of Songs* (1566; in *Complete Works*). Earlier devotional and mystical literature — for a time in Britain the genre *par excellence* by and for women (Joseph B. Collins, *Christian Mysticism*) — included the 1522 translation by Margaret Beaufort (Countess of Richmond) of Dionysius Carthusianus, *The Mirroure of Golde for the Synfull Soule* (see Rita M. Vergrugge,

"Margaret More Roper's Personal Expression in *Devout Treatise upon the Pater Noster*," in Hannay, *Silent but for the Word*, p.39; and P. Gartenberg and N. Thames Wittemore, "Checklist of English Women in Print"). On devotional aspects of Princess Elizabeth's poetry, see William P. Haugaard, "Elizabeth Tudor's *Book of Devotions*" (which does not, however, mention the "Glass").

18. William Grindal, a student of Roger Ascham (author of *The Scholemaster*), was probably Elizabeth's tutor in 1544. Ascham, himself her tutor from her sixteenth to her eighteenth year, argued for the use of "the double translation," his principal model being the letters of Cicero. Among other tutors to Henry VIII's children were Jean Belmain (Balmain) and Battista Castiglioni (Castiglione), who taught French and Italian. Translation was a traditional field for Elizabethan scholarship of the Renaissance (F. O. Matthiessen, *Translation*, and Charles Whibley, "Translators") and an especially important *métier* for women scholars and students (including the multilingual Lady Jane Grey); cf. John Florio's remark, in his translation of Montaigne's *Essayes*, (sig A2r), that "all translations are reputed femalls" (Lamb, "Cooke Sisters," p.116).

19. Published poets like Elizabeth — her metrical translation of Psalm 14 also appeared in 1548 — were rare in Elizabethan and Jacobean England. See Barbara Lewalski, "Of God and Good Women," n.2.

20. The general unavailability of the work has made it nearly impossible for students to pursue this topic in detail, though it seems plausible, as I suggested in *The End of Kinship*, that Shakespeare, for one, was influenced by the "Glass" in writing such plays as *Measure for Measure*.

21. Dormition, or *koimēmsis*, refers to the specific "dying" of the Virgin Mary: she passes from being the mature Mother of God the infant Son to being the infant Daughter of God the mature Father, as discussed in the body of church literature called the *Transitus Mariae* (*Patristic Greek Lexicon*, s.v. "koimēsis"). Cf. Marina Warner, *Alone of All Her Sex*, pp.88–89. The dormition of the Virgin Mary, though generally considered a doctrine of the Eastern church, is depicted prominently in such public buildings of Western Christendom as La Martorana in Palermo, Sicily (see illustration 5) and in such Western manuscripts as the twelfth-century Winchester Psalter in England (British Museum Cotton Manuscripts, Nero c iv, foli.29; see Sapl and Wittkower, *British Art and the Mediterranean*, 24.6, 7).

22. Elizabeth's letter to Catherine Parr, ms Cherry 36, fol.3v.

23. Harold Jenkins, at 3.4.6 in his edition of Shakespeare's *Hamlet*, notes

that only in the First Folio does Hamlet, about to enter Gertrude's chamber, call out, "Mother, mother, mother"; in the First Quarto the line appears as "Mother, mother," and in the Second Quarto it does not occur at all.

24. Deut. 25:5–6 (biblical citations not otherwise identified refer to the King James Version of 1611).

25. Simon Augustine Blackmore, "Hamlet's Right to the Crown," argues that "the diriment impediment to marriage with a deceased brother's wife was part of English Church doctrine since earliest times and was retained by the English secular authorities until the nineteenth century. As Ernest Jones (*Hamlet and Oedipus*, p.68) points out, "Had the relationship not counted as incestuous, then Queen Elizabeth would have no right to the throne; she would have been a bastard, Catherine of Aragon being alive at her birth." On *Hamlet* and the relationship between Henry VIII and Catherine of Aragon, see also Jason P. Rosenblatt, "Aspects of the Incest Problems in *Hamlet.*"

26. In *Henry VIII*, Shakespeare goes to extraordinary lengths to allay anxiety about Elizabeth's possibly illegitimate birth. "Ann Bullen," for example, is noticeably absent from the christening scene. Yet toward the end of the play the Porter suggests that Anne Bullen, who (like her sister Mary) had been Henry's mistress, was a "fornatrix," so that the Princess Elizabeth might be a bastard. When the Porter cries out, "What a cry of fornication is at the door!" (5.34–35), he refers in part to the crowd of common people; yet the smallest "fry" in the play is Elizabeth herself, who from the Catholic viewpoint is born of a "fornatrix."

27. Much relevant material here is included in Edward Fox's *Collectanea statis copiosa*, a basis for *A Glasse of the Truthe* (1532; attributed to Henry VIII). It included such treatises as Thomas Cranmer's *Determinations . . . That It Is Unlawful for a Man to Marry His Brother's Wife* (1531); see Ives, *Anne Boleyn*, pp.165, 167.

28. For Luther's marriage to the Cistercian Sister Catherine von Bora, see Thomas More, *Confutacyon with Tindale*, pp.48–49. For Rome's condemnation of Bale's marriage to Dorothy, see John Pits, *Relationum historicum de rebus Anglia*, pp.53–59; cf. Jesse W. Harris, *John Bale*, pp.22–23. For Elizabeth's work with Ochino, see Craster, "Unknown Translation."

29. The notion that bastards, especially those born from bigamous or incestuous relations, cannot inherit the throne gained some support from the fact that the children of Edward IV, as the offspring of a bigamous union, were unable to inherit. The issue was hotly contested in the 1540s. Upon the execution of Anne Boleyn, for example, although "parliament was required to

establish the succession on the new basis of Henry's new queen Jane Seymour . . . it also empowered the king to leave the crown by will if he had no legitimate issue, but the illegitimate son of the Duke of Richmond, in whose favor this provision is said to have been conceived, died shortly afterwards" (EB, s.v. "English History," pp.522d, 531d).

30. Two other counts may be mentioned: first, the rumor that the king was impotent (Paul Friedmann, *Anne Boleyn*, 2:280 n1; J. Dewhurst, "Alleged Miscarriages of Catherine of Aragon and Anne Boleyn"), and second, the view that the marriage was declared invalid *ab initio* on the ground of Anne's supposed marriage contract with Lord Percy.

31. See Friedmann, *Anne Boleyn*, 2:287, 351; and for the indictments of Anne for sibling incest and an account of the trial, 2:262–63, 278–81. The charge of adultery and incest with her brother, Lord Rochford, was made on May 2, 1536; Lord Rochford's wife was a principal witness for the prosecution.

32. See Friedmann, *Anne Boleyn*, 2:262–63, 278–81.

33. See Ives, *Boleyn*, illus. 27. The idea of Elizabeth as divine was fostered from the beginning, even as Anne was associated with Saint Anne, and there was a religious symbiosis of Mary's son and Anne's (expected) son in literary propaganda of the period (Ives, *Boleyn*, p.284).

34. The 1536 Act of Parliament ordered every man who had married his mistress's sister to separate from his wife and forbade all such marriages in the future. For Cranmer's views on the matter, see John Lingard, *The History of England*, 5:74, 540–42; and Friedmann, *Anne Boleyn*, 1:43, 2:323–27, 351–55. On the view that the "marriage was declared invalid *ab initio* . . . on the ground of the affinity established between Henry and Anne by Henry's previous relations with Mary [Boleyn]," see EB, s.v. "Elizabeth Queen of England."

35. See Frank A. Mumby, *The Girlhood of Queen Elizabeth*.

36. For Henry's views of Mary's illegitimacy, see *Calendars of Letters . . . between England and Spain*, 1534–35, p.57 (LP 7:214); cited in Ives, *Anne Boleyn*, p.271.

37. John Howard Fowler, "The Development of Incest Regulations," pp.12–13. For the Latin term, see Rabanus Maurus, *Concilium moguntium*.

38. *Jacob's Well*, 162/15; Jonas of Orleans, *De institutione laicali*, PL 106: 183–84.

39. On the Renaissance link between incest as the venereal disease of the body politic and syphilis as the venereal disease of the individual body, see my

Notes to Pages 14–16

End of Kinship, pp.31–33; and Walter E. Vest, "William Shakespeare, Syphilographer."

40. In A.D. 868, Church councils ruled that "we will not define the number of generations within which the faithful may be joined. No Christian may accept a wife . . . if any blood relationship is recorded, known, or held in memory" (in J. D. Mansi, ed., *Sacrorum conciliorum*, 15:875). Pope Julius I specified the seventh remove as the limit of diriment impediment to marriage (*Decreta*, no.5, PL 8:969). But there were enormous practical problems of record-keeping, and even where the numerical degree was both agreed upon and ascertainable, there were controversies about the correct method of counting. Thus Stephan of Tournai notes that "the counting begins with the brothers according to some and with the sons of the brothers according to the others" (*Summa decreti* 255). Cf. Charles Edward Smith, *Papal Enforcement*, chap.2.

41. Eph. 5:31–32; 1 Cor. 6:16 (cf. Gen. 2:24). On the kinship relationship engendered by sexual intercourse, see Gratian, *Decretum* 35, q.5, 10; Orlando Bandinelli, *Summa* 203; Stephan of Tournai, *Summa decreti*, 250; Bernardus Balbus, *Summa decretalium*, 168; and H. Feije, *De impedimentis et dispensationibus matrimonialibus*, chap.14.

42. Bale, "Conclusion," fol.40r.

43. For an interpretation in this context, see Seth Bernardete, "A Reading of Sophocles' *Antigone*," pt.2, p.11; and G. W. F. Hegel, *Phänomenologie*, in *Werke*, vol.6, chap.6.

44. There would have been many bibliothecal sources of information, including a French metrical account of how Anne was brought to trial and executed, the *Histoire de Anne Boleyne Jadis Royne d'Angleterre* of 1545, and perhaps early versions of the picaresque midcentury Spanish *Cronica del Rey Henrico*, in which one "Marguerita" — maybe a figure of Marguerite of Navarre — is the bawd who procures Smeton (Mark Smeaton) for Queen Anne. The *Histoire* is discussed in G. Ascoli, *La Grand-Bretagne devant l'opinion française*; the *Chronicle of King Henry VIII* (ed. M. A. S. Hume), pp.55–59, 68–76, refers to Marguerita; cf. Ives, *Boleyn*, pp.69–70, 375.

45. "You are welcome," says Hamlet to the twinlike Rosencrantz and Guildenstern, "but my uncle-father and aunt-mother are deceived" (*Hamlet*, Jenkins ed., 2.2.371–72). Insofar as Hamlet's mother, Gertrude, is married to Hamlet's uncle, she is his aunt. Similarly, because Henry had had sexual intercourse with Anne' Boleyn's sister Mary, and because by the doctrine of

carnal contagion a lover is, to all intents and purposes, a wife, Anne was Elizabeth's aunt as well as mother.

46. *Hamlet*, 1.2.156–57.

47. For a review of the evidence concerning the Elizabeth-Seymour liaison, see William Seymour, *Ordeal by Ambition*, pp.215–19, 225–26. Thomas Tyrwhitt, who was sent to Hatfield to extract the truth from Elizabeth, complained that Thomas Seymour, Mistress Ashley, Thomas Ashley, and Elizabeth told a story so close in so many details that they were "all in a tale" (see Elizabeth, *Letters*, p.9; cf. Elizabeth to Edward Seymour, Lord Protector, January 28, 1549, *Letters*, p.11). Elizabeth's relations with Thomas Seymour occasioned the syntactically complex letter she sent him soon after she left the Lord Admiral's household in July 1548: "You needed not to send an excuse to me for I could not distrust and not fulfilling your promise to proceed for want of good will, but only that opportunity serve not. Wherefore, I shall desire you to think that a greater matter than this could not make me impute any unkindness in you, for I am a friend not won with trifles, nor lost with the light" (*Letters*, p.8).

48. Elizabeth to Edward Seymour, January 28, 1549 (*Letters*, p.11).

49. I. F. Duff, "Die Beziehung Elizabeth-Essex," p.469.

50. Plutarch, *De curiositate*, chap.24, in Elizabeth, *Englishings*, p.139.

51. The centuries-old tradition of ascribing to Elizabeth various feelings about her family circumstances continues unabated among traditional scholars. Prescott, for example, tries to determine "how [Elizabeth] respond[ed] to the executions of her mother, Anne Boleyn, and her stepmother, Catherine Howard" ("Pearl," p.68). Religious or psychological speculation arising from such texts as the "Glass" would seem to be particularly compelling—at least where the rhetorical quality of such speculation is recognized.

52. There is some evidence that there was a copy of the book in Henry VIII's household; see *Letters and Papers . . . of Henry VIII*, 14 (1): 369. In 1544 Marguerite had not yet a great literary reputation; she was known as an author pretty much only by her *Miroir*, its companion religious poems, and a farce. See *Letters and Papers . . . of Henry VIII*, 18:128; Prescott, "Pearl," p.68.

53. Henry VIII opened negotiations to marry Marguerite of Navarre (then Duchess of Alençon) while he was entertaining the idea of divorcing Catherine of Aragon. Margaret's reply, made through Wolsey, makes clear that she refused to marry Henry because he had committed crimes against Catherine of Aragon. See Ames, Introduction to Elizabeth, *Mirror*, p.32, quoting *Margaret, the Pearl of Navarre* (Edinburgh, 1868).

54. Ames, Introduction to Elizabeth, *Mirror*, p.33.

55. Elizabeth, "Glass," fols.7v, 8r, 23v.

56. Elizabeth to Catherine Parr, MS Cherry 36, fol.3r.

57. Replacing consanguinity with a sort of amatory *alliance* of friendship had, in carnival style, begun to affect many levels of society in the sixteenth century; in conjunction with an amatory neo-Platonic view of the Christian exhortation to love (1 John 4:11–12), it seemed to encourage spiritual libertinism. Pierre Jourda, in his edition of François Rabelais, (*Oeuvres complètes*), suggests that the social structure of Rabelais's Island of Ennasin (*Pantagruel*, bk.4, chap.9; cf. "Essene") parodies such spiritual *alliances* as that between Marot and Anne d'Alençon; the Rabelaisian "Island of Alliances" is associable with the ideas of the one-time Franciscan Tourangeau de Tours. See Emile Telle, "L'Île des alliances," p.166; and Telle, *L'Œuvre de Marguerite d'Angoulême*, pp.299–312.

58. *King Henry the Eighth*, 5.4.60–61.

59. Chaucer, *Boece* 2.3.30–31, in *The Riverside Chaucer*, p.410.

60. Elizabeth, *Englishings*, p.54, translates Boethius, *Consolation*, 3.6. The first three lines in Latin read "Omne hominum genus in terris simili surgit ab ortu. Unus enim rerum pater est." When the great Alfred, king of the West Saxons, translated these famous lines in the ninth century, he changed "the Father of all things" into "the father and mother of the race." Albert B. Friedman, "'When Adam Delved,'" pp.220–21, comments: "Seemingly Alfred preferred the concept of a concrete biblical blood cousinry to the abstract mystical brotherhood of men, sons of a spiritual father, which his text, influenced by late Stoicism, intended."

61. D. Cox, "The Lord's Prayer," in Edward Farr, ed., *Selected Poetry . . . of the Reign of Queen Elizabeth*, 2:503.

62. For the proverb and its corollaries in England and elsewhere, see Friedman, "'When Adam Delved.'"

63. The inability of King Edward, Elizabeth's half-brother, to disinherit his half-sisters Mary and Elizabeth, hence to devise the succession to Jane Grey in 1552, would seem to prove this rule.

64. With the double meaning of "taboo" as both "unclean" and "holy," compare Latin *sacer*. Cf. Sigmund Freud, *Totem and Taboo*, p.18.

65. See *Measure for Measure*, 3.1.138–39. John Bale ("Epistle Dedicatory" [reproduced below, pp.83–92], fol.9r) translates the name Elizabeth as *Dei mei requies*, or "the rest of my God."

66. *Sponsa Christi* is a technical term used as early as Tertullian. See Je-

rome's relevant theory of the virgin as the bride of Christ and of "spiritual matrimony" (*Epistulae*, Letter 107, CSEL 55:298; cf. Demetrius Dumm, *The Theological Basis of Virginity*, p.74). For a modern version, see Pius XII, "Sponsa Christi." For an anthropological view of the institution of women marrying gods in Christianity and in other cultures, see Edward Westermarck, *The History of Human Marriage*, 1:403–6; and Mary Esther Harding, *Woman's Mysteries, Ancient and Modern*.

67. Aubin Louis Millin, *Antiquités nationales*, 3:28.6, on an inscription at Ecouis; my translation.

68. Ibid. Luther (*Tischreden*) retells such stories of incest. See Anatole de Montaiglon's note to the thirtieth tale in his edition of Marguerite of Navarre, *Heptameron*, 4:281–83, and Saintsbury's note in his translation, 3: 214–16.

69. Millin, *Antiquités nationales*, 3:28.6; my translation.

70. *Pericles of Tyre*, . . 65–72. The vital solution requires a kind of resurrection: wife and daughter, believed dead, are reborn from their living deaths in a religious institution and a brothel. Dramatically, the solution to the riddle of Antiochus involves assigning to Pericles and Marina the roles of Antiochus and Antiochus's daughter; beyond the resurrection of the two women, the plot enacts a final rebirth, as Pericles calls it, of the father, Pericles, from the daughter, Marina: "Thou that beget'st him that did thee beget" (5.3.195). In this atonement, Pericles foreshadows kinship relations in all the other romances.

71. Mark Taylor, *Shakespeare's Darker Purpose*, p.69, compares the riddle in *Pericles* with similar riddles in two of Shakespeare's sources: Gower's *Confessio amantis*, and Twine's 1594 translation of Apollonius of Tyre, *The Patterne of Painefull Adventures* — neither of which, however, plays up the spiritual nunnish-or-monkish quality of simultaneous parenthood, spousehood, and childhood in the same way that *Pericles* does. For Medrano, see Otto Rank, *Das Inzest-Motiv*, pp.334–35.

72. Rabelais, *Pantagruel*, bk.4, chap.9.

73. Elizabeth, "Glass," fol.26v.

74. Ibid., fol.43r–44r. For the poet-lover in this fourfold kinship role, see also such passages as "O my father, brother, child, and spouse" (fol.21r); "O what a sweet rest it is, of the mother, and the son together" (fol.26r); and "Now then that we are brother and sister together, I care but little for all other men."

75. Ibid., fols.13r, 19r–v.

76. Elizabeth, Letter to Catherine Parr, MS Cherry 36.

77. In the "Glass" the sinful soul is a fourfold traitor: the prodigal *child* who leaves the home of the father; the careless *parent* who fails to watch out for the child; the *sibling* who betrays the brother; and the *spouse*.

78. Bale, "Conclusion," fols. 39r, 40r.

79. Salminen (*Miroir*, p. 81) dismisses the fourfold kinship in Marguerite's poem as a strange myticism rather than a central principle: "Marguerite loses herself in a strange mysticism: she describes the union of the soul with the Savior with the aid of metaphors associated with kinship relations. She calls herself, one by one, the sister, mother, spouse, and daughter of God" (my translation).

80. Bale, "Conclusion," fol. 39r. A late instance of the Elizabethan four-fold-kin *topos* occurs in Aemilia Lanyer's reference in *Salve deux rex judaeorum* (1611) to a new Cynthia (i.e., Elizabeth I). Of her it is said that Jesus is "Her Sonne, her Husband, Father" (Travitsky, *Paradise*, pp. 99, 101); see also Lewalski, "Of God and Good Women."

81. In their specific emphasis on *fourfold* kinship, both Marguerite's *Miroir* and Elizabeth's "Glass" not only recall the Eastern Church's ideology of Dormition (which emphasizes Mary's role as Mother and Daughter) but move beyond it. Dormition is illustrated in such works as the twelfth-century mosaic in the church of La Martorana in Palermo, Sicily, where Jesus is shown giving new life to Mary's soul, which resembles a baby in his arms. (For other illustrations, see *New Catholic Encyclopedia*, 4:1017B). Julia Kristeva ("Stabat Mater," p. 105), citing Dante's well-known line "Vergine Madre, figlia del tuo Figlio [Virgin Mother, daughter of your Son]," says that "not only is Mary her son's *mother* and the *daughter* of Jesus [as in Dormition], she is also his *wife*. Thus she passes through all three women's stages in the most restricted of all possible kinship systems." But as Marguerite and Elizabeth emphasize, Mary is also the *sister* of God the Brother. And this Sisterhood, which makes equal siblings of all mankind, reaches beyond the restriction that Kristeva remarks.

82. Claire Lynch Wade takes Paul's famous statement "Where the Spirit is, there is liberty" (2 Cor. 3:17) to be the heart of Marguerite's *Prisons*, a poem that includes "a joyous mystical marriage of the soul at death" (Introduction to Marguerite of Navarre, *Prisons*, p. xv) and ends thus: "Où l'Esprit est divin et vehement, / La liberté y est parfaictement [Where spirit is divine and vigorous, / There liberty in full (perfectly) exists for us]" (fol. 348v, lines 4927–28). Robert Marichal (Introduction to Marguerite of Navarre, *Navire*,

p.16) similarly associates Marguerite's *Navire* with the Pauline doctrine as reinterpreted by Martin Luther.

83. Tale 30 in Marguerite of Navarre, *Heptameron* (trans. Saintsbury), 3:192, 200. For various sources, see Nicole Cazauran, "La trentième nouvelle de l'*Heptameron*," esp. p.624.

84. Some literary historians have sought to use the story that Marguerite was raped in the 1520s to elucidate her tales about rape, including those where religious Brothers rape laywomen and Sisters (e.g., tale 72), but they generally ignore the definition of spiritual incest as "sexual relations involving any Brother or Sister," and so they tend to overlook the relationship between the physical incest described in the *Heptameron* and the transformation of physical incest into spiritual incest depicted in the *Miroir*. On the presumed rape of Marguerite by Admiral Bonnivet, see Pierre de Bourdeille Brântome, *Les Dames galantes*, pp.422–23 (cited in Patricia Francis Cholakian, *Rape and Writing in the Heptameron*, p.9).

85. Tale 30 in Marguerite, *Heptameron*, 3:201, 195.

86. *Love's Labour's Lost*, 1.1.13, 150–51. Cf. 1.1.206–7: "It is the manner of a man to speak to a woman." Shakespeare very probably knew the work of Marguerite of Navarre; her influence is suggested by his depiction of academic celibacy in *Love's Labour's Lost*, whose Princess is modeled on Marguerite of Valois, her grandniece. See esp. A. Lefranc (*A la découverte de Shakespeare*, and *Sous le masque de Shakespeare*) and the endorsement of Lefranc's position in Richard David's introduction to his edition of *Love's Labour's Lost*, p.39.

87. Here there are biographical dimensions to Marguerite's concern with incest, as to Elizabeth's: for example, Marguerite's love for her brother, King Francis of France, is the subject of her greatest poetry. George Saintsbury remarks: "It has been asserted that improper relations existed between the brother and the sister," though the historical evidence is not conclusive on the side of either chastity or incest (introduction to Marguerite's *Heptameron*, 1:56). For the view that Marguerite loved her brother incestuously, see also François Génin, *Nouvelles Lettres de la reine de Navarre*, pp.3–12; and Jules Michelet, *Histoire de France*, 8:154–66. Against Michelet's view, see Jeanne Calo, *La Création de la femme*, pp.400–401. Cholakian (*Rape and Writing*, p.10) argues from the *Heptameron* itself that Marguerite "was the victim of a traumatic rape experience"; and in discussing tale 30, she feels called upon to say, "Of course, I am not arguing here that Marguerite de Navarre was ad-

vocating incest between mothers and sons or marriage between sisters and brothers" (p.154).

88. Ames, Introduction to Elizabeth, *Mirror*, p.42.

89. Ibid., p.42; A. Lefranc, *Les Idées réligieuses de Marguerite de Navarre*, p.15.

90. John Calvin, *Contre la secte phantastique et furieuse des Libertins qui se nomment spirituels* (1545), in *Opera omnia*, 7:145–248. For the antinomian beliefs of the spiritual libertines, see Williston Walker, *John Calvin*, pp.293–94. Calvin's attack offended Marguerite, and he wrote an ambiguously apologetic letter to her on April 28, 1545 (*Opera omnia*, 12:65). On Marguerite and the spiritual libertines, see too Gerhard Schneider, *Der Libertin*, esp. pp.81–84; and Jean Dagens, "*Le Miroir des simples ames* et Marguerite de Navarre."

91. Matt. 23:8.

92. OED, s.v. "Counsel," sb.2b; cf. Matt. 19:21.

93. Thomas Vautrollier, *Luther's Commentarie*, p.85, marg. (1577 ed.). Luther resented the canonical imposition of celibacy laws, which, given the conflation of intent and act that characterizes his notion of faith, were impossible for (almost) all human beings — including such monks and priests as himself — to fulfill.

94. OED, s.v. "Perfection," sb.4 (with Hamilton example).

95. Freud, *Totem*, p.6.

96. "Anyone who has trangressed one of these prohibitions," writes Freud (*Totem*, p.22; cf. p.35), "acquires the characteristic of being prohibited." Cf. Freud, "Taboo on Virginity" and "Obsessive Acts and Religious Practices."

97. Luke 14:26.

98. Marguerite, *Miroir*, lines 267–68. A translation of Matt. 12:50: "Quicumque enim fecerit voluntatem Patris mei . . . ipse meus frater, et soror et mater est." Elizabeth's translation of the verse: "Those that shall do the will of My father, they are My brethren and mother" ("Glass," fol.17r).

99. For a monk or a nun it is official Church doctrine and law that "concubinage or marriage to anyone is incest." See such documents as Council of Rome (A.D. 402), can.1, 2, in Carl Joseph von Hefele, *Conciliengeschichte*, 2:87; Pope Gelasius I (A.D. 494), letter to the bishops of Lucania, c. 20, in Gratian, *Decretum*, causa 27, q.1, c. 14; Council of Mâcon (A.D. 585), can.12, in Hefele, *Conciliengeschichte*, 3:37; Gratian, *Decretum*, causa 30, q.1, c. 5.10; and Oesterlé, "Inceste," in R. Naz, ed., *Dictionnaire de droit canonique*. For the reference to Thomas More, see his *Tindale*, pp.48–49.

100. Courtly love may have been a similar way to love one's sibling with-

out violating the taboo against physical incest. Indeed, "in the middle ages a sister was not infrequently the object of courtly love, partly, it appears, because the presence of the incest barrier served to re-inforce the knight errant's resolution to adhere to the ideal of chastity" (Henry A. Murray, introduction to Herman Melville, *Pierre*, p.55).

101. Sigmund Freud, *Civilization and Its Discontents*, pp.48–49.

102. "Il Canto di Frate Sole," in Francis of Assisi, *Gli scritti*, p.168; trans. as "The Canticle of Brother Sun," in *Saint Francis: Omnibus of Sources*, 130–31.

103. Bonaventure, *The Soul's Journey into God* (thirteenth century), p.93. Franciscans generally regarded Bonaventure, the "Seraphic [or Franciscan] Doctor," as the principal theological and philosophical spokesperson for their order.

104. See *Acta sanctorum*; and Martin P. Harney, *Brother and Sister Saints*.

105. Athanasius (?), *Vita Antonii*; and EB, s.v. "Monasticism."

106. Three days later, Scholastica died; in the course of time, Benedict joined her in a single grave. See Gregory the Great, *Vita S. Benedicti*.

107. Hartmann von Aue, *Gregorius*.

108. Leander, *Regula*, PL 5:331–32.

109. Leander, *Regula*, quoted in Montalembert, *The Monks of the West*, 2:188.

110. Damasus, *Epigrammata*, quoted in Harney, *Brother and Sister Saints*, p.20. Nor was concern with a sibling's chastity confined to men. Saint Lioba, seeking to serve her cousin Saint Boniface, wrote him thus: "God grant, unworthy as I am, that I might have the honor of having you for my brother." She closed the letter with the following suggestive verse: "May the Almighty judge, who made the earth / And glorious in His kingdom reigns, / Preserve your chaste fire warm as at its birth, / Till time for you shall lose its rights and pains" (quoted in Harney, *Brother and Sister Saints*, p.93; see also Willibald of Mainz, *Vita S. Boniface*). Boniface asked that at her death Lioba be buried in his grave, but the monks of Fulda did not carry out his request.

111. Quoted in Harney, *Brother and Sister Saints*, p.114.

112. Bernard of Clairvaux's *Sermones in Cantica Canticones* demonstrates this "dernière libération de l'âme" of which Paul preaches. See Marcel Viller et al., *Dictionnaire de la spiritualité*, s.v. "Bernard"; cf. John Bugge, *Virginitas*, p.90.

113. Ernst Robert Curtius, *European Literature of the Latin Middle Ages*, p.122.

114. Victoria Lincoln, *Teresa, a Woman*, pp.xxv, 10. Cf. Téofanes Egido, "The Historical Setting of St. Teresa's Life."

115. Teresa of Jesus, *The Book of Her Life*, IV, in *Complete Works*, vol.3.

116. Teresa, *Meditations on the Song of Songs*; and *Way of Perfection*, IV (cf. VIII), in *Complete Works*, vol.3.

117. Teresa, *Exclamation of the Soul to God*, XIV; and *Way of Perfection*, XXXVII, in *Complete Works*, vol.3.

118. John of the Cross, *Precautions*, V, in *Collected Works*, p.656.

119. Lincoln, *Teresa*, p.24; cf. Teresa, *Book of Her Life*, II.6; and *Rules for a Brotherhood*, in *Complete Works*, vol.3. To the list of saintly siblings might be added Heloise and Abelard, who lived together first in spiritual incest of a physical kind (he a Brother, she a laywoman), then as secret husband and wife. After Abelard was castrated at the command of Heloise's uncle, she became a Sister, and they lived as "brother and sister" — to quote the letters between them (Jean Leclerq, *Monks and Love in Twelfth-Century France*, esp. p.119).

120. David Knowles and R. N. Hadcock, *Medieval Religious Houses*, esp. pp.104–5, 194–95, 202.

121. At Fontevrault was found the oldest manuscript of Marguerite Porete's powerful *Mirror of Simple Souls*; see Dagens, "Miroir," p.288; and Henri Hauser, *Etudes sur la réforme française*. Marguerite Porete's antinomian influence on Marguerite of Navarre and the Siblings of the Free Spirit are discussed below.

122. Tale 30 in Marguerite, *Heptameron*, 3:202. Robert d'Arbissel, the founder of the abbey at Fontevrault, was himself accused of sleeping in the same bed with nuns; see Pierre Bayle, *Dictionnaire historique et critique*, s.v. "Fontevrault," 6:508–10.

123. EB, s.v. "Monasticism."

124. Rom. 8:23; cf. Rom. 8:15.

125. On Ochino and his stay in England from 1547 to 1553, see Karl Benrath, *Bernardino Ochino von Siena*, pp.172–99. On Elizabeth's 1547 translation, see Craster, "Unknown Translation," p.723; the autograph manuscript is at the Bodleian Library (M. H. Swaim, "A New Year's Gift from the Princess Elizabeth," pp.261–65).

126. For Bale's defense of his marriage, see *Scriptorum illustrium majoris Britanniae*, p.702; for Rome's condemnation, see Pits, *Relationum historicum*, pp.53–59; cf. Harris, *John Bale*, pp.22–23.

127. John Bale, *The Image of Both Churches*, chap.18, p.537.

128. "Rabelais's [bastard] children were granted the unusual privilege of an official legitimization by the Pope Himself" (M. A. Screech, *The Rabelaisian Marriage*, pp.19–20; cf. J. Lesellier, "Deux enfants naturels de Rabelais."

129. For Luther's critique of religious celibacy, see his "Exhortation to All Clergy Assembled at Augsburg," esp. pp.40–52, and "Exhortation to the Knights of the Teutonic Order."

130. "Love needs no laws," said Luther, sweeping away "those stupid barriers due to spiritual fatherhood, motherhood, brotherhood, sisterhood, and childhood"—or so Robert Brain, *Friends and Lovers*, p.94, has it (cf. Luther, "The Persons . . . Forbidden to Marry," p.8, and "The Estate of Marriage," p.24). Luther did not sweep away all barriers to marriage, however. He stressed the distinction between figure and letter, or spirit and body, and thus redefined the incest taboo in terms of a literal, or corporeal, principle.

131. *Ancrene Riwle* 106/21 (c. 1230), quoted from photostat copy of the Corpus Christi College (Cambridge) manuscript; from Hans Kurath, Sherman M. Kuhn, and John Reidy, eds., *Middle English Dictionary*, s.v. "Incest."

132. Richard Rolle, *Form of Living* (1425), 413.

133. John Lacy (?), *A Middle English Treatise on the Ten Commandments*, p.28.

134. John Lydgate, *Fall of Princes*, 2.4068–71. See also Robert of Gloucester, *The Life and Martyrdom of Thos. Beket*, line 757.

135. Geoffrey Chaucer, "The Parson's Prologue and Tale," line 908.

136. On the Benedictine orders and the idealist policies that More promulgates, see R. W. Chambers, *Thomas More*, p.136; and Thomas More, *Utopia*, pp. 281–82. Although More generally admired the Catholic orders and their doctrines (J. H. Hexter, *More's Utopia*, pp.85–90), he was not himself a monk or friar but a husband and legitimate father.

137. EB, s.v. "Celibacy."

138. More, *Tindale*, pp.48–49 (emphasis added). Cf. Luther's references to the "incestuous celibacy" of the papists (*Tischreden*, 2:138–39).

139. Matt. 23:8. Christianity proposes a universalist doctrine that both incorporates and transcends ordinary kinship with an extraordinary unifamilial kinship. Cf. Gal. 3:26–28: "For ye are all the children of God by faith in Christ Jesus. . . . There is neither Jew nor Greek . . . for ye are all one in Christ Jesus." Church fathers who urge Christians to follow out the implications of Matt. 23:8 in such a way as to call all men their "brothers" and to call *no one* by the name "father" include: Ignatius of Antioch, "To the Ephesians,"

10.3; Clement of Alexandria, *Stromata*, 7.14.5; Justinian, *Dialogue with Try-phon*, 96; and Tertullian, *Apologeticus*, 39.8–9.

140. 1 Cor. 5:1.

141. Adela Yarbro Collins, "The Function of Excommunication in Paul," p.253.

142. 1 Cor. 10:23, and Lev. 18:8. For this position on Corinthians, see E.-B. Allo, *Saint Paul*, p.121; and Hans Conzelmann, *1 Corinthians*, p.97. For the larger debate about incest and the Corinthians in particular, see Eugene Mangenot, "Inceste," pp.1544–45. For Christian reports of the non-Christian complaint that the early Christians were incestuous, see Eusebius, *Histoire ecclésiastique* (PG 20:408, 413, 416); and the Acts of Saint Epipode (PG 5:1458). Christian apologists counterattacked, claiming that the critics of Christianity were themselves incestuous (Mangenot, "Inceste," p.1546).

143. For a general account of the Brethren, see Norman Cohn, "The Cult of the Free Spirit." In Italy, Bernardine of Siena was affected by the Brethren; see his *Opera omnia*, 1:34, 536; 3:109; 4:544; 6:248. In Germany the Brethren influenced the philosophical Meister Eckhardt and the polygamist Anabaptists of Münster (see Telle, "Île," p.169; and EB, s.v. "Eckhardt"). The sixteenth-century Belgian David Joris, a prominent member of a local sect influenced by the Free Spirit, had an affect on Bosch, whose painting *The Garden of Earthly Delights* is said to depict the Free Spirit's "incestuous orgies" (Wilhelm Fraenger, *The Millennium of Hieronymus Bosch*, p.42).

144. This was also the motto of the spiritual libertines (Telle, *Marguerite*, p.297).

145. 2 Cor. 3:17.

146. Women were especially prominent as the theorists of the Brethren of the Free Spirit (e.g., the poet Hadewijch of Brussels). The "Homines Intel-ligentes" of Brussels were a local sect of the Free Spirit; their leaders Giles Cantor and William Hilderniss were condemned by Pierre Ailly, Bishop of Cambrai, in 1411. See Henry Pomerius, "De origine monasterii Viridvallis," p.286; and Ernest W. McDonnell, *The Beguines and Beghards*, p.502.

147. Similarities between the literary work of Marguerite of Navarre and Marguerite Porete include verbal parallels, as in the use of the term "distant close" or *loingpres* (see Dagens, "*Miroir*") and historical connections (see Joseph Bédier, "La tradition manuscrite"; G. Eekhoud, *Les Libertins d'Anvers*; and J. Frederichs, "Un Luthérien français devenu libertin spirituel"). See also Simone Glasson's Introduction to Marguerite of Navarre, *Prisons*, for the connection between that work and Marguerite Porete's *Mirror*.

148. The relation between Lutheran doctrine and the ideology of spiritual liberty as they converge in the court of Navarre is a subject of Frederichs, "Un Luthérien français"; and Eekhoud, *Les libertins d'Anvers*.

149. See F. T. Perrens, *Les libertins en France*.

150. For a discussion of various medieval Italian, Latin, and French versions, see Marilyn Doiron, "The Middle English Translation of *Le Mirouer des simples ames.*"

151. John Champneys, *The Harvest Is at Hand*.

152. Samuel Rawson Gardiner in his *History of the Great Civil War*, 3:380, writes of the Levelers: "They have given themselves a new name, Viz. Levelers, for they intend to set all things straight and raise a parity and community in the kingdom." Cromwell attacked the Levelers in a speech to Parliament in September 1654 (quoted in Thomas Carlyle, *Oliver Cromwell's Letters and Speeches*, speech 2): "Did not that Leveling principle tend to the reducing of all to an inequality." See EB, s.v. "Levelers." For the Ranters, see n.169 below.

153. Vernon L. Parrington, *Romantic Revolution in America*, pp.335–36, suggests that the basis for American Perfectionism lies not so much in French Romanticism or German Idealism as in a medieval utopian past that extends to the religious utopianism of the 1650s and to Roger Williams and beyond, and that Noyes and his Perfectionists were at one with the Diggers and Levelers of Commonwealth times. On American Perfectionism, see also Marc Shell, "Those Extraordinary Twins," esp. pp.43–44.

154. Sociologist Lewis Yablonsky, *The Hippie Trip*, p.290, describes a San Francisco ritual now called "the funeral of the hippie movement": the participants' "explicit idea was to bury the hippie image, as they put it, produced by the mass media, and to signal the birth of *The Free Man*." The Love Children wanted to be Brethren of the Free Spirit.

155. In the 1520s Lollards and other groups tracing their origin to Wycliffe came together with Lutheranism and thus became a sect to reckon with (EB, s.v. "English History," p.529c).

156. EB, s.v. "Anabaptists," p.905b; referring to an event of 12 April 1549.

157. Athanasian Christian Church doctrine claims that the Virgin Mary had no biological part in the making of her baby. In the first half of the ninth century, Theosterikos tells the following anecdote about the iconoclast emperor Constantine V: "Taking in his hand a purse full of gold and showing it to all he asked, "What is it worth? They replied that it had great value. He then emptied out the gold and asked, What is worth now? They said, Noth-

ing. So, said he, Mary (for the atheist would not call her Theotokos), while she carried Christ within was to be honoured, but after she was delivered she differed in no way from other women" (*Vitae Nicetae*, in *Acta sanctorum*, Ap.I, app.23; quoted in Edward Martin, *A History of the Iconoclast Controversy*, p.62).

158. See Bale's "Elucydacyon" in Anne Askew, *The First Examinacyon* and *The Lattre Examinacyon*.

159. Telle, "Île," p.169.

160. Regarding the view that Anne Askew may have been one of Catherine Parr's ladies-in-waiting, see *Writings of Ed[ward] VI*, 6:238; and EB, s.v. "Askew."

161. Quoted in McDonnell, *Beguines and Beghards*, p.497.

162. See Hartmann's interrogation at Erfurt by Walter Kerling, recounted in I. I. von Döllinger, *Beiträge zur Sektengeschichte*, 2:386.

163. Gordon Leff, *Heresy in the Later Middle Ages*, 1:378–79.

164. Ibid.

165. "Amye, amez et faites ce que tu vouldrez" (Marguerite Porete, *Miroir des simples ames*, fol.26v).

166. MS 71, St. Johns College, Cambridge, fols.28v–29r. This passage is apparently a gloss by the Middle English translator; see Doiron, "Middle English Translation," p.145.

167. Ibid., fol.7r: "Vertues, I take leeve of you for evermore," translating "Vertuz, je prens congé de vous a tousjours" — a statement condemned by the Council of Vienna of 1311–12, which treated *congé des vertues* as *licentiat a se virtutes*.

168. Ibid., fol.10r. This statement too was condemned at Vienne (France).

169. Abiezer Cope, a member of the Ranter sect, promulgated in England in 1650 the Brethren's view that "God dwelt inside them, as an inner light whose authority was above all laws. . . . Sin was thus made to disappear. The consequence was, for some Ranters, sexual license" (John Carey's Foreword in Nigel Smith, ed., *A Collection of Ranter Writings*, p.7). Cope described the state beyond "good" and "evil" in terms of "the mother Eternity, Almightyness, who is universal love" and to whose child dress and undress, incest and chastity, are alike — he knows no evil" (quoted in Cohn, "Cult of the Free Spirit," p.68).

170. Quoted in ibid., pp.59, 56.

171. Elizabeth, "Glass," fol.62v.

172. "Fay ce que voudras" (*Gargantua*, bk.2, chap.57). The liberty of Rabelais's abbey is often interpreted as mere "Epicurean" (i.e., gluttonous)

intemperance or desire for a heaven on earth (see, e.g., Joseph Spencer Kennard, *The Friar in Fiction*, p.58), but it also has a serious libertine aspect. Mikhail Bakhtin, *Rabelais and His World*, p.412, compares Thélème with the medieval parody *The Rules of Blessed Libertine*.

173. Marguerite Porete, *Miroir*, fol.26v (p.189): "Telles âmes roynes, filles de roy, seurs de roy, et espouses de roy."

174. Elizabeth, "Glass," fol.43r. Marguerite Porete's Middle English translator adds that "the soule is for a tyme departid fro al synne and is unyted to God bi unyoun—thanne is the soule fre. As for that tyme of unyoun, ful litel tyme it is. . . . A creature may be enabited bi grace in fredom foreuere; but to stonde contynuelli in fredom withoute synne, it may not, for the unstabilite of the sensualite that is alwei flittinge" (MS 71, St. John's College, Cambridge, fols.4v–5r).

175. See the charges against Marguerite Porete (1309) listed in *Grandes Chroniques de France*, 5:188.

176. English devotional works similarly depict Jesus as a female lover or as both a male lover and a female parent taken together. Among such works are the Middle English translation of Aelred of Rievaulx's *De vita ermitica*, 329; Julian of Norwich's *Revelations of Divine Love*, 58–60; and *On Ureisun of Ure Louerde*, p.2. A basic biblical text here, of interest to Marguerite of Navarre and Queen Elizabeth, is Saint Paul's letter to the Galatians, where he writes that "there is neither male nor female," but we become "one in Christ" (Gal. 3:28)—though in the Greek, "one" is here [*heis*] masculine (as in Eph. 2:14), not neuter (as in Eph. 2:14). Franciscan theologans often portray maleness and femaleness joined together, not in what we usually assume to be the closest union (marriage) but in relations that would normally be considered to impede that union: mother and son, or brother and sister (Ewert H. Cousins, *Bonaventure, and the Coincidence of Opposites*, p.20).

177. See Porete, *Miroir*, fol.13r–v. Elizabeth asks, "For what thing is a man (as for his own strength) before that he hath received the gift of faith ("Glass," fol.5r). Bale's "Epistle Dedicatory" refers to "the barren doctrine and the works without faith" (fol.7v). Marguerite of Navarre, in Elizabeth's translation, writes of the "thing a man cannot understand, unless he hath a true faith" ("Glass," fol.14r) and asserts that "if we have Him through faith then have we a greater treasure than any man can tell" ("Glass," fol.62v).

178. MS 71, St. John's College, Cambridge, fol.11r–v. One example of the mockery of "erotic communism" is Jean de Meun's contribution (c. 1275) to Guillaume de Lorris's *Roman de la Rose*, especially "Toutes pour touz e touz

pour toutes"; this is cited by Curtius (*European Literature*, p.6), who adds that here "the goddess Natura has become the servant of rank promiscuity." Bakhtin (*Rabelais*, p.412) discusses the medieval *Rule of the Blessed Libertine*, a parody of monastic laws similarly built upon sanctifying that which is forbidden.

179. Dollinger, *Sektengeschichte*, 2:664. See also Schneider, *Libertin*, p.60.

180. Martin Luther, in his *A la noblesse chrétienne de la nation allemande: La liberté du chrétien*, p.49, wrote that "the whole sum of Christian life is contained in this little book [on the liberty of a Christian]." Melanchthon, however, pointed out in his *Articles of Visitation* that Luther's doctrine of liberty was interpreted by some Protestant reformers as a charter for moral laxity; Melanchthon argued for the preaching of the Ten Commandments as a guide to the good works that are to follow true faith (cited in Franklin Sherman, Introduction to Martin Luther, "Against the Antinomians"). For a study of the relationship between the Brethren of the Free Spirit and French Protestantism, see Frederichs, "Un Luthérien français"; and for a general discussion of the role of the doctrines of the free spirit in the Reformation, see Romana Guarnieri, "Il movimento del libero spirito dalle origini al secolo xvi" and "Appendici," in her *Il movimento del libero spirito*, pp.114–49, 336–58. On the *Miroir* as Protestant in the reformist tradition of Guillaume Briçonnet and Simon Du Bois, see Salminen, *Miroir*, pp.40–65, as well as Lefranc, *Idées religieuse*; on its Protestant mystical aspects, see H. Sckommodau, "Die religiosen Dichtungen Margarete von Navarra."

181. See J. M. Cooper, "Incest Prohibitions in Primitive Culture," p.2. The term *liber* means both "son" and "free," the *Oxford Latin Dictionary* defining *liberi* as "sons and daughters, children in connection w[ith] their parents."

182. Thomas Elyot, *The Image of Governaunce*, 34; George Chapman, *Chapman's Homer: The "Iliad,"* 16.501.

183. W. Wilkinson, *A Supplication of the Family of Love*, p.34.

184. Ibid., p.19; John Rogers, *The Displaying of an Horrible Sect*, sig.15r.

185. *The Family of Love*, a comic play probably written by Thomas Middleton and performed by the Children of the Revels, contains a trial scene in which the Family's sexual freedom is institutionalized in law. See Simon Shepherd's introduction to his edition of the *Family*, p.iii; C. L. Cherry, *The Most Unvaluedst Purchase*; and Janet E. Halley, "Heresy, Orthodoxy, and the Politics of Religious Discourse."

186. *Monk* means "alone" (from Greek *monachus*). However, not all monks were *anchorets* living in solitude. Some were *coenobites* (from *koinos*, "common,"

and *bios,* ("life"), who lived in communities with one or another kind of *archē,* or rule. The *archon* might be a traditional *cenobiarch* in a universally fraternal and/or sororal community where all members, *including* the ruler, were "siblings" and called one another Brother or Sister. On the other hand, the *archon* might rule in a community of a strictly patriarchal or matriarchal sort where all members of the community were Brothers or Sisters *except* the ruler, who as Father or Mother Superior was everyone else's "parent." There was a parallel struggle in the Elizabethan and Jamesian period as to whether the "monarch"—meaning "alone rule" or "one ruling" (from *monarché*)—was essentially "parent" or "sibling."

187. Clement [Pseudo-], *Epistolae ad virginies,* PG 1:379–416, discussed in Bugge, *Virginitas,* p.72. See Matt. 23:19: "Call no man father."

188. Bugge, *Virginitas,* p.73.

189. Dumm, *Virginity,* pp.119, 121, citing Jerome, *Epistulae,* Letter 130, 14, in CSEL 56:119; and Gregory of Nyssa, *Vita S. Macrinae,* PG 46:969.

190. Dumm, *Virginity,* p.121, citing John Chrysostom, *De virginitate,* 73, PG 48:586.

191. Aristotle *Politics* 1.2.5 is generally the Christian ideologists' *locus classicus,* but it is a mistake to assume that this view of the ruler is universal. Indeed, it is generally absent in the nonuniversalist (and to Christendom of the period, politically and ideologically threatening) doctrine of Islam—perhaps, as Bernard Lewis remarks in *The Political Language of Islam,* because of its Christian connotation. Only in Turkish does a term meaning "father," *ata,* acquire a political connotation, and the image of the ruler as mother seems to have been equally abhorrent. If, however, the Moslem state has no parents, it certainly has children, and terms denoting sons and brothers are in common political use. These may be literal, indicating membership in a tribe or dynasty, for example; or figurative, indicating a relationship to the state. The term "brother," with its various equivalents, is common among those who are members of the same group, whether by allegiance or by kinship. And in Turkish usage "elder brother," *aga,* is a common term of respect for holders of authority. The best-known example is the *abna,* "sons," of the Abbasid dynasty, an elite group of slaves and freedmen, both soldiers and civilians, who served the state and thus freed it from dependence on Arab tribal support. See "Agha," by H. Bowen; and "Abna," by K. V. Zettersteen, both in *Encyclopedia of Islam.*

192. Introduction to *Menaphon,* in *The Works of Thomas Nashe.*

193. For the Elizabethan conjunction of "unrestrained violence and sex-

ual licentiousness," see William Saffady, "Fears of Sexual License during the English Reformation."

194. Stephen Gardiner, *Letters*, p.279.

195. J. Thomas Kelly, *Thorn on the Tudor Rose*, p.3.

196. For the executions, see Heinrich Mutschmann and Karl Wentersdorf, *Shakespeare and Catholicism*, p.43; for the rebellion, David Kaula, *Shakespeare and the Archpriest Controversy*, esp. p.71.

197. James I, *Trew Law* (in *Political Works*), esp. pp.64–66.

198. John Locke, *Two Treatises on Civil Government*, p.6.

199. Norman O. Brown, *Love's Body*, p.4.

200. Lawrence Stone, quoted in Susan Staves, *Players' Scepters*, p.114.

201. See "Français, encore un effort si vous voulez être republicains," in de Sade, *La philosophie dans le boudoir*, pp.179–245, esp. 221–22.

202. Bale, "Conclusion," fol.40v.

203. Bale, "Epistle Dedicatory," fols.3r, 4v, 6v–7r (biblical references omitted). Of this sort of attempt in the sixteenth century to replace the role of blood in the kinship structure with virtue — or "beauty" — Hermann Melville may provide the best commentaries in his *Pierre*, with its ambiguously illegitimate heroine Isabella/Elizabeth: "A beautiful woman is born Queen of men and women both, as Mary Stuart was born Queen of Scots, whether men or women. All mankind are her Scots; her leal clan are numbered by the nations." According to the narrator, "a plain-faced Queen of Spain [perhaps Queen Isabella I, called *la Católica*] dwells not in half the glory of a beautiful milliner's daughter," and people deserve to be excoriated for worshiping "Mary Queen of Heaven" yet "for generations refus[ing] cap and knee to many angel Maries, rightful Queens of France" — including many "immortal flowers of the House of Valois" (pp.46, 47, 56). Among the Maries that Melville may have had in mind are *Mary* Stuart, wife of King Francis, who was a Valois/Angoulême; *Mary*, Queen of France, née Tudor, who was daughter to Henry VII and Elizabeth, sister to Henry VIII, and queen to Louis XII of France, a Valois/Capetian; and *Mary* Tudor, called "Bloody Mary," daughter to Henry VIII and Catherine of Aragon. Melville was apparently an admirer of Robert Melville (1527–1621), who was a representative of Mary, Queen of Scots at the English court; among those who begged Elizabeth for Mary's life, Robert Melville later accompanied James VI to England (1603).

204. Bale, "Epistle Dedicatory," fol.7r; "Conclusion," fol.40r; "Epistle Dedicatory," fol.7r.

205. Luke 14:26.